*The Word
and the World*

The Word and the World

Explorations in the Form of Sociological Analysis

Michael Mulkay

Professor of Sociology, University of York

London
GEORGE ALLEN & UNWIN
Boston   Sydney

George Allen & Unwin (Publishers) Ltd,
40 Museum Street, London WC1A 1LU, UK

George Allen & Unwin (Publishers) Ltd,
Park Lane, Hemel Hempstead, Herts HP2 4TE, UK

Allen & Unwin, Inc.,
8 Winchester Place, Winchester, Mass. 01890, USA

George Allen & Unwin Australia Pty Ltd,
8 Napier Street, North Sydney, NSW 2060, Australia

First published in 1985

British Library Cataloguing in Publication Data

Mulkay, Michael
  The word and the world: explorations in the
  form of sociological thought.
1. Discourse analysis – Social aspects
I. Title
306'.4   P3012
ISBN 0-04-301196-9
ISBN 0-04-301197-7 Pbk

Library of Congress Cataloging-in-Publication Data

Mulkay, M. J. (Michael Joseph), 1936-
  The word and the world.
Bibliography: p.
Includes indexes.
1. Sociology – Research – Methodology.   2. Social
sciences – Research – Methodology.   3. Discourse
analysis.   I. Title.
HN24.M783   1985   301'.072   85-13439
ISBN 0-04-301196-9 (alk. paper)
ISBN 0-04-301197-7 (pbk. : alk. paper)

Set in 10 on 11 point Plantin by Columns, Caversham, Reading
and printed in Great Britain by Biddles Limited, Guildford, Surrey

In memory of
BOB REID
who got me into this
and for
P M
who helped to keep me going

Art is as natural an artifice as Nature:
the truth of fiction is that Fact is fantasy;
the made-up story is a model of the world.
John Barth, *Letters* (1979, p. 33)

Contents

Acknowledgement

Chapter five below is a revised version of 'The Scientist Talks Back: A One-Act Play, with a Moral, about Replication in Science and Reflexivity in Sociology', published in *Social Studies of Science* in 1984. I wish to thank David Edge, the editor of that journal, and Sage Publications for allowing me to reprint this material.

Preface

Because this book is an attempt to depart from the established conventions of sociological texts, an attempt to explore the opportunities afforded by new textual forms, I would have liked to have begun right here with some kind of 'anti-preface'. This would have helped to establish from the outset the possibility of employing new textual forms in the most unlikely of places. I have discovered, however, as I have tried out various formulations in my head, that 'the Preface' is a particularly resilient form. It seems difficult to tamper with, without creating misunderstandings and possibly giving offence. The main reason for this, I suppose, is that prefaces are normally used to draw the attention of a largely unknown audience of potential readers to the debt owed by the author to various persons who have contributed to the text, but whose contribution is deemed not to justify participation in its authorship. A central problem for any writer who seeks to play around with a preface is that, if s/he fails to express her debt sufficiently clearly to this impersonal audience, s/he is in danger of causing offence, not to that audience, but to her colleagues, helpers and friends.

The special constraints of 'the Preface' arise from its being a bridge between a form of direct, personal discourse among colleagues, helpers and friends, and a form of discourse directed at an indefinite and 'uninformed' audience. Thus one's expression of thanks must not only be clear to one's friends, who may well be relied on to treat even a literal denial of debt by the author as, given the context, 'actually an affirmation', but also to anybody else who happens to glance through the book's preliminary matter. Yet, at the same time, 'the Preface' is a peculiarly indirect form, in which the author tells a third party that s/he 'would like to thank' a second party, but seldom actually says 'thank you' to that second party.

Prefaces, then, are an unusual blend of personal dialogue and impersonal monologue which is worthy of detailed sociological study and which, through its combination of dialogue and monologue, prefigures one of the central themes of the book. The study of prefaces could also reveal, I am sure, something interesting about our treatment of textual ownership and responsibility. For in their prefaces, authors identify those contributions by others which have been helpful, influential, seminal, even indispensable, yet which are not treated as constituting that special textual status called 'authorship'.

But the discussion so far is clearly a digression. It is no more than a preface, in the form of a brief comment on prefaces, to the real preface, which now commences. Before I begin the real preface, however, let me just say that this preface to the preface, and the real preface to come, are the only parts of the book which have been written without considerable assistance from numerous colleagues, helpers and friends. The rest of the book, after the preface, which will follow shortly, would not have come into existence if these colleagues and friends had not been so willing to provide support and critical advice. The people I have in mind are Malcolm Ashmore, Gus Brannigan, Nigel Gilbert, Trevor Pinch, Jonathan Potter, Gordon Smith, Teri Walker, Steve Woolgar, Anna Wynne and Steve Yearley.

My friend and ex-co-author, David Edge, who did *not* comment on this text and who will not, therefore, appear in the preface, once went so far, in a 'preface' of his own, as to thank everybody he had met and read during the previous twenty years. I will not adopt such a comprehensive approach. Many people have affected my work profoundly who will not be mentioned in the preface. I will refer only to those who have commented on first drafts of various parts of this text (excluding, of course, the preface and the preface to the preface), who have helped me to improve it and, in some cases, to avoid serious error, and who have at the same time helped to sustain my enthusiasm through to the book's completion.

Actually, what I have just written is not entirely correct. Because I am not quite sure whether I need this preface to the preface, I think I'll have to ask Malcolm Ashmore, who is listed above as commenting on the main text but *not* on the preface to the preface, to give me his comments on what I am now writing. I can then thank him for this extra contribution in the preface itself. In addition, I'll thank Carole Barrowclough in the preface for doing all the typing so efficiently and with such good humour. I'll ask Dorothy Lane to type the real preface, so that neither Carole nor Malcom will be aware that I have thanked them, for typing the book and reading the preface to the preface respectively, until they read the printed book.

I am not sure that this solves all my problems, however. If Dorothy types the preface in which I thank Carole, do I need to get Carole to type another preface in which I thank Dorothy? Even more seriously, if Malcolm reads the preface to the preface, who will read the preface where I thank Malcolm for reading the preface to the preface? It cannot be Malcolm. But if it is somebody else, will they have to be thanked in another preface? Well, I shall cross that bridge when I come to it. What is absolutely clear is that I must thank the Social Science Research Council for awarding me a personal research grant for the year 1983–4. There can be no doubt that, without the grant, this book would not have been written. On the other hand, is it possible to thank an organization which no longer exists? I could, of course, thank the Economic and Social Research Council. But that body simply honoured a commitment made by its predecessor, of which it may or may not have approved. Perhaps the best policy would be to thank them both. However, the more I think about this preface, the more difficult it comes to appear and the more inclined I am to do without it altogether. Even the scientists who provide the data for much of this book are not easily thanked. For they contribute to the text under pseudonyms which hide their real identity. I should perhaps thank them most of all, particularly 'Jennings', who appears throughout Part 3, and the two men whose debate is examined in Part 1 of the book. But if I refer to the latter by their pseudonyms and express my thanks to 'Marks and (especially) Spencer', this is bound to lead to further confusion and, what is worse, perhaps to a certain levity.

In the light of these considerations, it seems to me best not to include a preface in the present text. I apologize to readers for bringing them this far, only to find themselves abandoned in mid-text. I also apologize to the people mentioned above who will not, alas, receive the thanks they deserve. But in my view the practical difficulties alone would prevent me from doing the job properly. Moreover, even the very short analysis at the beginning of what I should perhaps now call this 'preface to the non-preface' suggested that it is impossible to do anything new or interesting with such a structurally restricted and rigidly conventional form as 'the Preface'. My initial aim of devising a (possibly light-hearted) preface which by its own structure revealed something about the nature of prefaces is clearly unrealistic. Let me, then, do without a preface and turn to the much simpler task of listing the major contributors to the text which follows and writing an introduction.

List of Characters

Analyst, the
Anonymous Speaker, an
Auditor, the
Author, the
Black, Prof.
Book, the
Borges, Jorge Luis
Brannigan, Gus
Critic, Prof.
Elder, Prof.
Jennings, Dr
Marks, Prof.
Meta-author, the
Mulkay, Prof.
Nobel Representative
Pseudonymous scientists, various
Purple, Mrs
Purple, Prof.
Reader, the
Representative of the Nobel Committees
Scientist, the
Spencer, Dr
Sociologist 1
Sociologist 2
Sociologist 3
Statesman, Prof.
Student Representative
Textual Commentator, the
Younger, Dr

Introductions

I wish that you were with me now in my study, dear Reader, as I search for the words with which to introduce this volume. It would be so much easier if we could *talk*, because, in talking, I could answer any questions you wished to ask and provide an introduction designed specifically for you. One trouble with the printed word is that it commits you irrevocably to a particular sequence of words, when so many different texts are always possible and so many are always needed. The chapters which follow have many potential meanings and neither of us can know, at this moment of writing, which one will best meet your requirements, situated as you are at some as yet unrealized point in space and time. If we were talking together, I could elicit words from you around which I could weave a textual gloss suited to your specific needs; a gloss which would, as is imperative for all introductions, not only summarize what is to come but also assure and reassure you of its worth.

Unfortunately, I am condemned to rely on an introduction that takes the form of a written monologue. I have no choice but to offer a general purpose account – which is written for anybody, and therefore for nobody in particular – of what the book is about. Consequently it may well be that you will not find in this first chapter what you want; even though I could have given you the words you seek, if I had only known. Because you are a silent partner in this discourse, I must proceed in ignorance of your response to my text and you must proceed without knowing my reaction to your reading of that text.

Of course, the written monologue does have some advantages. It will enable me to carry on without interruption and without danger of contradiction. I won't have to deal with any questions I cannot answer. I will be able to make all those small changes in wording that are so often necessary to prevent one's argument collapsing in ruins. I will be able to make it quite clear that *this* is what the book is about. Yes, the written monologue confers a certain interpretative authority on its author. The more I think about it—

If you need me, why don't you invite me into the text?

Who said that?

I did. If you want a dialogue instead of a monologue, why don't you invent a potential reader to talk to?

I can't do that. This is a serious academic study, not a fairy story. My readers wouldn't like it if one of their number (especially an hypothetical one) were to get into the text. They wouldn't know what was going to happen next. Readers know what to expect from academic authors like me. We authors provide our readers with a single, coherent, understandable story about a particular segment of the world; at least, that's what we're supposed to try to do. If there isn't a single, coherent understandable story, then readers know whom to blame: the author. But readers cannot and do not trust other readers. It is well known that other readers often fail to understand the simplest of texts. They make irrelevant comments which miss the point and frequently raise silly questions. Now, if one of these unreliable readers (excuse me) were to get into the printed text, s/he could disrupt things for everybody else. If things went awry and the book developed serious flaws, readers would not know who was responsible. So, I thank you for the suggestion. I'm sure it was meant to be helpful. But I think I'll return to the comfort and safety of the conventional monologue.

I'm afraid it's not as simple as that. Now that I'm in the text, it will be difficult to get rid of me without my acquiescence. The only other alternative is to scrap what you've written so far and start again. Not only would that be textual abortion, but you may well just find yourself writing once again, 'I wish that you were with me now, dear Reader . . .' Indeed, the fact that you've let me go on talking seems to me to imply that you actually want me to remain in the text. So, please go ahead and introduce me personally to your book.

You make it sound as if the book is another person; whereas, in fact, it is no more than a collection of diverse and, in many ways, discrepant and socially generated discourses. Well, on second thoughts, that's a pretty good definition of a 'person' as well. So maybe it is all right to introduce the two of you. Reader, this is Book; Book, this is Reader. Book, why don't you tell our Reader about yourself?

The Book Speaks

How do you do, Reader. I'm pleased to have you peruse my pages. I think of myself as a sociological research monograph (made possible by a personal research grant from the ESRC to the

Author). As such, I have none of the author's qualms about using the form of the monologue. Indeed, an empiricist monologue seems to me to be the only form of discourse which is appropriate to my goal of showing you, in careful and systematic detail, what a particular part of the social world is like.

My central concern is the nature of scientists' discourse. To put it another way, I describe some of the interpretative practices observable in scientific discourse, whereby scientists attribute meaning to, and thereby constitute, their social world. This is a continuation of earlier work carried out on scientific discourse and scientists' interpretative methods by such authors as Latour and Woolgar (1979), Latour (1980), Woolgar (1980, 1982, 1983), Brannigan (1981), Yearley (1981), Lynch (1982), Gieryn (1983), Mulkay, Potter and Yearley (1983), Gilbert and Mulkay (1984), and Potter (1984). I have concentrated below on four topic areas and my text is divided up accordingly into four parts. In Part 1 I examine a technical debate; in Part 2, experimental replication; in Part 3, scientific discovery; and in Part 4, the celebration of scientific achievement.

Part 1 deals with an epistolary debate between two biochemists; that is, a debate that was transacted by letter. Letters are particularly convenient for discourse analysis because they provide a lasting register of naturally occurring interpretative exchange among participants. They allow unobtrusive observation of some of the fine detail of scientists' everyday interpretative work. As my text unfolds, the letters are supplemented by various other kinds of written document, by transcripts of interviews with scientists working within the area of biochemistry discussed in Part 1, by a tape-recorded conversation between the Author and one of the leading biochemists, and by the official records of the Nobel ceremonies.

In the first chapter of Part 1, the ten letters of a technical debate are examined at some length, initially along lines similar to those adopted in previous sociological discourse analysis (Gilbert and Mulkay, 1984). The starting point for the analysis is participants' distinction between fact and opinion, around which the whole debate hinges. A detailed description is given of how the two authors employ this distinction, how each author's discourse is organized to display its own factuality, and how the persistently asymmetrical organization of the letters leads to interpretative failure. The findings of this analysis are summarized as a set of rules for generating scientific letters in cases of dispute about technical matters. The analysis concludes with a discussion of the textual forms which are most appropriate for the presentation of scientific results and for the effective resolution of scientific debate.

A comparative assessment is given of the empiricist monologue which is characteristic of the research literature and the more personal dialogue which is possible in letters and face-to-face interaction.

This long opening chapter furnishes the interpretative background for the whole work and particularly for the two following chapters, which draw more selectively upon the same data. Chapter 2 explores a major issue identified, but not pursued, in Chapter 1, namely, the similarities and differences between epistolary dialogue and ordinary conversation. The approach adopted is to compare the letters with certain general conclusions about conversational structure which are available in the sociological research literature. It is shown that direct, spoken dialogue differs from written dialogue and that these differences have important implications for the form of epistolary debate. Nevertheless, certain basic features found in naturally occurring conversations reappear regularly in these letters. Moreover, re-examination of the letters in terms of concepts taken from conversation analysis provides the basis for a more formal explanation in Chapter 2 of why the epistolary debate was difficult to resolve and why participants were unable to bring this dialogue to a successful completion.

Chapter 3 takes the analysis further by employing 'analytical dialogue' to investigate the dialogue between participants which is embodied in the letters discussed in the first two chapters. It does this by presenting a second debate, this time between the analyst and one of the authors of the original set of letters. This analytical debate begins with an exchange of letters and culminates, for the purposes of this text, in a recorded conversation between the 'analyst' and the 'participant'.

In this secondary debate, the scientist is invited to comment on an analysis of the initial set of letters offered by the sociologist and on the sociologist's attempts to account for the previous dialogue's supposed failure. By bringing a participant into the analytical text, not only do we subject some of the claims proposed in Chapters 1 and 2 to a most unusual scrutiny, but we also make the results of this scrutiny directly available to the reader. It is taken for granted in Chapter 3 that participants are quite capable of doing sociological analysis and that both parties may come to learn through analytical collaboration. By reducing the distance between participants' and analysts' discourse, this secondary analysis is able not only to explore from an unusual perspective the relationship between these two discourses, but also to investigate the nature of dialogue and monologue in a practical way. In so far as this analytical exercise is successful, it should imply the possibility of a set of rules for generating dialogue which provides an effective alternative to those rules previously extracted from the original epistolary debate between biochemists.

One recurrent concern in the biochemists' letters is the replicability of their various experimental findings. The topic of experimental replication is discussed briefly in Chapter 1, but its extended treatment is reserved for Part 2, Chapters 4 and 5, where the structure of discourse about replication is described and documented in some detail. Sociologists' as well as scientists' replication accounts are used in these chapters to illustrate the potential irony of the relationship between analysts' and participants' discourse (Woolgar, 1983; Yearley, 1984).

Chapter 4 examines some of the interpretative outcomes which scientists can accomplish through their replication-accounts. Particular attention is given to the way in which scientists use replication-accounts to attribute and to deny scientific originality. It is shown that the scientists under study regularly employ a complex and diverse accounting repertoire which enables them to construe given experiments as either the same or different, depending on the interpretative context, and to depict a given experiment as an 'original confirmation' or as a 'mere replication', in accordance with the other interpretative work being undertaken. In short, replication is shown not to be an attribute of scientists' experiments, but to be an aspect of scientists' context-dependent interpretative work.

Chapter 4 goes on to explore the implications of the preceding demonstration of the variability of scientists' replication-accounts for analysts' own discourse. It does this by applying its conclusions to its own text and to prior sociological work on replication. This procedure of analytical self-reference can be seen as a limited form of textual dialogue. It leads to the further conclusion that Chapter 4's initial findings can equally well be treated as a mere replication of prior sociological work on replication, as original confirmation of that work or as a basic contradiction of that work. This recognition of the possibility of attributing multiple meanings to the analytical text, as well as to participants' texts, links back to the discussion and exploration of 'analytical dialogue' in Part 1. For one of the main advantages of analytical dialogue is that it allows more than one voice, and more than one interpretative stance, into the analytical text on an equal footing.

The first chapter on replication in Part 2 shows that such an approach is needed in dealing with this topic, in order to cope with the potential multiplicity of analysts', and members', accounts. The second chapter on replication (Chapter 5) is designed specifically to meet this need. It takes the form of the text for a play in which both analysts and participants take part as interpretative equals in a discussion of scientific replication. This quasi-fictional text is offered as a supplement to the genuine participant–analyst dialogue presented in Chapter 3. It is another alternative to the conventional, univocal form of sociological analysis. The text of the play is an attempt to re-present the divergent forms of replication-account employed by both analysts and participants, to show how such accounts can be used, and to do this without assuming that any one speaker's accounts are superior to any other's.

Part 3 below resembles Parts 1 and 2 in employing both monologic and dialogic forms of analysis to examine a given body of textual material. But its topic, that of scientific discovery, is different. The topic of 'discovery' is related to that of 'originality' examined briefly in Part 2. In Part 3 we see that members' discovery-accounts, like their attributions of originality, vary in accordance with the surrounding interpretative work being carried out in a given text. In the first chapter of Part 3 (Chapter 6), several of participants' 'discovery-accounts' are examined in detail. The analysis builds upon previous work on members' 'folk theories of discovery' (Brannigan, 1981). It is shown that the two major folk theories of discovery generate quite different kinds of interpretative outcome and are used in different interpretative contexts. Whereas the folk theory of scientific 'genius' is typically used in celebratory accounts, the alternative members' theory of 'cultural maturation' seems more suitable for, and appears to be used for, expressing opposition to other candidate discoveries.

The analysis of scientists' theories of discovery makes use of, and depends on, a distinction between analysts' and members' theories of social action. This distinction also appears in the sociological analysis of experimental replication, where it is customarily used to enable the analyst to claim interpretative superiority over the participant; that is, whereas members' accounts are treated as defective 'folk theories', analysts' accounts are treated as accurate 'scientific theories'. In other words, in the sociological analysis of both replication and discovery, analysts regularly claim interpretative dominance over participants, even though their secondary analyses are dependent on participants' prior interpretative work. Such a view of the relationship between analysts' and members' accounts is often employed in the sociology of science and in sociological texts in general. The second chapter on discovery (Chapter 7) explores the practical implications of this view. It uses the topic of 'discovery' to investigate whether monologic or dialogic discourse is likely to provide a form of sociological analysis which can be helpful in a practical sense.

Consider, for instance, a situation in which sociologists were asked to help some scientists to resolve certain practical difficulties which the latter had experienced in recognizing a particular discovery. Can the sociologist employ his supposedly superior analytical monologue actually to help scientists to improve their defective 'folk reasoning' and thereby to cope more effectively with their practical problems? Is it possible for the sociologist to sustain his claim of interpretative superiority when he moves outside the safe confines of his analytical discourse into a more practical context?

Such questions provide the point of departure for the second analysis of discovery. This chapter once again takes the form of a quasi-fictional, imaginative discourse, featuring both participants and analysts. The model this time, however, is not the drama, but the formal inquiry into scientific fraud. In Chapter 7, we have an imaginary inquiry into discovery, based upon participants' and analysts' spoken and written words on this topic. The broad conclusion is that the analyst's claim of interpretative superiority is ill-founded and that the nature of conventional, monologic sociological discourse seriously limits the possibility of any helpful practical application of sociological knowledge. It is suggested that the dialogic form of sociological analysis, along the lines of that employed in Chapter 3, where analyst and participant carried out a collaborative analytical dialogue, may furnish a more practically helpful analytical practice.

The single chapter in Part 4 provides an analysis of the ritual celebration of scientific achievement. It is shown that the Nobel ceremonies take the form of an orderly circulation of laudatory discourse from non-Laureates to Laureates and from Laureates to the wider scientific community. Participants' reliance on a narrowly restricted evaluative repertoire is also illustrated. This chapter shows how Nobel discourse turns the celebration of personal achievement into a collective affirmation of the activities and accomplishments of scientists in general. In addition, this concluding chapter explores another possible form for sociological analysis; that of the parody. This analytical parody leads to a final discussion of the meaning of the overall text in which numerous textual agents from previous chapters, as well as participants in the Nobel parody, take part.

Thus, dear Reader, my chapters deal with five inter-related themes. In the first place, they investigate and describe certain recurrent forms of scientific discourse which occur in connection with technical debate, experimental replication, discovery and celebration. Secondly, they examine the relationship between participants' and analysts' discourse; between participants' and analysts' interpretative practices. Thirdly, they explore the difference between monologue and dialogue; in both particpants' and analysts' discourse. Fourthly, they seek to devise and to try out new kinds of analysis which are more dialogic in form than conventional research texts. Finally, an attempt is made to begin to investigate whether analytical dialogue can be put to use for practical purposes.

These themes are woven together throughout the whole text in a complex manner. The text is not presented as a linear, univocal argument, but as a series of overlapping, multi-levelled interpretative sequences representing, and themselves open to, multiple readings. The dominant underlying concern is to try to develop a new kind of analytical discourse which is not modelled on the one-dimensional scientific research text, but draws upon and uses creatively other forms of discourse in such a way that the interpretative complexity of both participants' and analysts' textuality can be more fully realized.

Reader and Author Discuss the Book

Well, Author, that's very interesting, but I'm not sure that I properly understood all that the Book had to say. Is it possible for me to ask him some questions?

I'm afraid not. That's the trouble with books, research reports, and so on; once they've made their statement, that's it. As I pointed out earlier, there's no way you can come back at them with specific questions and elicit a response geared to your particular concerns. There is a built-in rigidity in such texts. Did you notice how, although the Book was emphasizing towards the end the availability of multiple readings of any text, whether a member's or an analyst's text, he made no attempt to draw attention to what this implied for his own summary of the chapters to come, namely, that his summary is just one possible analyst's reading? Did you also notice how he quickly stopped talking to you personally and dropped into the impersonal mode of a conventional research report: 'it was shown that', 'these chapters examine', and so on? Despite his apparent recognition of the multiple meanings of discourse and action, he offers a single, purportedly literal reading of his own text.

Surely that's your fault, not his! You're the author. The Book will say anything that you want him to.

I'm afraid it isn't as straightforward as that. In the first place, I don't know exactly what I want to say until I begin to collaborate with the Book on producing what will eventually turn out to be *his* text. Then, once we've started, he quickly becomes the dominant partner. Every new statement that I try to make has to be reconciled with both the form and the content of *his* prior statements. The further we proceed, the less freedom I seem to have. One reason for this is that, once he has taken over my words, he makes them seem to be, not my freely created verbalizations, but his representations of phenomena out there in the world; a physical object, a social action or a text. As the Book takes control, he increasingly creates the illusion that any further statement on my part must fit neatly with his version of these supposed external realities. Similarly, now that I've allowed you into the text, I cannot control you completely. There's little doubt that, as a textually independent contributor, you will insist on differing from me in certain respects. Furthermore, the rules of conversational turn-taking will require me to let you have your say. Thus you will necessarily bring to the text a degree of interpretative diversity which I would otherwise have avoided.

I see. You seem to be arguing that the choice of textual form constrains the content of your analysis to such an extent that you cannot be held to be fully responsible for its content. But if the Book refuses to answer my questions and you deny responsibility for the Book's contents, who will explain to me what the Book really means?

I'm not sure that anybody can do that. But I could give you *my* answers, as a kind of proxy for the Book.

That suits me fine. My first question is about monologue and dialogue. Am I right in thinking that you want to abandon the monologic form completely in both written and spoken texts and replace it with various forms of dialogue?

No. I doubt whether we could do away with monologues completely, even if we wanted to. But I do believe that the sociological research literature has become unnecessarily dominated by a particular kind of empiricist monologue, derived from the natural sciences, and that this restricted form of analytical discourse has prevented sociology from being as fruitful as it could otherwise have been and, indeed, can still be. In my view, however appropriate the empiricist monologue may be for the natural sciences, and that itself is a matter of dispute, this analytical form is in many ways the least suitable for sociological analysis. In other words, I believe that sociology needs more than topics, data, theories and methods; it also needs a form of analytical discourse which is appropriate to its analytical perspectives. If you accept, as

I do, that every 'social action' and every 'cultural product' or 'text' has to be treated as a source of or as an opportunity for creating multiple meanings, or further texts (Gilbert and Mulkay, 1984), then forms of analytical discourse which are designed to depict the singular, authoritative, supposedly scientific meanings of social phenomena can never be entirely satisfactory. They must be supplemented by new analytical forms which use two or more textual voices to re-present and display the ever-present possibility of interpretative multiplicity. Of course, both dialogic and monologic forms rely on conventions of discourse. Neither form is superior in any ultimate sense. There is no point, therefore, in trying entirely to replace one form with the other. However, the two forms do enable you to do rather different things. I have tried to explore these different things in this book, not only by devising different kinds of analytical dialogue, but also by using given collections of textual material as the basis for both monologic and dialogic analysis. This procedure promotes fairly direct comparison and evaluation and it enlarges our conception of what can be done, analytically, with sociological data. In short, I'm not rejecting monologue in favour of dialogue; rather, I'm extending the range of analytical discourse to include forms not previously considered appropriate.

That sounds very attractive in principle, but it ignores the important distinction between fact and fiction. Sociology surely resembles biochemistry or the other natural sciences in being concerned with fact rather than with fiction. I realize, of course, that facts are 'theory-laden'; scientific facts are not lying around to be garnered like ears of corn. Nevertheless, there is a fundamental difference between the texts of an empirically based academic discipline and the products of fiction and literature. It sounds as if the Book's more 'imaginative' texts, the play, for example, or the imaginary inquiry, are moving uncomfortably close to the fictional end of the spectrum.

It's interesting that you should focus upon the distinction between fact and fiction, because the participants in the epistolary debate examined below also use these terms and, like you, they prefer facts to fictions. Unfortunately for them, however, it's not so easy to make a clear-cut distinction in practice; partly because, as you yourself acknowledge, the statement of any fact presupposes a certain amount of prior interpretative work which 'goes beyond the facts' and which is, in this sense at least, a 'fiction'. In addition, what we recognize as fiction always has a factual component. A novel or a play would simply make no sense to us if it bore no resemblance to what we take to be the real world. Even 'Little Red

Riding Hood' can be taken to represent certain basic realities facing little girls in the peasant communities of mediaeval Europe (Zipes, 1983). And literature is often distinguished from other fiction by the profundity of the truths which it reveals (Potter, Stringer and Wetherell, 1984). So it does always seem to be possible, at the very least, to extract certain facts from supposedly fictional texts. Moreover, in practice, as my biochemists discover, rather painfully, fact and fiction can be very hard to separate. For they find that what is fact for one of them is no more than fiction for the other.

Aren't we in danger of confusing two different meanings of 'fiction'? That is, the word can refer to a text or to a textual genre that does not attempt to describe actual happenings, as in 'Little Red Riding Hood', or it can refer to a claim that deals with supposed events in the real world, but which is false. I presume that you are advocating the use of fictional genres, but that you are not suggesting that sociologists should make a point of proposing false statements about the social world.

Yes, you're right. My failure to make this distinction was confusing. Whereas the biochemists I mentioned were trying to distinguish between fact and fiction in the sense of true and false statements about the world, I am trying to distinguish between different forms of discourse that we can use to talk and write about the world. Your last comment enables me to emphasize that there is no necessary, or even close, connection between the use of a fictional form, such as imaginary dialogue, and the endorsement of false statements about the world.

I think that sociologists', and others', avoidance of fictional forms has largely rested on the assumption that 'facts' are symbolic expressions which have a one-to-one relationship with 'reality'. It seems to me, however, that we never have access to that supposed reality. It is always mediated by some kind of symbolic representation (Mulkay, 1979). There's no way of separating reality from the symbolic realm of human discourse and no way in which reality as such can be used to check our factual claims. Thus, both facts and fictions are interpretative creations. The propositions of factual texts are no more a direct representation of the real world than are the contents of fictional texts. Both kinds of text are imaginative reconstructions of the world, in so far as that world is mediated through our own and others' interpretative work. My view is that 'fact' and 'fiction' are not distinguished by some radically different relationship with an independently real world, or even by some radically different use of empirical evidence, but are rather labels which we attach to forms of discourse which formulate and present their propositions through significantly different conventions.

Fact and fiction, then, are for me forms of discourse (Hanson, 1969), neither of which has a privileged relationship to the world in which we are interested. Given that I am proposing below that we should explore the sociological possibilities that are opened up by new forms of discourse, it is inevitable that I shall be recommending forms which are not at present seen as suitable for empirically based sociological analysis (see Latour, 1980). Because 'factuality' is an aspect of discourse, my exploration of new forms of discourse will involve a move away from orthodox conceptions of factuality. In proposing new forms of analysis, I am necessarily proposing a redrawing of the boundary around 'factual discourse'. The discourse of much sociological research, it seems to me, is founded on a nineteenth-century conception of the relationship between fact and theory (i.e. scientific discourse) and the world; it embodies a traditional conception of scientific rationality. Only by changing and extending the scope of our analytical discourse can we create new forms of interpretative rationality which are designed for and appropriate for the study by human actors of meaningful human action.

OK. I will accept that one can talk validly about social action in many different ways and that the discourse of the social sciences, modelled on that of the more advanced sciences, is only one way of representing the social world. I will also accept that these other forms of discourse can have a factual component. After all, as we both know, the natural sciences used dialogic forms at least up to the writings of Galileo. But, surely, there are three distinctive features of technical scientific discourse which may well be irretrievably lost by your approach: first, scientific claims about the natural world often embody original discoveries about that world which, secondly, can be validated by experimental replications. Thirdly, much scientific knowledge is further validated by successful practical application. It seems to me most unlikely that fictional forms of discourse can ever generate discoveries, can ever be replicated or can ever give rise to effective practical application. Thus the great disadvantage of your proposed move towards dialogic and fictional forms is that it will make discovery, replication and hence successful practical advance quite impossible. I recall, from what the Book said, that you deal with these three topics below. So I suppose you have some kind of answer to my criticism.

I'm very pleased that you've raised these issues. I was hoping that you would. Replication and discovery are, as you say, dealt with extensively below. I think it will become clear in Parts 2 and 3 that discovery and replication are much more complex than you imagine. As far as discovery is concerned, I suggest that non-scientific discovery occurs all the time, even in the realm of fictional discourse. However, such non-scientific discovery is absorbed fairly quickly into everyday discourse and as quickly becomes invisible. In other words, one characteristic of non-scientific discovery is that it is seldom recognized or celebrated as a discovery for long. It soon becomes 'what everyone knows' (Brannigan, 1981). In contrast, scientific discovery is culturally segregated and is constantly reaffirmed and celebrated by scientists; even though the existence or nature of each supposed discovery is highly problematic for those involved and even though the meaning of each discovery will be subsequently transformed out of all recognition. Consequently, I think it is quite misleading to propose that scientific discourse is to be preferred because it has a monopoly over discovery. I suggest that scientific discourse sustains the appearance of continual discovery by means of a particularly numerous and intense series of ritual celebrations.

As far as replication is concerned, I see no reason why one cannot replicate, that is, confirm previous conclusions, by means of more dialogic and imaginative forms. I hope that it will become clear in subsequent chapters that quite 'different' textual forms and arrangements of words can be taken to substantiate the 'same' conclusions. (I place the words 'same' and 'different' in quotes, because I will later suggest that sameness/difference is itself a subtle interpretative accomplishment.) In short, I want to propose that dialogic forms of analysis enable us to extend our analytical scope, without preventing us in any way from replicating or confirming prior conclusions, if we so wish.

With respect to practical application, my argument is even stronger. I suggest that whereas analysis formulated in terms of the empiricist monologue creates an interpretative relationship between analyst and participant which is inappropriate and which hinders practical implementation, certain forms of analytical dialogue can be of direct practical benefit to participants.

In this connection, it is worth thinking about the notion of 'applied social science', which notion is modelled on the situation taken to be characteristic of the natural sciences. The customary idea of applied science seems to be that after the scientist has established a reliable body of knowledge about a natural domain, that knowledge can then be put to practical effect by, or with the guidance of, the scientist (Potter and Mulkay, 1983). The critical part of this view of applied science is, in the present context, that the scientist alone is taken to be competent to decide what can and cannot be done in practical terms. Only the scientist can identify the natural limits within which the layman can exercise choice in practical matters.

This model is derived from areas of investigation where the object of study, say electro-magnetic radiation or the migration of birds, is assumed not to contribute in any active way to the creation of scientific knowledge. Furthermore, these interpretatively inert objects of study are often not available to the layman and for this reason the layman is seldom able to challenge the scientist's technical expertise. Thus the only person who can speak reliably about or on behalf of such phenomena seems to be the scientist. The discourse of the scientist is privileged because the phenomena are taken to be *objects* of study or of manipulation and because laymen are taken to be technically uninformed and incompetent. In general terms, it is taken as reasonable and appropriate that the scientist working on such phenomena should claim a special privilege for his technical discourse and should claim the right to legislate about technical matters relating to his field. Both laymen and the objects of study are deemed to be incompetent to challenge the scientist's authoritative discourse on practical matters.

However, this view seems much less appropriate when it is displaced to the realm of social action. For in this case the object of study, that is, meaningful action/discourse, is not only available to but is actually provided by those social actors to whom the sociologist may try to give practical advice. In other words, the objects of study for sociologists are neither inaccessible to the layman nor devoid of meaning for the layman. Consequently, it seems much less appropriate for the sociologist to claim the right to legislate on practical matters related to his technical discourse. The discourse of the sociological analyst and that of the layman are inevitably much more closely linked than is the case today in the natural sciences. Not only does the layman provide the initial interpretative material for the sociologist, but he is also capable of understanding, modifying or repudiating the sociologist's gloss on that material. In short, the sociologist's version of the social world is in many respects dependent on and at the same interpretative level as participants' versions (Yearley, 1984). When offered practical advice by the sociologist, the layman is always able to talk back.

It is difficult, then, to see how the sociologist can ever appropriately claim the kind of interpretative privilege in practical matters which the natural scientist asserts. Yet traditional sociology, when it imitates scientific discourse, is likely to approach the possibility of applied social science in a manner similar to the natural sciences. In so far as sociologists claim to know the facts about some part of the social world, in so far as they claim to know how some area of social life really works, they seem also to be claiming the right to identify the limits of practical intervention, whatever the layman may say in response. Implicit in the discourse of sociology as a social science, it seems to me, is the idea of sociology as a basis for interpretative domination in practical matters.

There is, I believe, an alternative to this Comtean conception; and that is of sociological analysis as a collaborative dialogue between analyst and participant. This has already been mentioned as one of the forms of analytical dialogue which is explored below (Chapter 3). Through such collaborative dialogue it may be possible for analyst and participant to converse together and to learn from each other, with neither party claiming interpretative dominance.

It *may* be, of course, that such a dialogue can only take place under exceptional circumstances and that the joint exploration of a common topic by interpretatively equal analysts and participants can occur very seldom. But I'm not so sure that this is so. I suspect that this kind of collaboration lies partly hidden behind the text of many sociological studies. I've always thought, for example, that the gang leader Doc should have been given much of the credit for Whyte's *Street Corner Society* (1955); but that, of course, would have been taken to contravene the supposedly essential distinction between analyst and participant. I recommend, therefore, that we become less reluctant to allow participants to speak openly through our own texts. I recommend that we abandon the customary practice of either taking over certain of participants' accounts and presenting them as our own or seeking to reveal the inadequacies of participants' accounts, and that we adopt new analytical forms which help us instead to display the variety of versions of social life which are always possible. Collaborative analytical dialogue is one such form which could deal with issues of practical interest to participants and, by involving them actively in sociological interpretation, might change their understanding, their discourse and hence their action; as well as helping us to avoid reifying our own empiricist versions of the social world. In this sense, the analysis itself could be, for both participant and analyst, an effective form of practical engagement.

Well, maybe. I can't really assess your remarks until I've read the Book and seen your approach in operation. I don't yet fully understand what you mean by 'analytical dialogue' and 'collaborative analysis'. It is becoming clear that I'm not able to sustain a proper dialogue with you at the moment, because you know the chapters below in detail and I do not. Consequently, our conversaton is not between interpretative equals.

I seem to be in danger of the kind of interpretative subjection that you mentioned a little while ago.

Yes, you're right. I did launch into a monologue instead of talking to you properly. Let's take that as a sign to stop now. I think that it is time for you to turn to the Book itself. You will recall that earlier the Book described some of the main features of its own text. Let me rephrase those remarks, in more dialogic terms of course, as a request: please don't approach the text expecting a conventional linear analytical development. The Book doesn't try to proceed from A to Z by means of a clearly accumulating argument. You should find that the text is constantly moving backwards as well as forwards; what comes later in the sequence is often intended to illuminate and redefine what has gone before. The Book is also intended to operate at several levels, to refer to itself whilst appearing to refer to other texts, and vice versa, to exemplify its own analysis, and to treat all texts, itself included, with quiet irony. You must of course, make of the text what you will, as I know that you will. Nevertheless, please try to imbue it most of all with the qualities of invention, subtlety and humour.

PART 1

Dialogues

1

Dialogue and Textual Agency: a Self-Commenting Discourse Analysis

This chapter examines the texts of a set of ten letters exchanged between two biochemists during the period September 1975 to June 1976. The letters were concerned with resolving what was described as a 'difference of opinion' about the technical issue of the stoichiometry of respiratory chain systems in mitochondria. For the purposes of this exercise in discourse analysis, it will not be necessary to understand all the technical details or theoretical ramifications of the debate contained in these letters. Whatever scientific commentary is required will be provided as the analysis unfolds.[1]

The stoichiometry letters have been said by those closely involved to have been unsuccessful. They are said to have been unsuccessful in the sense that the objective of 'resolving a difference of opinion' over stoichiometries appears not to have been achieved; and indeed the letters end with no apparent alteration in the incompatible claims of the two authors. Moreover, several years later both authors were still publishing papers defending their initial answers to the central question explored in the letters. The letters can also be said to have been unsuccessful in the sense that close observers sometimes describe them as having become increasingly bitter and a source of bad feeling.

If the 'failure' of this informal exchange of letters were unusual, one could easily treat it as being due to special features of this case which are unlikely to be repeated elsewhere. One might perhaps suggest that the letters were unsuccessful because there was a clash of personalities or because the scientific issues were exceptionally complex and therefore difficult to solve. However, every collection of letters dealing with initially unresolved scientific issues which I have obtained appears to have the same negative outcome; in no instance do the parties involved appear to have reached scientific agreement through this informal means of communication. In addition, one of the authors of these letters in due course explicitly asked me to examine the processes of informal communication in science, with the objective of helping him to understand why such communication was so seldom successful. It seems reasonable, therefore, to take as one point of departure in analysing the stoichiometry letters the possibility that there are recurrent problems with informal communication among scientists which may be evident, to some degree, in these letters.

It seems clear that a sequence of letters must involve participants in an explicit dialogue; that is, each author's contribution must be addressed directly to one or more other potential authors and designed in a way which encourages, or at least allows, a personal response to the previous contribution. It is important to note that this epistolary form of discourse is different from that used in scientific research papers. For example, the latter are usually written as impersonal monologues which are addressed, not to any specific scientist, but to a diffuse audience of interested specialists. Whereas experimental papers in the published literature formally report on various aspects of the natural world, letters tend to focus more openly on the arguments, claims and objections of particular scientists. In other words, the dialogic form of discourse essential to an informal exchange of letters necessarily differs in certain respects from the monologic form typical of the research literature. In this chapter, I will examine how the technical dialogue contained in the stoichiometry letters is textually organized, how it develops over time, how far conventions of discourse appropriate to the monologic research literature are introduced into the dialogue, and finally, whether this examination throws any light on the supposed failure of these letters.

Textual Commentator[2]   Dear Reader, at this point a new voice enters the present text; what the author would presumably call a new 'textual agent'. My goal is to make visible to you aspects of the present text which its author, without my help, is likely to ignore or suppress as irrelevant to his purpose, and which, therefore, will be withheld from or not appreciated by you, the Reader. The focus of our analyst's attention in the introduction above is firmly upon the letters which he is about to examine in detail. Consequently, he writes in a way which draws attention to the textual organization of these letters and away from the organization of his own text. Yet it is only by organizing his own text in a particular way that he is able to reveal to us what he wants to say about the texts of his scientists' letters. Indeed, it follows from his own analytical position, as I am sure will become clear below, that his own observations of the nature of scientists' discourse are inseparable from the interpretative work he carries out upon their texts as he constructs a text of his own.

I have observed our analyst at his desk from the moment he took up his pen and I will stay with him throughout the writing of this chapter. I will tell you some of the things which he, as he engages in analysing others' texts, forgets to say about his own practice of textual production.

The first thing that is apparent to me is that he does not yet have a clear idea of what he is going to write. That, I think, is what he means by calling the first version of this text a 'working paper'. (Of course, this heading will have disappeared by the time the analysis appears in print, even though its content may have changed very little.) Although he writes above that 'I will examine how the technical dialogue contained in the stoichiometry letters is textually organized', we must not imagine that he has already observed in the stoichiometry letters a clear structure which he is now about to describe. Rather, the writing of this chapter is itself his way of revealing a textual structure which is not yet fully evident to him, despite his tendency to write as if it is already there to be described. Thus, although the author's text presupposes that the letters have a describable textual organization, it is only through the successful completion of this chapter that this structure may be made accessible to the author as well as to us.

The author has, of course, carried out a great deal of preparatory work. In preparation specifically for this chapter, he has read through the letters numerous times as well as reading the research papers mentioned in the letters and the remarks made in interviews about the letters by interested parties. Each time he has gone through the letters he has made detailed notes on what he takes to be their textual organization. For example, he has done such varied things as examining the ways in which pronouns have been used in the letters; noting any occasions on which participants have agreed to alter their research papers in response to points made in the exchange of letters; and describing the use participants have made of such recurrent dichotomies as fact/opinion, simple/ complex and observation/interpretation.

It is clear that our analyst does not intend to use all this material here. For he has selected out for special attention a sub-set of notes headed 'dialogue', 'fact/opinion' and 'textual agency'. Drawing on these notes our analyst, like the scientists whose texts he is studying, has organized his opening paragraphs around certain dichotomous contrasts. Our analyst has relied mainly on the distinctions between informal and formal scientific communication, successful and unsuccessful discourse, and dialogue and monologue. Thus, in the same way that he can claim to reveal the organization of scientists' discourse, I can claim to do likewise with respect to his developing text. This is to be expected. All texts can be seen to be organized in terms of such semantic contrasts and other recurrent and describable interpretative devices. It is through the use of such devices that meaning is created, whether in scientists' letters or in discourse analysis. Thus our analyst has set himself the task of extending and building upon the semantic resources carried over from his notes into the opening of this text, in a way which makes possible an orderly description of certain features of the stoichiometry letters which the analyst himself at present only vaguely grasps.

Let us follow him into the unknown.

Fact, Opinion, Apology

Author   One way of organizing this chapter would be to summarize now the main sociological conclusions to be drawn from the stoichiometry debate and then to present extracts from the scientists' correspondence in a way which systematically illustrates these conclusions. This procedure would enable me to construct a relatively concise, clear and simple text of my own. But it would also, I think, tend unduly to impose the structure of my analysis upon the original scientific debate. Although the account I give of this debate must inevitably involve interpretation on my part, I want to stay as close as possible to participants' actual discourse. Consequently, I have chosen to examine the letters in detail one by one in chronological sequence. I will describe and comment on the textual organization of each letter in turn, thereby building up a gradual picture of the development of the complete dialogue, in a manner analogous to that experienced by the correspondents themselves. This means that the present chapter will be unusually long and complex. By the end, however, if I am at all successful, you will have been given the chance to catch more than a glimpse of the textual world of the debating scientists. My aim is to immerse us both in a particular kind of discourse and to help us both to understand intimately its character and its limitations.

Letter S1   Dr Peter Spencer to Professor Albert Marks, 30 September 1975 (eight paragraphs in length)
In this first letter, Professor Marks is addressed as 'Dear Al' and the letter is signed 'Warmest regards, yours sincerely, Peter'. This personal note is continued in much of the body of the letter, the first paragraph of which is as follows:

May I say how glad I was to see you again, after so long, at the meeting at Fasano. So I was all the more sorry that you were offended by my remarks about the need to distinguish between facts and opinions in the matter of the $\rightarrow H^+/O$ or $\rightarrow H^+/2e^-$ stoichiometry of respiratory chain systems and the $\rightarrow H^+/P$ stoichiometry of ATPase systems. Certainly, no offence was meant, especially since, having dabbled in theoretical matters a good deal, it may be suggested with some force that I myself may be especially susceptible to the trouble that comes from mistaking opinions for facts!

This opening paragraph takes the form of a direct, personal dialogue between Peter Spencer and Al Marks. The paragraph is dialogic in the sense that Spencer expresses sentiments which are addressed to Marks alone: 'I was glad to see you', 'I was sorry to have offended you'. This personal form of address is appropriate because Spencer is referring to a specific incident in which they were both involved; and also because personal feelings are being expressed, gladness for example, and a personal matter involving the two of them, namely, offence and apology, is being explicated.

The discourse of the first paragraph is organized around several simple dichotomies, the most obvious of which are gladness/sorrow and fact/opinion. These oppositions provide the main resources which Spencer uses to bring off the apology contained in paragraph one and to specify the supposed 'offence' which makes the apology necessary. The author of this paragraph, or, more correctly, the 'I' voice in the text, takes it as already known to both parties that Marks was offended by some remarks made by Spencer at the Fasano conference 'about the need to distinguish between facts and opinions. . .'. Although the precise nature of what could have been construed as offensive about these remarks is never made explicit, the final sentence of the paragraph shows that Marks is taken to have been offended by an apparent suggestion that he had 'mistaken opinions for facts' in the stoichiometry matter. This reveals that, for Spencer in S1, as well as, it is presumed, for Marks, 'fact' is the preferred category. To treat as a 'fact' what is really only an 'opinion' is taken to be a mistake; and to be accused of having made such a mistake can be construed as offensive. The whole organization of paragraph one rests on the assumption that fact is superior to opinion.

The effect of the final sentence in this passage is accomplished by Spencer's making his own discourse self-referring. He proposes that the remark uttered at Fasano could equally well be applied to him, because he has been especially inclined to 'dabble in theoretical matters'. (The text here seems to treat both 'theoretical matters' and 'opinions' as more or less equivalent to 'removed from the facts'.) It is suggested that the remarks at Fasano cannot really have been a condemnation of Marks's actions, because this condemnation would automatically include some/many of the speaker's own actions. Thus the force of Spencer's claim that no offence can have been meant depends on the assumption that scientists never (or very rarely) speak so as to condemn their own scientific views or actions. Spencer's claim seems to be: 'I cannot have intended my remark about fact and opinion to be offensive, because the remark applies at least as much to me as it does to you and clearly I would not say offensive things about my own scientific views.' It has been suggested elsewhere that scientists persistently take for granted the propriety of their own actions and the correctness of their own (scientific) claims (Gilbert and Mulkay, 1984). In paragraph one, Spencer takes the existence of this interpretative pattern for granted and employs it to repudiate what he takes to be Marks's view of his remarks at Fasano.

Paragraph one, then, works to remove a possible interpretative inequality between Marks and Spencer. It conveys that, despite what happened at Fasano, Spencer is not now claiming to have special access to a privileged 'factual discourse' about stoichiometry as opposed to Marks's 'mere opinion'. In this way, the personal issues discussed in the opening paragraph are used to prepare the way for the technical dialogue which follows. Not only does the focus on personal matters in paragraph one enable Spencer to address Marks in the direct, dialogic manner, so that it becomes possible to acknowledge that there are personal differences of scientific opinion, but it also enables him to establish, before he turns to the detail of the technical issue, that he and Marks are to be equal partners in the ensuing dialogue.

This dialogic equality is confirmed in the short, second paragraph of S1, where Spencer formulates the 'twofold purpose' of this letter: 'First to say again that I am sincerely sorry that I gave offence; and second to try to identify, and possibly resolve, what appears to be a difference of opinion between us.' An equality of interpretative status is assumed in the latter part of this sentence. Both Spencer and Marks are described as having 'opinions' about the stoichiometry issue. Neither of them is credited with having access to the facts. The purposes of the letter, apart from that of making an apology, are said, in the first place, to be that of identifying these opinions; presumably this means that Spencer and Marks should each use the letters to make their views clearer to the other party and to make sure that they have an accurate grasp of the other's views. Secondly, an attempt is to be made to resolve the apparent difference of opinion. Assuming that the 'apparent' difference turns out to be genuine, and taking for granted participants' distinction between fact and opinion, this seems to amount to deciding which set of opinions is factual and which is mere opinion. Thus paragraph two envisages that Spencer and Marks will engage in a combined attempt as *equals*, through a *direct person-to-person debate*, to decide which of their divergent sets of opinions should be *recognized as factual* and hence given *scientific superiority*.

The third paragraph takes up the task of clarifying the apparent difference of opinion. It consists of a concise formulation of what Spencer takes Marks's position to be in relation to the stoichiometry issue. In order to clarify the nature of this debate for non-biochemists, let me offer a brief and highly simplified outline of the scientific issue under investigation.

The Scientific Problem

The overall biochemical process which Spencer and Marks are studying is called 'oxidative phosphorylation'. In the process of oxidative phosphorylation energy is obtained from the oxidation of molecules derived from carbohydrates and fats. This energy is used to synthesize the biologically important molecule ATP (adenosine triphosphate). Oxidative phosphorylation takes place within units called 'mitochondria', which are small, peanut-shaped particles located in cells of living organisms. The basic events of oxidative phosphorylation are thought to occur in the vicinity of the inner membrane of mitochondria. Various kinds of movement across that membrane are taken to be essential to the processes whereby energy is made available for the production of ATP. The membrane and the basic processes of oxidative phosphorylation are schematically represented in Figure 1.

In this figure, we see that hydrogen atoms (made up of protons and electrons) from carbohydrates and fats are carried by molecules of NADH to a system of enzymes in the membrane. These enzymes are linked together to form what is known as the 'respiratory chain' (on the right of the figure). In the process of respiration, which is carried out by the respiratory chain, the protons and electrons of the hydrogen atoms become separated. It is thought that the electrons travel in pairs and that each pair of electrons crosses the membrane three times, each time at a different 'site' in the respiratory chain. At each crossing, a number of protons are transported from inside the membrane to the outside.

As a result of these processes of 'translocation', there is a build-up of protons and electrical potential on the outside of the

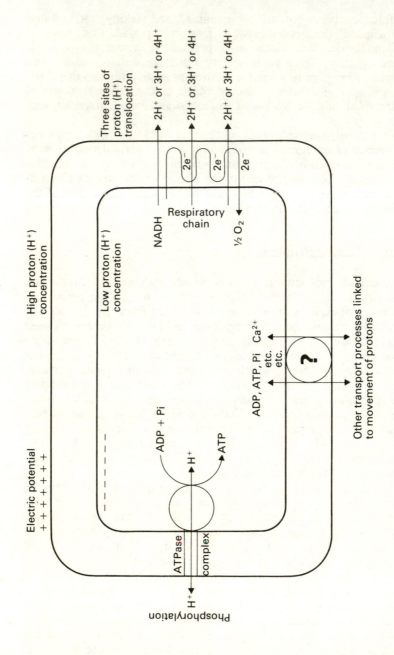

Figure 1 *Oxidative phosphorylation and the problem of stoichiometry.*

membrane. This gradient in proton concentration and electrical potential tends to force the protons on the outside back through the membrane. The energy of this gradient across the membrane drives the process of ATP synthesis. The protons return across the membrane through the ATPase (ATP-making) complex (on the left of the figure). As they do, they provide the energy necessary to join together ADP (adenosine *di*phosphate) and inorganic phosphate (Pi) to form ATP.

The issue with which Spencer and Marks are concerned in these letters is that of *how many protons cross the membrane to form each molecule of ATP*. The answers to this question are given in the form of ratios or quotients of various kinds. For example, the $\rightarrow H^+/2e^-$ ratio refers to the number of protons (H^+) which cross the membrane ($\rightarrow$) with each pair of electrons ($2e^-$) at each of the three sites in the respiratory chain. After their third trip back and forth across the membrane, the pair of electrons are taken to combine with oxygen in the matrix of the mitochondria to form H_2O. Thus a second measure of the movement of protons is the ratio of protons to oxygen consumed. This $\rightarrow H^+/O$ ratio will necessarily be identical with the $\rightarrow H^+/2e^-$ ratio. Finally, for our purposes, the number of protons which return from outside the membrane through the ATPase complex to form ATP can also be measured. Because ATP is taken to be formed by the combination of ADP and phosphate, this measurement is given as the H^+/P ratio. This ratio is not necessarily the same as the two previous ratios. The study of such ratios in chemical reactions is called stoichiometry.

During the ten years or so before these letters were written, Spencer had formulated the chemiosmotic theory of oxidative phosphorylation. The account given above of the process of oxidative phosphorylation employs the terminology and basic assumptions of that theory. Spencer had reported in several experimental papers that the three stoichiometries described above were equal to 2·0 and he had developed various details of his theory on the assumption that 2·0 was the correct figure. The stoichiometry of 2·0 had subsequently been confirmed by other researchers. During the early 1970s, Marks had written a number of papers which had some bearing on the proton stoichiometries, and at the Fasano meeting in 1975 he produced experimental results which, he claimed, showed that the $\rightarrow H^+/2e^-$ stoichiometry was not 2·0 but 4·0. It was in the discussion of these results that the 'difference of opinions' crystallized which Spencer seeks to address in this exchange of letters. One of the central problems in measuring the proton stoichiometries lies in the fact that there are a large number of other movements across the membrane, which are taken to be linked to the 'primary' movement of protons involved in ATP synthesis. Much of the technical discussion focuses on the issue of how to make allowance for these other movements (see Figure 1).

Preparation for a Dialogue

In paragraph three of S1, Spencer formulates a version of Marks's position on the stoichiometry issue. In this formulation he maintains the dialogic form of the preceding paragraphs.

> I understood, from what you said in your paper on $Ca^{2+}/\sim$ and $\rightarrow H^+/2e^-$ stoichiometry at Fasano, that you interpret your current work (along with your earlier studies) to mean that the $\rightarrow H^+/2e^-$ ratio . . . averages out very close to 4·0 . . . You associated yourself with Barnes in suggesting that the $H^+/2e^-$ values obtained in your research were not in agreement with the $\rightarrow H^+/2e^-$ quotients of close to 2·0, obtained by other research workers, and that the latter value was an underestimate attributable to technical difficulties associated with the complexities of the ion [ion = charged particle, e.g. H^+, Ca^{2+}, e^-] movements accompanying the translocation of H^+ ions by the respiratory chain.

'I' (Peter Spencer) continues to address his statements directly to 'you' (Al Marks) as he deals with these technical matters. Spencer uses this personal mode of address to emphasize that both parties are involved in complex interpretative work which could, it is implied, be mistaken. 'I understood', writes Spencer, 'from what you said', that your views are as follows. This formulation recognizes that the author might have misunderstood what had been said, in the same way that Marks has previously been depicted as misunderstanding what was said at Fasano. Similarly, Marks's supposed view of the $\rightarrow H^+/2e^-$ stoichiometry is presented in terms which emphasize that it is a personal interpretation of, one possible meaning extracted from, experimental work which could, in principle, be given different meanings: 'I understood that you interpret your work to mean that the ratio is very close to 4·0.'
Attention is also drawn to the possibility of alternative interpretations by the reference to the 'quotients of close to 2·0 obtained by other research workers'. Thus the continuation of the form of personal dialogue in this paragraph enables the author to attribute a particular technical formulation to his potential partner in the dialogue and to bring out the fact that such technical views,

in this case those of the recipient, depend on interpretative work which may be open to criticism.

By the end of the third paragraph, therefore, the ground has been prepared for a direct technical dialogue between interpretative equals about the correctness of the interpretative work which is required in reaching definite conclusions with respect to the $H^+/2e^-$ stoichiometry. At this point, Spencer begins a new paragraph with the first explicit request for dialogue: 'I would be very grateful if you would be prepared to discuss this matter with me privately through the post. . .' This is followed by three further paragraphs in which the author assumes that there will be a positive answer to his request and in which he returns to the task of preparing for the dialogue to come. More specifically, these paragraphs are devoted to making sure that both parties are using the stoichiometry quotients in the same manner. Spencer admits, however, that although 'it is obviously vital to make quite certain', there is 'little room for doubt' that they are using the same definitions. Hence, he concludes that there almost certainly is a real difference of opinion to be resolved. He then adds a final technical reminder: the quotients 'are derived coefficients, interpreted from experiments, and are not actual unprocessed values taken from experimental data that may include effects of systems other than the ones considered above, for which the quotients are supposed to be characteristic'.

There is an important contrast between Spencer's definition of the $\rightarrow H^+/2e^-$ quotient in the preceding paragraph and the phrasing of this methodological *caveat*. The quotients are defined initially as 'the *actual number* of protons' crossing the membrane. But we are then told that the quotients 'are *not actual* unprocessed *values*'. It appears, then, that although the issue to be resolved is how many protons actually cross the membrane, the actual number of protons is not the same as the number of protons actually observed. Thus the quotients are said to be both actual numbers of protons and derived coefficients dependent on scientists' interpretations. There appears to be a potential disjuncture here between the initial definition of proton stoichiometry, which treats the quotients as describing actual elements in the biochemical system of ATP production, and the methodological conception of these quotients, which treats them as describing necessarily derived/interpreted elements in that system.

Moreover, the methodological conception appears to treat the ATP system itself as an artificial, experimentally constructed system. As Spencer points out, the synthesis of ATP in mitochondria is assumed to be intimately linked to processes such as transport across the membrane of ATP, ADP and phosphate.

Thus he seems to be saying that the meaning attributed to what can be observed about proton translocation in mitochondria must always depend on how one interprets the effects of other related systems. In other words, the facts about the actual numbers of protons which Spencer is involved in establishing in the course of the proposed dialogue are taken by Spencer himself to be complex interpretations about facets of an idealized, experimentally constructed system.

Spencer's aim seems to be to abstract from the complex, multifunctional and interdependent movement of protons and other ions across the mitochondrial membrane that movement of protons which is responsible for ATP synthesis. This 'primary system of ATP synthesis', as it is sometimes called, can never be 'observed' outside the biochemists's laboratory. Yet it is a measurement taken from this idealized experimental system that Spencer in S1, and Marks in later letters, term the 'actual number of protons'. There seems to be an implicit paradox built into the discourse about the factual/interpretative nature of the $\rightarrow H^+/2e^-$ stoichiometry which, as we will see, comes increasingly to provide a central focus for the ensuing dialogue.

Spencer's first letter ends, as it began, on a personal note: 'Please forgive me if this seems long-winded, but I am anxious to prepare the way for a successful and enjoyable dialogue.' In this discussion, I too have treated S1 as a preparation for dialogue. I have tried to make sense of its textual organization within its own frame of reference. This does not mean, of course, that the comments above provide the only possible or only legitimate reading of S1. My reading is organized so as to generate an understanding of the accomplishment of success and failure in informal scientific communication. An indefinite number of alternative readings, focused around different concerns, are clearly possible. I could, and probably will, produce other analyses which make somewhat different use of the text of S1. In so far as these analyses differ from the present chapter, the meaning given to S1 will necessarily alter. Another possibility is that some participants might treat S1, for instance, as 'another example of Spencer dogmatically resisting experimental evidence which disproves his theory'. However, such a reading differs from mine in several respects: it takes sides in the scientific debate; it attributes particular kinds of motives and actions to the participants in order to explain the text; it assumes special knowledge of what the text really means; it rejects certain parts of the text as insincere or rhetorical; it implies that the real meaning of S1 can be established by reference to definitive readings of other relevant texts (i.e. utterances as well as documents).

In contrast, my reading focuses as closely as possible on the internal characteristics of S1 as a text. It is concerned, in the terms of semiotics, with the play of signifiers within the text. My concern is to describe what is established within the text of S1 and how. Readings which go beyond my own are possible; but they would, I suggest, have to take into consideration the sorts of textual features to which I have drawn attention. For instance, a reader might deny that Spencer was really apologizing in S1. Nevertheless, he would have to recognize that S1 contains an arrangement of discourse which conveys an apology. Thus, my analytical reading of these texts is not undermined by the possibility of alternative readings. Rather, such alternative readings are irrelevant to my concerns; except in so far as they provide, in turn, additional texts to be internally deconstructed.

I have treated S1, in its own terms, as a preparation for technical dialogue. I have tried to describe some of the ways in which the resources of scientific and everyday discourse are organized to accomplish this preparation. I have suggested that in preparing for further discourse, S1 focuses on establishing the discursive framework within which further technical debate might take place. Specifically, I have proposed that S1, within the confines of its own text, does the following things:

(1) It consistently adopts a style of address appropriate to direct, personal debate.
(2) It proposes a personal debate between interpretative equals.
(3) It removes an interpretative asymmetry which may have been created previously and which would have pre-judged the outcome of the proposed dialogue.
(4) It assumes a distinction between factual discourse and opinion.
(5) It assumes that factual discourse is scientifically superior to opinion and that the aim of the dialogue is to establish which of the competing positions on stoichiometry is factual.
(6) Thus it assumes that, if the letters are 'successful', they will establish the kind of interpretative inequality which is avoided in S1.
(7) It makes use of the assumption that scientists take for granted the correctness of their own scientific views.
(8) It formulates the author's understanding of the recipient's scientific position.
(9) It accomplishes this formulation in a manner which emphasizes the interpretative character of the recipient's position.
(10) It provides two versions of the meaning of stoichiometry quotients which appear potentially difficult to reconcile, in that one version treats stoichiometries as firmly within the

factual realm, whilst the other appears to treat stoichiometries as necessarily interpretative and closer to the category
of 'opinion'.

S1 is a particularly rich text for discourse analysis, because it is
more concerned with establishing the grounds for discourse than
with actively engaging in the stoichiometry debate as such. As we
examine the way in which S1 sets out the framework for an
informal dialogue, we can already see some of the difficulties which
lie in store; how far is it possible to maintain interpretative equality
whilst demonstrating the inadequacy of the other's scientific
assertions? How far is it possible to sustain a personal mode of
address whilst claiming to report on the actualities of the
biochemical phenomena? How far is it possible to bring about
significant changes in others' technical formulations if others'
discourse is premised on the validity of these formulations? How
far is it possible to establish unequivocally how many protons
'Actually cross the membrane', when the assertions of all parties
can be treated as interpretations formulated with respect to
artificially constructed systems?

Let us see how Spencer and Marks deal with these problems in
practice in the rest of the letters.

Dialogue Rejected

*Letter M1.   Professor Marks to Dr Spencer, 12 November 1975 (six
paragraphs in length)*
In his reply to S1, Marks initially continues the form of direct,
personal address begun by Spencer. Marks also takes over, with
some modification, certain elements from the structure and content
of Spencer's letter. For instance, he too begins with an apology, in
this case for being so slow to reply. He also refers to the pleasure
derived from their reunion at Fasano, and he expresses sorrow
about their having come 'to an apparent disagreement, particularly
because we also would like to "separate fact from fiction" with
regard to the stoichiometry of H^+ ejection during mitochondrial
electron transport'.

Marks's alteration of Spencer's distinction between 'fact and
opinion' to 'fact and fiction' plays a significant part in the textual
organization of M1. In the first place, it clearly strengthens the
opposition between the two categories; opinions may sometimes be
correct, but fictions are necessarily quite distinct from the facts. As
M1 unfolds, we see that it is organized around this distinction in
that one of the letter's main textual accomplishments is to show

that Spencer's attribution of scientific meaning to his experiments is based on a fiction; whereas Marks's attribution of meaning is required by the facts. As this accomplishment proceeds, the personal pronouns through which Marks himself has appeared as a personal agent in the text of the letter tend to disappear and Marks comes to be replaced as the main textual agent by the supposed experimental facts themselves (Latour and Woolgar, 1979; Knorr-Cetina, 1981; Gilbert and Mulkay, 1984).

In the second paragraph of M1, immediately following the statement that both parties want to separate facts from fiction, Marks maintains the direct dialogue between himself and Spencer as he corrects one of the latter's statements in S1. Spencer had written that 'the $\rightarrow H^+/2e^-$ values obtained in your [Marks's] research were not in agreement with the $\rightarrow H^+/2e^-$ quotients of close to 2·0, obtained by other research workers'. Marks clearly repudiates this part of Spencer's attempt to formulate his [Marks's] position:

> I might say at the outset that we have been able to reproduce quite easily your basic oxygen-pulse experiments of 1965–1967, with identical results, i.e. with $\rightarrow H^+$ site ratios (which we also define, by the way, as the number of H^+ ions ejected per pair of electrons per energy-conserving site) close to the value of 2·0 which you reported. So there is no difference between us on this particular fact. But where we may differ is in the meaning of the value 2·0 obtained under the conditions you employed.

In the course of this direct exchange, Marks portrays himself as rectifying a mis-formulation on Spencer's part. Spencer is treated as having taken their difference of opinion to involve a disagreement at the observational level. Marks responds by stating that there is no observational disagreement, in the sense that he obtains the same measurements as Spencer when he observes under the same experimental conditions. That Spencer's experimental conditions generate (apparent) stoichiometries of 2·0 is described as an agreed fact. But Marks stresses that this experimental fact has no conclusive implications for the 'true value' of the $\rightarrow H^+/2e^-$ stoichiometry. This 'fact' is formulated by Marks as a statement of what biochemical observations follow from a given experimental set-up. The scientific meaning of this observational regularity, however, is taken to be open to various, different interpretations, depending on how well one understands what is actually happening in that experimental set-up.

At this point in M1, Marks separates fact from scientific meaning and emphasizes that the scientific meaning of experimental facts

involves interpretation in the light of the experimental conditions
adopted in the experiment in question. By separating 'fact' from
'meaning' and 'observed values' from 'true values', Marks depicts
Spencer and himself as necessarily being involved in an interpretative activity. It appears from the last quotation above that the
main task of the participants in this debate is not to establish the
facts, but rather to identify the meaning or correct interpretation to
be given to the facts. In this passage, Marks seems to depart from
the previous statement about seeking to distinguish fact from
fiction. For now he is presenting himself as trying to establish the
correct meaning of facts which are agreed and, therefore,
unproblematic.

Marks's statements in M1 about the variable meanings which can
be given to an observational regularity have significant consequences for his dialogue with Spencer. Once he has textually
established that experimental facts are open in principle to different
interpretations, Marks is able to reveal how Spencer has come to
adopt a wrong interpretation. Put in the simplest possible terms,
Marks proposes that Spencer failed to make proper allowance for
the movement of calcium across the mitochondrial membrane and
that this failure led him to underestimate the number of protons
actually being transported:

> In brief, we were led to question whether your observed value of
> $2 \cdot 0$ represents the true value of the primary H^+ pumping process
> coupled to electron transfer, or whether it reflects in part the
> occurrence of other ion movements [in particular the movement
> of calcium] that were not measured in your early experiments.

In order to appreciate in detail how Marks employs his
distinctions between fact/scientific meaning and fact/fiction as
resources in the technical debate, it is necessary to look a little
more closely at the nature of the scientific argument. Let me
provide a version of Marks's criticisms of Spencer's experiments
which is designed for non-biochemists.

Both parties accept that electron transport along the respiratory
chain within the mitochondrial membrane moves positively charged
elements (positive ions) from inside the membrane to the outside.
Their aim is to establish how many positively charged hydrogen
ions (H^+, protons) are moved across the membrane by each pair of
electrons; but they both accept that observation of proton
movement is difficult because the movement of other ions is linked
in various ways to the process of electron transfer. Marks focuses in
the Fasano paper on the movement of calcium ions (Ca^{2+}) from
outside to inside the membrane. Ca^{2+} transport must be taken into

consideration when trying to measure the $\rightarrow$H$^+$/2e$^-$ stoichiometry, because it brings positive charges back across the membrane. Thus in measuring how many positive charges actually cross the membrane as a result of electron transfer, allowance must be made for those which may have returned across the membrane in the course of Ca^{2+} transport. Marks proposes in the Fasano paper and in M1 that Spencer has underestimated the number of positive charges brought back by Ca^{2+} transport and is, therefore, also under-estimating the number of H$^+$ transported by electron transfer. Marks suggests that when one properly understands the nature of Ca^{2+} transport, one comes to see that for every 2H$^+$ measured in Spencer's experiments, another 2H$^+$ have returned across the membrane and have gone unobserved. Thus, the 'true value' of the $\rightarrow$H$^+$/2e$^-$ quotient per site is not 2·0 but 4·0.

I had once accepted the hypothesis, as you have, that Ca^{2+} is transported through the mitochondrial membrane by an electrogenic antiport with one H$^+$, i.e. with net movement of only 1 positive charge. Such a mechanism seemed to be the simplest way of rationalizing inward transport of 2Ca^{2+} at the expense of the electrochemical potential generated when 2H$^+$ are ejected. However, this view of the Ca^{2+} transport process is a 'fiction', if I may use the word; in any case it never had any experimental support. Wood's experiments, which we were able to repeat and have refined further, clearly point to an electrogenic uniport process of Ca^{2+} transport, as do certain other experiments reported by Slim and Berger. We therefore feel we must interpret our results on the basis of the electrogenic uniport pattern, involving net transport of two positive charges in the form of Ca^{2+}. Our data on accumulation of 2Ca(BOH)$_2$ per site therefore indicate that electron transport causes ejection of 4H$^+$ per pair of electrons per site, or a total of 12 in the complete chain from NADH to oxygen.

In this passage, Marks makes use of his prior distinction between fact and fiction. The hypothesis about calcium transport which supposedly informs Spencer's interpretation of his experiments is said to be a fiction and to be without experimental support. At this point in the text, Marks abandons the contrast between 'facts', which have no clear scientific implication, and 'meaning' which necessarily involves contingent interpretation. This latter distinction had enabled Marks to acknowledge Spencer's experimental facts without accepting his interpretation. However, in asserting the validity of his own interpretation, Marks selects a different terminology for comparing the two sets of views; that is, he distinguishes between 'fiction', which does not depict the real world, and 'facts', which by implication do depict the real world. By using this alternative treatment of experimental 'fact', Marks can portray the basis for Spencer's interpretation as imaginary; whilst implying that, in contrast, his own interpretation simply reflects the experimentally demonstrated realities of calcium transport.

I am suggesting, then, that Marks uses two different conceptions of 'fact' in M1. These are created by placing the term 'fact' within two distinct dichotomies. The two dichotomies and the two conceptions of 'fact' are used to contribute in differing ways to the textual demolition of Spencer's stoichiometry quotient. The fact/scientific meaning dichotomy is treated by Marks as equivalent to his distinction between observed values and true values. It enables him to insist that although Spencer has identified a fact or observational regularity, the true scientific meaning of that fact has yet to be demonstrated. Having established that all facts have to be properly understood Marks has the interpretative space in which to show how Spencer can be scientifically incorrect, despite having got his facts right.

It seems possible, in principle, that Marks could, at this point in M1, have redefined the central objective of the stoichiometry dialogue as being not the establishment of 'the facts' about stoichiometry, but rather the formulation of an acceptable interpretation. If he had departed in this way from the initial distinction, carried over from Fasano, between fact and opinion, it might have been possible for him to sustain for much longer the dialogue between interpretative equals formally implemented by Spencer in S1. It might have been possible for him to treat Spencer and himself as equally engaged in complex interpretative work which, in principle, could never be reduced to the establishment of unproblematic facts.

Marks, however, does not take up this apparent option. Instead, as we have seen, he turns to his alternative fact/fiction dichotomy and, in the long passage quoted above, Spencer's fiction is contrasted with a position which Marks appears to be virtually forced to adopt by the unquestionable biochemical facts. As Marks moves from his repudiation of the fictional view of calcium transport to the formulation of the correct view, so the pronoun 'I', through which Marks speaks directly to Spencer, gives way to increasingly impersonal linguistic forms: 'Wood's experiments . . . clearly point to . . .'; 'We therefore feel we must interpret . . .'; 'Our data . . . indicate . . .'; 'These observations strongly indicate . . .'; 'Moreover, the fact that [other] ion-transporting ATPases . . . transport 3 or 4 positive charges . . . forms an important general argument for a H^+/site value greater than 2·0.'

In these phrases, the agents which formally express themselves are, preponderantly, not Marks or other interpretative agents, but experiments, data, observations and facts. Marks here adopts what has been called the 'empiricist repertoire' of scientific discourse (Gilbert and Mulkay, 1984); he becomes, as a result of the linguistic forms employed, part of the audience for his own text. The text presents the experiments, data, observations and facts as pointing to, indicating and addressing arguments *to* Marks. Marks is depicted in his own text as part of an audience which appears to be in receipt of the discourse of the biochemical world itself. As the text takes on the form of an impersonal monologue simply reporting the facts of the matter, the author himself inevitably withdraws from the text and is, consequently, unable to continue the direct, personal dialogue with Spencer. Such dialogue is now formally impossible because Marks has been replaced by other textual agents. Moreover, dialogue cannot be further sustained in M1 because Marks and Spencer are no longer interpretative equals in this text. Spencer is deemed to operate on the negative side of an interpretative dichotomy, so that even his reliable observations are rendered meaningless by their location in a discursive realm of fiction; whilst Marks, in contrast, when he appears in the text, writes from within the privileged domain of factual discourse. Personal dialogue between equals is no longer relevant for Marks, because his case has ceased to be a personal one; it is, rather, identical with that of the experiments, data, observations and facts.

Marks's withdrawal from the dialogue with Spencer, which is implicit in the style of his discourse in the central part of M1, is made explicit in the two concluding paragraphs.

You have suggested that we might have an exchange of letters regarding these questions. I am of course in total agreement that we should keep our communication lines open. However, I do not wish to engage in a round-robin exchange of letters. In my observations the exchanges of letters with Perry and Watson were not completely satisfactory. Rather than write long letters describing experimental details, I would prefer to communicate our findings to you in the form of drafts or reprints of papers submitted.

In this penultimate paragraph, Marks rejects Spencer's invitation to exchange views informally on a personal basis, on the grounds that a previous exchange of letters was 'not completely satisfactory'. He seems to imply that he does not expect such an exchange to be of much value to those involved. He then expresses a preference to continue to communicate 'in the form of drafts or preprints of papers submitted'. In other words, the judgement expressed here seems to be that direct, personal dialogue about stoichiometry is likely to be less satisfactory than communication via the impersonal, empiricist form of monologue which is characteristic of the research literature and which, as we have seen, actually tended to replace personal dialogue as M1 proceeded.

In these comments on M1, it may appear that I have been somewhat critical of Marks. But this is not so. My discussion will only seem to have been critical if Spencer's conception of direct, personal dialogue between interpretative equals is accepted as the ideal form of scientific discourse. It is possible that the empiricist monologue favoured by Marks may have significant advantages in practice over personal dialogue. After all, the former has gradually replaced the latter over time as the dominant form of scientific discourse and there may be important reasons why this is so. Furthermore, we do not yet know whether Spencer himself can sustain the dialogue for which he prepared the ground in S1. Perhaps we will learn more about the difficulties of pursuing scientific debate in dialogic form if we turn to Spencer's second letter in which he must, presumably, do more than just prepare the way for the stoichiometry debate.

Textual Commentator Excuse me for butting in again, dear Reader, but I simply have to draw your attention to the construction of the present text, in much the same way that our analyst is doing for the texts of dear Peter and dear Al. Our analyst has suggested not only that Al Marks has contravened some of the basic grounds for dialogue which are formulated in S1, but also that, in writing sometimes as if his technical formulations simply re-present the actualities of biochemical phenomena, Marks contradicts his own recognition elsewhere in M1 that scientific meaning is a complex interpretative achievement. Although our analyst denies that he is criticizing Marks's textual practice, he does seem to be suggesting that there are inherent contradictions or paradoxes built into the forms of discourse which the two biochemists are using.

However, our analyst's text seems to exemplify these contradictions just as clearly as those of his biochemists. He maintains that 'factuality' is accomplished by participants through certain forms of textual organization. These empiricist forms of discourse, he suggests, involve a hiding away of interpretative contingency and the adoption of a terminology which seems to allow the phenomena under study to speak directly through the author's text. But in identifying these forms of discourse in, for example, Marks's letter, our analyst employs the very same forms and accomplishes the 'factualtiy' of his reading of M1 through the systematic organization of his own text.

For instance, he has written above: 'In this passage, Marks makes use of his prior distinction between fact and fiction.' The actual words used by Marks quoted by the analyst were: 'this view of the Ca^{2+} transport process is a "fiction", if I may use the word; in any case it never had any experimental support'. Clearly, our analyst has interpreted Marks's words in order to establish their analytical meaning. Although Marks does not actually use the word 'fact' here, he is described by the analyst as 'making use of the prior distinction between fact and fiction'. The analysts' own textual work is evident.

The careful organization of his text is critical in allowing our analyst to construct his interpretation of the biochemists' letters. By choosing words in a particular manner, he is able in this instance to link Marks's description of the Ca^{2+} hypothesis as a 'fiction' to all the interpretative work which is carried out on fact/fiction and fact/scientific meaning by the analyst in this text as well as by Marks in M1. Yet the form of our analysts' assertion denies this implicit interpretation and its dependence on the detailed organization of the analytical text. For 'In this passage, Marks makes use of his prior distinction between fact and fiction' is couched as a simple impersonal description of the facts of the matter, of what the text undeniably says. Thus what is depicted by the analyst as a textual feature of M1 exists for the analyst, and for us, only through the interpretative work embodied in the organization of this present text. In his own textual practice, our analyst seems constantly to use forms of discourse which violate his own apparent view that meaning, whether it is the factuality of experimental results or the content of a written text, is itself necessarily a product of textual organization.

Dear Reader, does this not throw doubt upon the tenability of his analytical position?

Analyst Dear Commentator, although these remarks are formally addressed to a putative Reader, I assume that I, the author and analyst, can be that Reader. I want to propose, in reply to your concluding question, that your comments, far from throwing doubt on my analytical position, only serve to confirm it. For it would be totally incompatible with my claims regarding the textual construction of meaning if I were able to write a text which did *not* depend for its meaning on subtle organizational features. Of course the present chapter accomplishes its end through the interplay of signifiers within its own text! That certain of its features are empiricist and resemble those used by biochemists to accomplish factuality is equally to be expected. Avoidance of the empiricist repertoire does not make one's analysis less dependent on textuality; nor does use of empiricist forms necessarily prevent one from recognizing the interpretative nature of one's discourse.

You have chosen to comment on the present text as it is being formed. Your intervention makes this text more reflexive. You display some of the interpretative work on which it depends and you draw attention to parallels between its textuality and that of the biochemists' letters. But constant textual reflexivity is not obligatory. Textual reflexivity does not make a text any less reliant than other forms of discourse on the ordered interplay of signs. Nor does analysis of others' discourse necessarily imply a denial of one's own textuality. So, no more interruptions, please. Let us return to our biochemists.

Textual Representation of Dialogue

Letter S2.   Spencer to Marks, 17 November 1975 (sixteen mostly long paragraphs, including two postscripts)
This is a long letter and it will not be possible to examine it here in quite as much detail as the two previous letters. The first thing to be noted is that both authors subsequently mention that M1 and S2 must have crossed in the post. Thus S2 seems to have been written by Spencer without knowledge of Marks's reply to the first letter of the series. S2 is not a response to M1, but a continuation of Spencer's attempt to set the dialogue in motion. In S2, however, instead of preparing the way for a possible debate, Spencer enters into the fray and presents a detailed appraisal of certain aspects of Marks's interpretative work on stoichiometries.

Spencer begins by asking whether Marks had received S1. He then goes on to say that Marks would probably like to know that Barnes, with whose views Marks was said in S1 to be 'associated', was visiting Spencer's laboratory shortly 'in the hope of resolving the conflict of views about the $\rightarrow H^+/2e^-$ or $\rightarrow H^+/O$ stoichiometry of the mitochondrial respiratory chain . . .'. Spencer then uses these forthcoming discussions as an occasion for inviting Marks to send Barnes and himself any comments that might help them 'to make an accurate appraisal of the relevant facts and opinions'.

Having renewed the invitation to Marks to participate in the informal debate, and having reaffirmed the relevance of the distinction between facts and opinions, Spencer proceeds to remind Marks of the theoretical significance of the stoichiometry issue. He does this in a rather unusual way, by recreating some of the dialogue in which they had both taken part at Fasano.

Huxley's guidance of the evening discussion of the $\rightarrow H^+/2e^-$ question at Fasano brought out the great importance of deciding whether you are right in your contention that the Ca^{2+} uptake experiments show that the $\rightarrow H^+/2e^-$ quotient per energy transducing 'site' in the respiratory chain is $4\cdot0$. If your opinion is correct, the value of $2\cdot0$ found in my lab, and used as the basis of the present formulation of the chemiosmotic hypothesis, must be wrong. You may recall that Huxley asked me at Fasano whether I thought the chemiosmotic hypothesis would be invalidated if our value of $2\cdot0$ for the $\rightarrow H^+/\sim$ quotient in the respiratory chain were found to be wrong. I replied that, if I were frivolous, I would say 'no', but that, as I was serious about trying to develop a useful chemiosmotic rationale, I would answer 'yes'. When I went on to agree with Huxley that, in abstract principle, the chemiosmotic coupling concept was not wedded to any particular $\rightarrow H^+/2e^-$ value, Bill Fennell expressed concern that one seemed to be ready to consider shrugging off the serious consequences that would ensue if our $\rightarrow H^+/2e^-$ values were indeed found to be contrary to the facts.

Although this seems to me to be somewhat of an academic question at present, I must say that my sympathies are very much with Bill's point of view . . .

In this paragraph, Spencer offers us a picture of informal, person-to-person dialogue at the Fasano meeting. Not only are different scientists described as taking up radically different positions on the stoichiometry issue and on the scientific meaning of the various observations, but it is accepted that a specific individual is capable of coherently proposing quite divergent views. For Spencer depicts himself as capable of adopting various positions on the meaning of stoichiometry findings and his specific responses to this issue are portrayed as depending on more basic factors such as his decision to be 'serious' rather than 'frivolous', on his concern to develop 'a useful chemiosmotic rationale' rather than to defend the chemiosmotic theory merely at the level of 'abstract principle', and on his 'sympathies' with participants' 'point of view'.

In this passage, to a considerable extent, claims about scientific meaning are treated as being dependent on various kinds of individual human choices. Spencer here uses the language of scientific dialogue. He allows for the contingency of scientific discourse; for its ultimate dependence on human judgement and volition. The meaning of experimental observations appears not to be given in those observations themselves, but requires further interpretative work which is linked in a complex manner to various intangible considerations. The development of the stoichiometry debate appears to depend in this passage, to a considerable degree, on open-ended interpretative activity involving free interpretative agents.

However, this representation of the dialogic creation of scientific meaning is combined in S2 with an alternative conception. Consider the assertion, with which Spencer expresses 'sympathy', that serious consequences would ensue 'if our $\rightarrow H^+/2e^-$. values were indeed found to be contrary to the facts'. In this formulation, the language of dialogue disappears. This reference to 'the facts', in relation to which participants' quotients can be ultimately assessed, seems to imply that there is, after all, some particular and potentially available formulation which captures the way in which mitochondria really operate independently of scientists' activities and interpretations. 'The facts', when used in this way, are not another cogent interpretation of the available evidence; they express the nature of things and are used to repudiate all claims with which they are taken to be incompatible. When a scientist's quotient does not coincide with this ultimate validator, it seems that it must be abandoned, along with any theoretical interpretation which depends upon it. Clearly, in the passage quoted immediately above, as in M1 and S1, the author moves between such an 'empiricist' view of scientific meaning and the more interpretative conception employed by Spencer to depict direct personal dialogue. Nevertheless, although the two conceptions are used, it is the former to which authors are more strongly inclined when presenting their own views, and as S2 proceeds the impersonal, empiricist voice of 'the facts' comes to dominate, as it did in Marks's textual rebuttal contained in the previous letter.

Critique and Presupposition

In M1, we saw how Marks concentrated on some of the interpretative work which lay behind Spencer's stoichiometry claims and undermined that work within his own text by showing it to be inconsistent with 'the objective facts'. In S2, Spencer's procedure is similar; although, unlike Marks, Spencer does not link his criticisms to a presentation of new experimental results.

My general defence of our $\rightarrow H^+/2e^-$ value of 2·0, at Fasano, was that the respiratory pulse experiments that we employed to measure the $\rightarrow H^+/2e^-$ value were relatively simple, and that the variables which might have invalidated the result if they had been unknown and uncontrolled were comparatively easy to identify and to control . . . As Barnes showed in his paper at Fasano, there are a number of complicating factors that may influence the apparent $\rightarrow H^+/2e^-$ values . . . In the main papers on the $\rightarrow H^+/2e^-$ stoichiometries from my lab we discussed these complicating factors, and showed how to avoid being misled by them.

The Ca^{2+} translocation experiments, on which you base your estimated value of $4 \cdot 0$ for the $\rightarrow H^+/2e^-$ quotient, seem to me to be considerably more complex than our proton pulse experiments, and to be decidedly more susceptible to errors from unidentified variables or deficiencies in the general rationale.

This passage is taken from paragraphs four and five of S2. The text is still organized as a direct dialogue. However, Spencer and Marks are not, textually, equal partners in this dialogue. For Marks's views alone are carefully and persistently depicted as dependent on implicitly questionable interpretation. Marks's claims and measurements are always described in phrases such as 'apparent values', 'estimates' and 'contentions'. In this text, then, in exact opposition to M1, it is *Marks's* dependence on interpretative work which is highlighted; whilst Spencer's reliance on interpretation is portrayed as negligible. Indeed, as we see in the quote above, Spencer's 'general defence' of his value of $2 \cdot 0$ is that it is obtained from experiments which are so simple that their scientific meaning is unambiguous; whereas Marks's experiments are much more complicated and therefore susceptible to interpretative errors. Much of the rest of S2 is taken up with the demonstration of just how complex and difficult to interpret is the 'type of experiment' used by Marks.

This strategy, adopted by both authors, seems to be related to the dual conception of scientific fact which has appeared in every letter so far. The interpretative conception of 'fact' is used in criticizing one's opponent. The interpretative basis of the latter's views is made visible and emphasized as the author formulates the inconsistencies, uncertainties and mistakes perpetrated by his opponent. It is always possible for the author to find such errors, because the opponent's claims are inevitably assessed in relation to the author's differing conception of the facts and their scientific meaning.

In contrast, when formulating his *own* views, each author minimizes the interpretative work apparently involved. As a result, each author's position comes to appear in the text of each separate letter as indistinguishable from the observable realities of the biochemical world. It seems likely that this strategy, which reappears throughout the stoichiometry debate, is not knowingly chosen or even recognized in these terms by participants, but is a consequence of their use of common forms of critical discourse.

Because Spencer's textual demolition of Marks's typical experiment is quite general in character, we need only look at the broad outlines of his argument. He begins by suggesting that estimates of the $\rightarrow H^+/2e^-$ quotient become suspect if the initial experimental conditions and the final experimental conditions are not identical. If the final experimental state differs from the initial state, it is suggested, it becomes difficult to attribute any observed changes to the experimental variable. In Marks's experiments, it is proposed, the final experimental condition 'must always be different from' the initial condition: whereas in Spencer's experiments this is not so. 'The important question is, therefore, how different will the final State 4 condition be from the initial State 4 condition and how might this contribute (positively or negatively) to the translocation of Ca^{2+}?'

This question is addressed rhetorically to the two individual scientists engaged in the debate. However, the voice which replies is an authoritative impersonal voice which appears to know all the answers. This passage begins with a collective 'we' that seems to treat both participants as likely to endorse the apparently neutral description to follow. The impersonal voice then takes over and gives an account, which is textually independent of either participant, of what is really going on in Marks's experiments.

We can answer the above question qualitatively as follows. Before adding the Ca^{2+} pulse, the mitochondrial suspension would have been respiring in State 4 with a given protonic membrane potential $\Delta p = \Delta\psi - Z\Delta pH$, which was keeping respiration in the inhibited state. When the (small) Ca^{2+} pulse was added, Ca^{2+} would enter down the electric gradient and collapse the electric membrane potential $\Delta\psi$. But ΔpH, unlike $\Delta\psi$, would not be directly affected by the entry of the Ca^{2+} ions. However, the immediate effect of the collapse of $\Delta\psi$ would be to depress Δp and release respiratory inhibition, so that respiration and outward proton translocation would accelerate up to the State 3 rate. The consequence of the accelerated rate of respiratory proton translocation would be that *both* $\Delta\psi$ and $-Z\Delta pH$ would increase until Δp was brought back to its initial value. But, as only $\Delta\psi$ would initially be depressed by the entry of the Ca^{2+}, the final value of $\Delta\psi$ would be less than the initial value, and the final value of $-Z\Delta pH$ would be correspondingly greater than the initial value. This is the essential point: the increment in $-Z\Delta pH$, corresponding to the internal pH rise induced by entry of the pulse of Ca^{2+} in the usual well-buffered mitochondrial suspension, would define a shortfall in the recovery of $\Delta\psi$. As it is the electrical gradient (and not the pH gradient) that pulls the Ca^{2+} into the mitochondria, it is evident that the shortfall in the recovery of $\Delta\psi$ after entry of the Ca^{2+} pulse represents electrical energy used in Ca^{2+} uptake that is not restored by the respiratory pulse, and that this shortfall in $\Delta\psi$ must correspond to a shortfall in the extra oxygen used. In other words, your $\rightarrow Ca^{2+}/O$ quotients would be expected to exhibit super-stoichiometry of a different kind from that which you have so far identified.

One does not need to understand the technical details to be able to observe how, in this passage, Spencer's voice is replaced for an uninterrupted twenty-four lines (on the original copy) by a distinct and apparently independent voice which seems to offer a simple description of the experimental facts. However, in the last quoted sentence, we find that this unidentified textual agent has all along been addressing, not Spencer, but Marks alone: 'In other words, your $\rightarrow Ca^{2+}/O$ quotients would be expected . . .' The phrase 'in other words' indicates that the final sentence contains a summary of the preceding twenty-four lines; and we find that the summary is addressed to Marks. The impersonal, objective textual agent points out to Marks that he has made an interpretative error. This agent, although textually distinct from Spencer, clearly provides detailed support for the latter's general argument. Whereas it is Spencer who makes the general interpretative point that Marks-type experiments are likely to be difficult to interpret, it is the impersonal voice, in telling us precisely how such experiments work in detail, that reveals exactly where Marks has misinterpreted the facts.

Textually, then, the separation of the two voices, or the two textual agents, restricts the extent to which Spencer seems to be actively engaged in an interpretative clash with Marks. It is not, textually, Spencer who discloses Marks's error. It seems, from the text of S2, that Marks's mistake is inherent in the disjunction between the facts of the biochemical world and his misinformed interpretations. Spencer's text is organized in a way which displays to us that the revelation of Marks's error, although it occurs in a letter written by Spencer, is not due to Spencer's own interpretative work. S2 conveys to us that Marks's errors exist, whether or not Spencer happens to write about them.

On the photocopy of S2 in my possession, Marks or one of his colleagues has commented on the passage quoted above and on the next two pages of detailed analysis. The last part of the quoted passage is noted to be 'illogical' and subsequent of Spencer's statements and equations are marginally rejected or marked with question and exclamation marks. It appears from this textual gloss that the apparently factual parts of S2 can be read both as highly interpretative and, in their turn, as involving glaring errors. It is not the case that apparently factual texts are devoid of interpretation. It is rather that the interpretative work which can be attributed to them is partly hidden by the form of the text. In S2, and throughout this exchange of letters, the interpretations underlying the empiricist sections of text produce conclusions which, without fail, support the central claims about stoichiometry advanced by the author of that particular text.

The authors of these letters organize each text in such a way that it serves to substantiate their overall position. One way in which each author does this is by taking for granted the factuality of his own central conclusions and by employing them implicitly in constructing the argument in support of these conclusions. Let me offer an example from S2. We have already noted how, in paragraph five, Spencer states that, before Marks had even begun his stoichiometry experiments, Spencer and his colleagues had identified the factors which make such experiments difficult to interpret and had 'shown how to avoid being misled by them'. We can see that Spencer is here presupposing, in claiming to know what the complicating factors are and how they can 'mislead', *excatly what is at issue* in these letters, namely, his understanding of how such experiments actually work and, consequently, his knowledge of the 'true stoichiometry'. Throughout the correspondence, each author somehow manages to portray all relevant considerations in such a way that they seem to require the author to remain committed to his central position. This is what I mean by suggesting that the basic view of each author seems to be presupposed in all of his interpretative work.

There is an indication in the final paragraph of S2 that Spencer recognizes the asymmetrical organization of his letter to which I have been drawing attention. In this paragraph, Marks is addressed in personal terms and an attempt is made to prevent a possible 'misreading' of the preceding text:

I do hope that this letter does not seem to you to be unsympathetic or destructive. The object is simply to try to reach a mutually acceptable understanding of the facts and concepts in our field. I put my point of view at some length here to invite you to show where I have got the facts wrong, or where my reasoning or judgement may be at fault. In keeping with your chairman's introduction at Fasano, you may detect some 'passion' here between the lines. But if so, please be assured that its source is none other than good will.

There is an implicit recognition in the first sentence that, from Marks's perspective, S2 is almost entirely negative; that Marks's work on Ca^{2+} transport is made to seem scientifically worthless; and that the conclusions of S2 are entirely in accord with Spencer's own claims. The fact that Spencer then decides to restate the objective identified in S1 of 'reaching a mutually acceptable understanding of the facts and concepts' appears to indicate that, even for Spencer himself, the present text may seem to have deviated from the aim of balanced debate between interpretative equals. Thus Spencer acts in this paragraph to redress the interpretative imbalance in his own text by inviting Marks, in turn, to show where he has 'got the facts wrong' or made some other error. In stressing that there is 'none other than good will' behind the present text, the author's textual voice seems to be addressing once again the possible offence which can be caused by comparing one's own appreciation of the facts with another person's defective opinions. This passage may reasonably be paraphrased as saying: 'It may *look* as if I've been distinguishing my facts from your opinions, as I seemed to do at Fasano. But its not like that at all. In reality, I've presented my case as strongly as possible, in order to give you the chance of pressing your own case by revealing the inadequacies of my strongest formulation. Out of this process of vigorous critical debate, we can expect to establish a correct, and therefore mutually acceptable understanding.'

It is important to note, however, that even this implicit process of generating mutual understanding out of an exchange of selectively critical, asymmetrical, empiricist texts, which is offered to Marks to counteract the onesidedness of the preceding paragraphs, is very different from the personal debate between textual equals which seemed to have been recommended at the outset.

Textual Asymmetry

Letter M2.   Marks to Spencer, 17 December 1975 (six paragraphs in length)
Spencer's long letter criticizing Marks's experimental and infer-ential procedures receives in M2 a comparatively brief reply. The reply is short because, as in M1, Marks avoids becoming involved in any detail in the technical debate initiated by Spencer.

After the usual opening apologies, Marks writes in paragraph two as follows:

> My colleagues and I greatly appreciate the trouble you have taken in your analysis of the problems involving the use of Ca^{2+} uptake in the measurement of the H^+/site ratio. I recognize it as a more quantitative statement of the general argument you advanced quite a few years ago when you visited us here, at which time we discussed this question. Today we know a great deal more about the process of Ca^{2+} transport and its effect on the state of the mitochondria and I believe we can now answer this criticism. However, rather than respond to this matter in detail in this letter, I should like to point out again that we have carried out a re-evaluation of the H^+/site ratio by the oxygen pulse method, utilizing K^+ in the presence of valinomycin, rather than Ca^{2+} as mobile cation. We have also developed a third approach in which the steady-state rates of H^+ ejection and electron flow are compared. By the latter approaches we have also obtained values of H^+/site substantially in excess of $2 \cdot 0$ and approaching $4 \cdot 0$, results which confirm the conclusions we derived from our experiments on the stoichiometry of uptake of Ca^{2+} and BOH.

Although Marks maintains here that he and his colleagues greatly appreciate the trouble taken by Spencer in S2, he declines to respond in detail to Spencer's arguments. Marks makes it clear, however, that this must not be taken to imply that he *cannot* answer Spencer's criticisms. He describes the content of S2 as another version of an argument which Spencer had advanced 'quite a few years ago'. The power of Spencer's repeated criticism is weakened by contrasting it with the growing knowledge about Ca^{2+} transport which enables 'us' now to see its limitations. Thus in this paragraph, the individual scientist Spencer is treated as engaged in a dialogue with a 'we' who now 'know a great deal more' about the topic in question. It is unclear whether this 'we' refers merely to 'my colleagues and I' or to some wider body of scientists. Whichever it is, it is a group which, textually, *knows* about the processes of Ca^{2+} transport and from which Spencer seems to be excluded.

The impersonal collection of knowledgeable researchers implicit in M2 inevitably includes Marks, the textual first person. Paragraph two, then, provides a further example of the way in which the correctness of the author's position is assumed in the structure of these texts and of the way in which impersonal textual agencies speak on behalf of the author in a manner which creates interpretative inequality. The interpretative inequality of paragraph two is used to enable Marks to avoid having to examine Spencer's criticism in detail. He takes it as sufficient to have drawn to Spencer's attention that it is answerable in principle. Then, having briefly registered this point, he adopts his customary more positive approach of re-stating his own experimental findings.

The second half of the paragraph is organized to make Spencer's criticisms of the Ca^{2+} experiments appear irrelevant by emphasizing that the same H^+/site values are obtained with three different experimental methods. Thus, not only is the S2 argument out of date, but it focuses on only one of three kinds of experiment, all of which support Marks's central claim and undermine that of Spencer. In this way, the text deflects the criticisms advanced in S2 without ever getting involved in the type of experimental interpretation which is the central topic of S2. M2 sustains Marks's claims and rebuts Spencer's criticism about undue interpretative complexity without ever bringing Marks's supposed interpretative work into his own text for reconsideration. In these letters, each author avoids explicit mention in his own texts of the underlying interpretation which his adversary seeks to 'bring into the open' and to rectify.

In paragraph two, a form of personal dialogue is sustained. The text employs the pronoun 'I' and a 'we' which seems, through much of the paragraph, to refer to 'my colleagues and I'. Furthermore, the paragraph is initially addressed directly to Spencer through the pronoun 'you'. The third paragraph, however, re-states Marks's preference for less personal and less dialogic forms of communication: 'we are most willing to send you copies of our manuscripts prior to publication. Accordingly, I am enclosing two preprints.' The rest of paragraph three and the whole of paragraph four are devoted to summarizing, for Spencer's benefit, the results of these papers, the texts of which are formally addressed to the research community at large.

Paragraph four focuses on a technical issue which has not yet been mentioned in this epistolary debate, but which is treated as critical in one of the enclosed papers: 'The manuscript submitted to PNAS points out that earlier measurements of the H^+/site ratio carried out with the oxygen pulse and reductant pulse methods have not taken account of the movement of other relevant ions in the system, particularly phosphate.' The argument about phosphate proposed in the PNAS paper is directly analogous to the previous argument about Ca^{2+} transport. Marks suggests that there is an uncontrolled movement of phosphate across the mitochondrial membrane which is brought about by the oxygen pulse method used in Spencer's experiments. He maintains that, because the return of each phosphate ion across the membrane 'causes re-uptake of one of the ejected protons' which Spencer is supposed to be measuring, 'the measurement of the H^+/site ratio as you described underestimates the H^+/site ratio'. Marks states that when the reagent NEM is used to inhibit the movement of phosphate, 'the H^+/site ratio increases substantially above $2 \cdot 0$'. Consequently, as a result of these new experiments on NEM and phosphate, and because 'of the consistency between the three different approaches in the PNAS article, we have concluded that the true H^+/site ratio of the primary proton pumping mechanism is certainly at least $3 \cdot 0$ and may be as high as $4 \cdot 0$'.

Paragraph four explicitly continues the dialogue with Spencer. But impersonal formulations increasingly replace Marks's own personal voice. For example, 'the manuscript' points out certain errors in previous experiments. The experimental procedures used by Marks are described in a neutral manner, as if the descriptions are simple, literal accounts, involving no interpretative work on the part of the experimenter. Furthermore, it is the consistency between the three distinct experimental approaches which, finally, requires Marks and his colleagues to conclude that the 'true H^+/site ratio' is more than $2 \cdot 0$.

The implicit argument here about experimental triangulation is not spelled out. The assumption seems to be that, if three different types of measurement give a value greater than $2 \cdot 0$, then the true value must be greater than $2 \cdot 0$. The consistency between the three different measures is taken to show that the observed value is truly characteristic of the biochemical phenomena in themselves and is independent of any particular measurement procedures. Thus triangulation is a way of externalizing the writer's discourse and of making that discourse appear to be independent of the writer's interpretative work. In M2, it enables Marks, after he has deflected Spencer's criticisms of one aspect of his work, to reaffirm the conclusions of that work and to present those conclusions as simply unavoidable, as being required by the phenomena of the bio-chemical world.

In paragraph four, although there has been a dialogue in process, it has been markedly unequal, in the sense that Spencer has been confronted by textual agents assuming, in various ways, some degree of interpretative superiority. However, in the next and penultimate paragraph, Spencer is invited to contribute to what is depicted initially as a more equal exchange of views: 'My colleagues and I would be most interested to have your comments on our experiments and their interpretation.' A distinction is made here between the experiments and their interpretation which seems to indicate that Marks recognizes that Spencer's assessment of the scientific meaning of his (Marks's) experiments might be different from his own and might point out errors on his (Marks's) part. In other words, as the text explicitly adopts the dialogic form so it seems formally to allow for a separation between observations and their, possibly fallible, interpretation by particular scientists. As is repeatedly the case in these letters, adoption of linguistic forms expressing interpretatively equal dialogue is accompanied by the separation of observation from interpretation, of fact from opinion; and also by acceptance of the idea that dialogue is mainly concerned with resolving differences at the interpretative level.

However, in this paragraph, as elsewhere in the letters, the possibility of such dialogue is quickly put in doubt by the writer's assumption of interpretative superiority and by an implicit denial of his own dependence on contingent interpretation. After the invitation quoted above, paragraph five continues:

> We also hope that you may find it useful to repeat them in your laboratory. We experienced no difficulty in obtaining values very close to $2 \cdot 0$ in repeating your classical oxygen pulse experiments under the precise conditions you defined and with the same extrapolation procedure. For this reason, we believe that you will be able to confirm our measurements quite easily.

There are two phrases here which are particularly difficult to interpret: 'you may find it useful to repeat' and 'you will be able to confirm our measurements'. One reading might be that Marks is simply stating that if Spencer copies Marks's experimental procedures closely, he will get the same readings. This seems to be equivalent to claiming that one has performed one's own experiments carefully. On this reading, Marks is merely claiming to be as experimentally careful as Spencer, in the sense that his recent experimental observations are as repeatable as Spencer's earlier observations. But in what sense will Spencer find this 'useful'?

Spencer has already stressed in S1 that the raw observations their experiments produce cannot, in themselves, decide the stoichiometry issue. In addition, Marks claims to have repeated Spencer's observations, without being obliged to accept Spencer's interpretation. Yet Marks seems to imply here that it will be *Spencer* who benefits in some way from confirming his (Marks's) measurements. It seems to be implied that this experimental replication will have some consequence for Spencer's understanding of the H^+/site ratio. Thus the second possible reading is that Marks is suggesting that if Spencer does repeat his (Marks's) experiments, he will be more inclined to accept the interpretations that go with them; even although Marks's repetition of Spencer's work had exactly the opposite effect. Whereas on the first reading, the interpretative difficulty was to understand how Spencer would find it useful merely to repeat Marks's data, on the second reading it becomes difficult to understand why mere observational repetition should in any way alter Spencer's interpretation.

Nevertheless, whichever of these, or other, readings is adopted, the general import of this concluding passage to M2 is clear; namely, that further experimental work on Spencer's part can only lead him towards Marks's current position. Thus immediately following an apparent invitation to open and equal dialogue, the text reasserts the privileged position of Marks's discourse about the realities of the $\rightarrow H^+/2e^-$ ratio.

The Merging of Observation and Interpretation

Letter S3.   Spencer to Marks, 30 December 1975 (eleven paragraphs in length)

S3 is one of the most consistently dialogic letters in the series. Not only does Spencer address many of his remarks directly to Marks, but Spencer himself continually appears as a textual agent: 'Your letter and your PNAS paper gave me the impression', 'My colleague and I recognized', 'We found that NEM', 'According to our observations', 'I do not understand your reductant pulse experiments', 'I would incidentally point out', and so on.

In accordance with this use of dialogic form, the text emphasizes that the differences which separate the two participants are interpretative, rather than factual, in character. The text also comes close, at one juncture, to treating their opposing claims as interpretatively equal. Nevertheless, even in this relatively dialogic text, the discourse is primarily organized in a way which minimizes the author's interpretative work and highlights the doubtful nature of the recipient's interpretations. Neither in S3, nor in any other letter in this sequence, does the author ever draw attention to or admit an 'own mistake'. Although both parties treat their partner as a generally competent scientist and thereby imply that he is not prone to making experimental errors, although both authors stress that stoichiometry experiments are complex and thereby imply that they themselves could have overlooked something important, and although an author occasionally invites the other, as did Spencer in S2, to 'point out my mistakes', in every text the author alone manages to emerge as an immaculate agent who has never actually made the slightest error bearing upon the issue in question. Thus the occasional textual accomplishment of direct, balanced, interpretative dialogue is swamped by the textual dominance of interpretative asymmetry and an implicit postulate of author correctness.

The main scientific topic of S3 is that of the movement of phosphate and its inhibition by NEM, which had been introduced into the debate in M2. Marks had argued in that letter that the movement of phosphate across the membrane was accompanied by a movement of protons. He maintained that this movement, which had not been controlled in previous experiments, reduced the number of protons measured and led to an underestimate of the number of protons carried across the membrane in the course of the primary process of respiration. Spencer responds by claiming that 'the effects of the translocation of phosphate' had been recognized in two of his earlier papers and that they 'could be minimized rather easily by lowering the temperature'. Spencer means by this that he gets the same results at high temperatures, where phosphate movement occurs, as at low temperatures, where it is inhibited. Hence he concludes that phosphate movement does not affect the results.

These assertions are presented confidently and without qualification. 'We recognized these effects' and 'we showed that they could be minimized'. However, this initial, entirely negative response leads to a new paragraph, which begins with a balanced and formally neutral presentation of the interpretative divergence.

Your interpretation of your observations with NEM is not consistent with our interpretation of our observations at 5° – and some explanation seems to be required.

This is a strongly dialogic formulation. The stress is on differences of interpretation. Two equal partners are recognized. And the possibility of either or both parties being in error seems to be allowed by this summary statement taken in isolation. However, the opportunity for full dialogue implicit in this passage is not pursued. For although Spencer himself continues to appear as a major textual agent in what follows, he acts only to identify what are taken to be the definite or probable defects of Marks's experimental procedures and interpretative work. At no point in S3 is the possibility of defective work by the author taken seriously.

For example, Spencer immediately provides an explanation of their difference of opinion about phosphate movement and its inhibition by NEM which, although presented tentatively, treats Spencer's conclusions as its point of departure and explains away Marks's conclusions as arising from a failure fully to understand the operation of NEM.

I think, from our own experience of the use of NEM, that the explanation is that NEM does more than simply inhibit the phosphoric acid porter.

Reference is made to several of Spencer's published papers and Spencer's personal voice gradually fades from the text. At first it is replaced by 'we' and then by an impersonal descriptive voice which simply informs Marks how NEM actually operates and draws attention to possible negative implications for Marks's interpretation of his experimental results.

We found that NEM, at a concentration of 0·3mM, inhibited the succinate dehydrogenase by some 80% and inhibited the 3-hydroxybutyrate dehydrogenase activity by virtually 100%. The reaction of the NEM with the mitochondrial components does not go to completion under normal experimental conditions (such as you seem to use), and it is possible that additional trivial effects of NEM on the apparent $\rightarrow H^+/O$ quotients may arise from this circumstance.

For the next five paragraphs, Spencer proceeds to identify a series of supposed experimental faults in those parts of Marks's work which he professes to understand, whilst claiming that there are certain experiments which he does not understand or about which there is insufficient information to allow a proper assessment. Each paragraph starts with a phrase employing a personal pronoun, but in every case the text is quickly taken over by the impersonal descriptive voice exemplified in the second sentence of the last quotation. Thus, by the end of these paragraphs, not only do we have a plausible explanation of how Marks has arrived at the wrong conclusions in his NEM experiments, but we have a catalogue of probable and possible procedural errors which serves, textually, to undermine confidence in Marks's work on this topic.

As S3 moves towards its close, Spencer introduces various kinds of summary remarks. A point which he repeats in several different ways is that the differences which they are seeking to resolve are not observational differences, but differences of interpretation.

You will see from these comments that . . . I am not questioning your experimental observations, but only the interpretations you place upon them . . . Generally speaking, I would not want to dispute your suggestion that we would get much the same results as you do if we were to repeat your experiments under substantially similar conditions . . . It is not over the raw experimental data that we disagree, but over the interpretations that we put upon them.

In these statements, Spencer makes a clear distinction between observations and interpretations. Observations are treated here as being scientifically neutral. Only through active interpretation can observations achieve scientific meaning. This separation of observation from interpretation enables Spencer to emphasize the complexity, uncertainty and incompleteness of Marks's interpretations, without denying the reliability or accuracy of his experimental results. Spencer's overall strategy in these letters, as exemplified here, is to separate observation from scientific interpretation in principle, to stress that the dialogue should be primarily concerned with the latter, and then textually to demolish Marks's interpretative work.

The treatment of his own claims, however, is radically different. For in the case of Spencer's own claims, observation and correct interpretation regularly coincide. In other words, Spencer 'observes' a $\rightarrow H^+/2e^-$ ratio of 2·0 and this is taken to be the correct ratio. This coincidence of observation and interpretation is accomplished by minimizing the degree to which Spencer's results appear to involve interpretation. Spencer's experiments are depicted, in his own letters, as remarkably simple, and therefore easy to keep procedurally correct and easy to interpret. Because Spencer's measurements are presented as virtually independent of interpretative work, it appears unnecessary to interpret Spencer's observations in order to accept them as the correct values. Despite the separation in principle between observation and interpretation, Spencer's observed values become, in his own texts, inseparable from the correct values; and any interpretation which proposes a different $\rightarrow H^+/2e^-$ ratio is deemed to be wrong.

> . . . the observed value of $2H^+$ per $\sim$ that we have found experimentally has not yet seriously been undermined by other more reliable or relatively more extensive experimental data.
> . . . Your *J. Biol. Chem.* paper with its footnote and PNAS addendum only tend to confirm my view that you are coming from 'super-super-stoichiometry' through 'super-stoichiometry' toward the actual stoichiometry of $2H^+$ per 'site' that is characteristic of the respiratory chain.

Spencer's observed value of $2H^+$ consistently provides the resting-point for his discourse. Having demonstrated the uncertainties and defects of Marks's interpretations, Spencer returns time after time to his own 'simple observations'. Thus the original distinction between fact and opinion (observation and interpretation) is persistently dissolved, in Spencer's texts, in his own favour. He uses this distinction to show, textually, that whereas Marks's interpretations are mistaken and are therefore mere opinion, in his own case observation and interpretation, opinion and fact, coincide and thereby represent 'the actual stoichiometry of the respiratory chain'. In this kind of strong, explicit formulation, Spencer's scientific assertions become textually indistinguishable from the discourse of the biochemical world itself. In such formulations, the author appears as no more than a neutral medium through which the actual biochemical phenomena express themselves.

Discourse Strategies and Irony

Letters M3.   Marks to Spencer, 26 February 1976 (fourteen para-
graphs in length)
This letter is Marks's longest and most substantial contribution to the debate. I do not have the final, signed version of this letter, but only a type-written draft. The draft takes the form of a series of itemized rebuttals of Spencer's previous criticisms. Items 1–6 deal with points raised in S3. There then follows a rejection of Spencer's argument in S2.

The defensive character of M3 arises from the significantly different discourse strategies adopted in these letters by the two authors. On the one hand, Marks has previously stayed close to the empiricist format of the research paper. He has enclosed copies of such papers with each letter; he has referred Spencer directly to their experimental results; and he has devoted most of his efforts in the letters to summarizing the papers' main points. His strategy has been to persuade or overwhelm Spencer with the weight of his own empirical evidence. He has not chosen to use the letters to write critical reviews of his opponent's interpretative work. Marks's critique of Spencer's experiments has been implicit in, or closely linked to, his presentation of his own findings. Marks has so far opted to emphasize the factual character of his own conclusions, rather than to draw attention to his adversary's interpretative failures.

On the other hand, as we have seen, Spencer has stressed the interpretative nature of the debate and has accordingly dwelt at length on Marks's supposed interpretative defects. Consequently, at this point in the debate, whereas Spencer's position is textually strong, in that he has both undermined Marks's claims and reasserted the factuality of his own observations, Marks is faced with a long list of unanswered criticisms. In M3, he acts to redress this critical imbalance by taking Spencer's points one by one and refuting them.

We cannot examine M3 in detail. Its itemized form means that it consists of a series of separate, technical comments, rather than a unified overall argument. Of course, each technical comment serves to 'show' that, in every case, Spencer's criticism was misguided. As a result Marks goes further than before towards revealing and challenging in detail various parts of the interpretative work which can be attributed to Spencer's supposedly simple and straight-forward experiments.

Consider, for example, Spencer's argument that, long before Marks had investigated the effects of phosphate on the H^+ quotient, he (Spencer) had already controlled for the effects of the translocation of phosphate by varying the temperature and had shown that phosphate movement was irrelevant. Marks replies as follows:

> The experiments from which you concluded that phosphate influx causes no significant interference does not prove this point. They were carried out with 2mM B-hydroxybutyrate as respiratory substrate. This concentration of B-hydroxybutyrate is already sufficient to lower the observed $H^+/\sim$ ratio of $2 \cdot 0$, at 25°, even in the presence of NEM, due to entry of the acid.

Marks is claiming here that when Spencer carried out his experiments investigating the effects of phosphate movement, he used a substrate (the reagent added to set in motion the process of respiration) which in itself generated artificially low readings of proton translocation. In other words, it is argued that whereas Spencer's use of NEM would have inhibited phosphate movement in this experiment and would have produced a (in Marks's view) correct ratio of $3 \cdot 0$ or more, the use of this particular substrate at this concentration in the same experiment would tend to lower the ratio artificially back to $2 \cdot 0$ again. Hence Marks, in defending his own experimental claims, is led to perform the same kind of textual demolition on Spencer as the latter had performed on him. Both authors clearly employ the same tactic. They identify some features of their opponent's experiment which appears not to have been considered in one or more of their experimental papers and they then show that this feature has important and negative interpret-ative consequences.

In M3, Marks consistently rejects Spencer's prior criticisms in this manner, that is, he introduces additional considerations to those mentioned in Spencer's texts and he uses these new interpretative resources to reverse Spencer's critical conclusions.

Not only does he deal with each of Spencer's main points, but he also responds in general terms, on behalf of his colleagues as well as himself, to Spencer's various suggestions about possible procedural oversights.

> We have very carefully checked all the technical details of the type you mentioned. After all, we would not dare to publish data questioning observations and conclusions that have been in the literature for over ten years and which have appeared to be supported by other investigators, without the most rigorous questioning of our methodology and assumptions in the light of today's knowledge regarding mitochondrial ion movements. We have expected that you would raise questions regarding method- ology and assumptions. However, most of your comments concern rather trivial points that are second-order in importance. We had hoped for more substantive responses regarding our main conclusions.

This passage is the only general comment in M3 on Spencer's previous letters. It is interesting, in the first place, because it employs what we have seen to be a typical interpretative asymmetry in these letters. For Marks depicts himself as publishing *data*, in contrast to other scientists who have published *observations and conclusions*. We have here, in condensed form, the recurrent tendency of these authors to hide their own interpretative work and to emphasize that of their adversaries.

But perhaps of greater interest is the second half of this passage in which Marks rebukes Spencer for failing to provide 'more substantive responses' regarding his 'main conclusions'. Here, Marks himself is seen to be dealing in conclusions, rather than just data. It is recognized, implicitly, that he is involved in an interpretative confrontation. Moreover, in maintaining that he had expected that Spencer would 'raise questions regarding method- ology and assumptions', Marks is not only accepting that the scientific meaning of his data depends on how such procedures and assumptions are interpreted; he is also recognizing that the typical strategy in informal scientific debates is to focus upon and textually to undermine the other party's background suppositions.

In this passage, then, Marks treats interpretative confrontation as typical of informal scientific debate and uses this typification to condemn Spencer for not coming up to expectations. There is, of course, a certain irony in Marks's statement that he had hoped for more substantive responses regarding his main conclusions. For, in the first place, Spencer's previous letters are clearly organized as if they do present significant comments on Marks's work. Indeed, they claim to show that Marks is fundamentally wrong. Secondly, the relatively long text of M3 is devoted entirely to answering Spencer's previous criticisms. Thus Marks is able to treat Spencer's previous comments as lacking in substance only after engaging in a great deal of counter-interpretation. Finally, the claim that Marks had 'hoped for' stronger criticism of his work can be taken as somewhat at odds with the fact that neither party to this debate ever accepts any substantive point offered by the other. In the next letter, Spencer appears to respond to the potential irony of Marks's request for more substantial criticisms.

Letter S4.   Spencer to Marks, 23 March 1976 (two paragraphs in length)

In the previous letter, Marks actively grappled, for the first time, with Spencer's criticisms of his work. As a result, M3 faced Spencer with a whole new range of interpretative considerations to be taken into account in any further contribution to the debate. Given Spencer's strategy of deconstructing Marks's claims, rather than advancing new claims of his own, M3 presented him with a major task of reassessment. S4 is a short letter in which Spencer asks for time to carry out this task and for certain experimental details which, he implies, are missing from Marks's research papers, yet necessary for their proper evaluation.

> A good deal of study and thought will be required before I can comply with your request to 'comment more substantially' on your findings; and some of my reactions will have to await the publication of the experimental details of your recent work, mentioned in your letter. But, meanwhile, I thought I should do some 'revision' . . . To help me study the experimental protocols, could you please tell me what value you used for the solubility of oxygen in the aqueous media in those experiments . . . I would be especially grateful for a quick reply, so that I can get on with the homework that you have set me . . .

This letter furnishes the only instance, in this series of letters, of what appears to be genuine dialogue, in that Spencer personally acknowledges that Marks's arguments are leading him to think again. It is notable, however, that this acknowledgement, so contrary to the usual tenor of these letters, is not done in an ordinary, matter-of-fact manner. Instead, Spencer places two of the critical phrases in quotes; namely, 'comment more substantially' and 'revision'. The first of these phrases is taken over from M3. Spencer uses it in S4 to indicate that he is, in some sense, taking Marks's request seriously. The central point of S4 is that Spencer needs more time and more information if he is to meet Marks's request.

However, the quoted word 'revision' is not taken over from Marks. The use of quotation marks in this case has some other significance. One effect of the quotation marks is to signal that this is a rather unusual word to be used in the context of technical debate between two eminent scientists and to suggest that the word is not to be read quite literally. The quotation marks around the word 'revision' also draw attention to the central metaphor of 'teacher/pupil' around which S4 is organized. For Spencer describes himself as having to carry out 'a good deal of study and thought' as well as 'revision' in order to complete the 'homework' which Marks has set him.

This terminology cannot be accepted literally. Spencer is not Marks's pupil in the ordinary sense of that word, nor has Marks set him homework. These phrases, then, represent Spencer's relationship to Marks in a figurative, playful or not-entirely-serious manner. Thus Spencer does portray himself in S4 as trying to match up to Marks's expectations about offering some substantial, rather than trivial, comments. But, by adopting a playful style, he avoids admitting any interpretative superiority on the part of Marks that this might be seen to imply. By using the teacher/pupil metaphor to exaggerate the intellectual challenge posed by M3, Spencer is able to write a letter which accepts the scientific significance of Marks's arguments, whilst simultaneously giving the impression that Marks's apparent interpretative strength is something of an illusion. The double irony of S4 is that, at the one juncture in this debate where Spencer was given a clear opportunity to implement his proposal in S1 for full interpretative dialogue (by acknowledging in a straightforward manner the plausibility of some, at least, of Marks's arguments and the need for careful reappraisal), he treats his own dialogic response ironically and thereby avoids fulfilling the normal requirements of dialogic exchange (see Woolgar, 1983).

We must not be too hard on Spencer, however. We must not forget that Marks has never accepted that he is engaged in a dialogue, has never hidden his preference for communicating via the formal research literature, and has never ceased to advance his own claims in markedly empiricist terms. It seems hardly likely, therefore, that any apparent interpretative concessions by Spencer would have been reciprocated by Marks. Given the interpretative asymmetry built into Marks's discourse, it seems only too likely that any clearly dialogic response by Spencer would have been treated as an indication that he was at last coming to recognize the 'true' stoichiometric values.

Letter S5. Spencer to Marks, 4 June 1976 (six short paragraphs in length)

I do not have a copy of M4. From Spencer's comments in the next letter, it seems merely to have been a note giving the experimental details on oxygen solubility figures that Spencer had requested in S4 and enclosing some more offprints of Marks's experimental publications. S5 similarly makes no contribution to the technical debate. It is a brief acknowledgement of receipt of Marks's oxygen solubility figures, followed by some general remarks.

In paragraph three, Spencer restates 'the conclusion that we are very much in agreement at the level of the raw experimental data. This confirms my view that it is at the level of interpretation that we mainly disagree.' Spencer had written virtually the same words in S3. This assertion seems to be part of his general strategy of focusing on interpretative differences rather than factual differences. The next paragraph is as follows:

I heard from [a fellow biochemist] that you feel that I have ignored your data. May I assure you that this is really not the case – indeed, it could hardly be so, since your data and our data do not seem to me to be in conflict (except, perhaps, in a few minor respects).

This paragraph epitomizes the basic divergence in discourse strategies between the two authors. Marks's data are repeatedly summarized in the letters and presented as equivalent to the true stoichiometric values. The data, of course, have to be interpreted. But Marks treats his own interpretative contribution as simply that of allowing for, and controlling the effect of, that complex set of variables which prevents direct observation of the true values. Marks's strategy, in the letters, is to bombard Spencer with research papers, and summaries of research papers, whose data clearly reveal the true values. Thus, in not accepting Marks's estimation of these values, Spencer is deemed to be 'ignoring the data'.

For Spencer, in contrast, Marks's data are treated as the product of complicated and ill-understood experimental set-ups, which differ from his own simple and coherent experimental designs and which are, therefore, beset by interpretative difficulties. Moreover, they do not generate the values which he knows, from his own experiments, are 'actually characteristic of the respiratory chain system'. Spencer never challenges the reliability or accuracy of Marks's data: for this is irrelevant to his argument. As he stressed in S1, the debate is not about 'actual unprocessed values taken from experimental data', but about 'derived coefficients, interpreted from experiments'. Spencer has continually applied this view to Marks's data throughout the letters. Those data are accepted by Spencer as reliable and accurate. But this is, for Spencer in these letters, quite independent of their scientific meaning. Thus Spencer's strategy has been continually to challenge Marks's interpretative work and to try to show that the apparent values obtained by Marks are not the actual values.

As we have seen, the experimental procedures and interpretations of both scientists are such that their data or observed values coincide with what they take to be the true value. Both scientists treat the interpretative work embodied in their own experiments as merely eliminating the effect of complicating factors in such a way that the true state of affairs is experimentally revealed. It is for this reason that the researchers can always present their own conclusions as if those conclusions were no more than data or mere observation. Yet, at the same time, they can always treat the other's data as scientifically meaningless in themselves and as furnishing only apparent, rather than true, values.

Accordingly when, as in S5, we find Spencer rejecting the accusation that he has 'ignored Marks's data', we must recognize that this phrase has a radically different meaning for the two authors. For Marks, Spencer can be taken to be guilty, in the sense that he has not changed his own incorrect interpretations in accordance with what Marks's data have shown to be the case. Spencer, however, can claim to be innocent, in the sense that he accepts the reliability and accuracy of Marks's reported measurements (data) and is conscientiously seeking to understand how those measurements are produced by Marks's experimental procedures. Despite their use of a common technical vocabulary and a common vocabulary for talking about their experimental activities (fact/opinion, observation/interpretation, data/scientific meaning), these scientists are, much of the time, talking past each other. They each endow the same apparently simple and recurrent phrases with significantly different meanings as they employ these phrases within interpretative frameworks provided by their divergent technical claims and discourse strategies.

The Final Irony

Letter M5.   Marks to Spencer, 22 June 1976 (seven paragraphs in length)
This is the last letter of the series. In it, the debate continues exactly as in previous responses. Marks encloses another preprint and devotes the two main paragraphs to summarizing its content.

Before he deals with the technical details of his paper, Marks adopts a strongly dialogic form in referring back to some general remarks previously made by Spencer.

> My colleagues and I are very glad to learn that you are not in disagreement on our experimental observation and that our differences are more matters of interpretation. However, we now also hope to persuade you that our interpretation of these experiments is reasonable, and that there is in fact an interfering movement of endogenous phosphate that causes serious under-estimation of the H^+/site ratio in the experiments as you originally described them.

Thus in the tenth and last letter of the series, as in the first, the stated aim is to eliminate the distinction between interpretation (opinion) and fact through open dialogue. Marks professes to hope that Spencer will be persuaded that his interpretation has captured the facts of the matter. M5 is designed to bring about this persuasive coup, not by challenging the accuracy of Spencer's observations nor by showing that there was a fault in his reasoning, but once again by showing that there was a relevant process occurring in his experimental system for which his reasoning had not allowed. In M5, Marks returns to Spencer's attempts to control for the movement of phosphate by varying the temperature. He refers at the beginning of the next quote to a section in one of Spencer's published papers.

> On page 1152 you indicate that the results of oxygen pulse experiments carried out at $5°$, which yielded H^+/site ratios identical to those observed at $25°$, satisfactorily excluded phosphate movements as a source of underestimation of the H^+/site ratio, on the entirely reasonable grounds that phosphate transport across the mitochondrial membrane should have been slowed sufficiently at $5°$ to eliminate or at least reduce it as contributing to the observed H^+/site ratio. However, we believe that this conclusion is not warranted . . . Thus in your experiments you appear to have eliminated phosphate movements by working at $5°$, but have then replaced the effect of phosphate by adding a relatively high concentration of the weak acid BOH, which can carry a proton in. We are confident that if you repeat the experiment with succinate as substrate at $5°$ in the absence of BOH you will confirm our observation that the H^+/site ratio is $3·0$ as in Fig. 11 of our paper.

At the end of this passage, which is almost the end of the debate,

Marks has once again succeeded in textually demolishing Spencer's interpretative work and in establishing that the facts of the biochemical world are encapsulated within his own discourse. Marks's confident recommendation that Spencer can 'confirm our observation that the H^+/site ratio is $3 \cdot 0$' by repeating Marks's experiment seems to disregard his acceptance at the start of M5 of Spencer's view that their differences are essentially interpretative. From Spencer's position, experimental replication cannot 'confirm the observation that the ratio is $3 \cdot 0$'; it can only 'confirm that the apparent experimental value is $3 \cdot 0$'. In the words of S1, the actual value cannot be observed, it can only be inferred indirectly from what is observed. However, in Marks's discourse at the end of M5, as indeed periodically in both authors' discourse, the writer's dependence on fallible interpretations is ignored. The author's own 'correct interpretations' are textually removed from view and are presented as the 'facts of the matter', to be simply observed as such by any other competent observer.

It is ironic that Marks ends the sequence of letters by treating his quotient as observable and as open to confirmation by exact experimental replication. For in M1, Marks's very first contribution to the debate was to insist that his own ability to repeat Spencer's observation of $2 \cdot 0$ in no way required him to accept that $2 \cdot 0$ was the true value. Once again we see how observations are treated merely as uninterpreted data when they are furnished by one's adversary, yet as indistinguishable from biochemical reality when employed within one's own texts.

As we have noted, the kind of textual confidence to be found towards the end of M5 has been exhibited before by both authors. It does not signal, in any way, the end of the debate. As I mentioned in the introduction, both authors can be observed several years later in the formal literature defending their ratios of $2 \cdot 0$ and $4 \cdot 0$. Despite his assertion of confidence in this letter, Marks does not treat his current experiments as conclusive even in the text of M5. For at the very end of the letter, Marks includes a one-sentence rebuttal of one of Spencer's earlier criticisms and he promises that it will not be long before he sends Spencer the results of an experiment which measures the H^+/site ratio by means of another new approach. Despite his strong claims for the persuasiveness of his case, Marks ends M5 on the assumption that his partner will not have been persuaded.

It seems that the professed objective of this dialogue, that is, an agreed statement about the facts of the matter, is neither accomplished nor ever textually assumed to be likely in the course of these ten letters. It is in this sense that the dialogue seems to have been a failure.

Some Rules for Generating Scientific Letters

In the introduction to this chapter, I suggested that there may be regular features of informal debate in science which are responsible for scientists' frequently describing such debate as unsuccessful. In this section, I am going to extract from the preceding discussion what I take to be the main recurrent features of the debate contained in these letters. I will suggest that the features we have noted above begin to reveal some of the difficulties inherent in the interpretative forms which scientists use when they take part in informal scientific discourse by means of letters.

What I intend to do now is to formulate a set of rules for constructing letters of the kind examined above. I am in no way implying that Marks or Spencer actually followed these rules when writing these letters. The rules have been extracted by me *ex post facto*. Indeed, the rules have a certain ironic quality in the sense that participants would probably be quite unwilling to accept that their letters were written in this way. In this respect, they reflect the typical opposition between participants' and analysts' accounts (see Woolgar, 1983; Gilbert and Abell, 1983). The rules are, therefore, to be regarded as an analysts's method of summarizing and making sense of his own analysis. However, I suggest that they could be used to generate recognizable contributions to epistolary debates similar to the one we have been examining.

Rule 1   Avoid debating technical issues in letters, unless you wish to challenge the basis for another researcher's experimental claims.

Rule 2   If your experimental claims are being challenged, constantly refer your critic to your research papers. These papers, because they are textual monologues and are not addressed to the specific points raised by your critic, will enable you consistently to present your conclusions as simply required by the evidence.

Rule 3   When asserting the factuality of your own conclusions in informal letters, model your discourse on the impersonal mode of exposition employed in the research literature. However, some modification of this mode will have to be made in order to cope with the personal authorship and direct personal address required in letters.

Rule 4   Pre-suppose the factuality of your own conclusions in every letter. Treat your own formulations as, ultimately, identical to the realities of the phenomena under investigation.

Rule 5   Organize every letter so that your own central claims are clearly confirmed. Never mention any of your own specific experimental or interpretative errors.

Rule 6   When challenging others' claims, focus on their interpretative work and show how it fails to deal adequately with the complexities of the actual phenomena. When identifying others' mistakes, take for granted your own understanding of the phenomena in question.

Rule 7   Re-formulate others' views in your own letters in versions which enable you most easily to deconstruct and undermine those views. Make visible those aspects of your adversary's interpretations which have been textually hidden and show how, because these interpretations are demonstrably incomplete or misinformed, the meaning given to his observations must be revised.

Rule 8   Emphasize the distinctions between fact/opinion, observation/interpretation and apparent value/true value when challenging others' claims. Make sure, however, that your own conclusions about the true values coincide with your observations. In this way ensure that the results of your own interpretative work can be presented as fact, and those of your adversary as mere opinion.

Rule 9   Emphasize that the replicability of others' observations in no way confirms the conclusions they have drawn from these observations. Do not refrain, however, from proposing that replication of your own observations will serve to confirm that those observations reveal the realities of the natural world.

Rule 10   Pay attention to the personal implications of your letters. Begin and end each letter on a friendly personal note. Try to pre-empt any possible accusations of personal antagonism, lack of co-operation or uncritical commitment to your own view.

Rule 11   Use the personal format of a letter to concentrate attention on the inadequacy of the recipient's position. Address him constantly in the texts of your letters, but withdraw from the text yourself as often as possible so that the other party continually finds himself engaged in an unequal dialogue with the experiments, data, observations and facts. When faced with these 'non-interpretative' textual agents, your opponent must always lose; at least, when he is confronted with them in *your* texts.

Rule 12   If, despite, adherence to these rules, some kind of concession to your opponent's claims becomes unavoidable, keep that concession as general as possible. Present your negative admissions in an ironic or playful manner, in this way implying that no genuine concession has been made.

Dialogue, Textual Practice and Failure

My aim, in formulating the conclusions of my analysis as a set of rules for constructing texts within an informal scientific debate, has been to bring home most forcibly just how difficult it is to resolve scientific issues through such texts. For it seems that adoption of these rules by those involved in a scientific debate would prolong any initial differences of opinion indefinitely. In so far as these rules capture the textual practice embodied in the stoichiometry letters, and perhaps in other similar exchanges, they provide some indication of why this kind of debate is so often deemed to be unsuccessful. 'Failure' is guaranteed by the divergence between the ostensible goal of resolving differences of opinion and the textual practice which makes this virtually impossible.

This conclusion is to some extent simply a product of my own procedure in constructing these rules. For the rules reproduce the textul practice of a debate in which no resolution of the scientific issues was achieved. Thus the rules provided above are designed to generate texts which lead to confrontation and scientific stalemate. I do not know how widespread this form of textual practice is and I cannot suppose that I would necessarily have obtained the same set of rules if I had examined a different collection of letters. However, many of these rules resemble the conventional practices used to generate the formal research literature; for example, rules 3, 4, 5, 8, 9 and 11. It seems likely, therefore, that other epistolary debates among scientists will draw upon these same empiricist textual conventions. Yet what is particularly interesting about the rules and the original stoichiometry texts is that participants' failure to resolve their differences seems to have arisen precisely from their use in the letters of these empiricist textual practices. If this is so, we are left with an intriguing question: why is it that textual practices similar to those employed in the formal literature produce informal texts which are deemed to be unsuccessful?

I want to suggest that the 'failure' of the stoichiometry debate, and possibly of other similar debates, is built into the very discourse of the letters. We saw earlier, particularly in some of Spencer's letters, how the kind of direct, personal address which is possible and to some extent required in letters tends to be accompanied by a strongly interpretative treatment of the scientific issues. For example, we saw how Spencer initially emphasized that he was inviting Marks to join him as an equal contributor to an essentially interpretative task. In subsequent letters we saw how, as long as direct, personal dialogue was maintained, the outcome of the debate was not treated as having been decided in advance, but as depending on open-ended interpretative activity involving free, and in principle equal, interpretative agents.

I want to suggest that, when scientists engage in direct, personal dialogue, something like this version of scientific debate is taken to provide the appropriate rules of discourse. This is evident in the letters in several ways; for example, in the way in which both authors emphasize their respect for the other's views in the personal passages at the beginnings and ends of letters; in Spencer's description of informal dialogue at Fasano in S2; and most revealingly, in his account in S1 of why Marks should not have taken offence at what happened at Fasano. Spencer's argument in S1 was that, whatever Marks might have thought, he had not claimed a privileged, factual status for his own discourse at Fasano, and, hence, that he had not contravened the 'rules' of informal discourse. My suggestion is that it is a central principle of informal scientific discourse, whether in letters or in conference discussions, that the attribution of factual status to a scientist's claims should be an outcome of interpretative debate among equals and should not be presupposed in any scientist's discourse. I am not, of course, claiming or implying that scientists normally comply with this rule. I am suggesting only that something like this rule may be used by participants to portray actions as appropriate/offensive in the course of direct, personal communication.

It seems likely that, in face to face interaction, participants can respond directly to what they take to be deviations from proper interpretative equality. In written texts, however, such an immediate response is impossible. Consequently, in the letters, although we find sporadic reference to the ideal of maintaining interpretative equality in pursuit of the facts, the textual practice, freed from immediate interactive control, regularly moves in a radically different direction. The ideal of interpretative equality and personal discourse is overwhelmed in the letters by reliance on textual practices close to those of the research literature. In other words, whereas the letters are treated as involving, in principle, personal discussion between interpretative equals, the textual practice becomes predominantly impersonal and asymmetrical as contributors assert their own privileged access to the realm of factual discourse. It seems likely that it is this unusual assertion of an interpretative ideal in conjunction with a markedly empiricist practice in the letters which contributes to scientists' describing such letters as 'unsatisfactory' and 'unsuccessful'. As in the stoichiometry letters, the personal agents present in the text profess to follow a procedure which can be seen as strikingly at variance with their textual practice.

Given that authors' letters have a strongly asymmetrical structure, it seems likely that, in depicting letters as 'unsatisfactory' and 'unsuccessful', participants are comparing other parties' supposed deviation from the ideal of symmetrical dialogue with what they take to be their own compliance. Given that each author presupposes the correctness of his own position, the complaint that the letters 'failed to resolve the scientific issue' may become equivalent to 'the other party failed to recognize the facts of the matter as I see them'. Thus, for example, we find Marks apparently complaining to a colleague that Spencer is too committed to his own ideas to give proper recognition to Marks's experimentally demonstrated facts. It seems, then, that scientists' complaints about the letters' failure themselves depend on a juxtaposition of the ideal of interpretative equality with the very practice of interpretative asymmetry that we have observed to be dominant in the letters. Without the ideal, there would be no grounds for complaint about other scientists' partiality. But without use of the empiricist mode in one's own discourse and the consequent interpretative asymmetry, it would be impossible persistently to locate the 'failure' in the discourse of one's partners. Moreover, quite apart from participants' allocation of blame for the failure of the debate, it is their persistent use of the empiricist mode to advance opposing claims which prevents them from achieving any sustained interpretative dialogue and, thereby, from reaching an interpretative agreement.

Empiricist Discourse and Technical Agreement

We have, then, a tentative explanation of why epistolary debate tends to be treated as unsuccessful. But, we may ask, does it not follow that the formal research literature will be equally beset by problems? In particular, would we not expect the empiricist mode of discourse employed in the formal literature to generate the kind of intellectual stalemate which occurred in the stoichiometry letters? Certainly there can be no doubt that the conventions of the research literature are often treated critically, humorously or ironically by scientists (Gilbert and Mulkay, 1984). In this sense, the formal literature is often deemed to be unsatisfactory. It seems to me, however, that it does not generate constant interpretative difficulties within its own framework of discourse. In this sense it is unlike the letters examined above and provides a more coherent form of textual practice. I suggest that this coherence has been achieved because, in the research literature, technical consensus is accomplished textually, as opposed to the letters, where the objective of technical consensus is supposed to be accomplished intertextually. Let me explain what I mean by this.

The dialogic form of informal letters involves participants in a debate which can only be satisfactorily resolved through the production of a technical formulation which is personally agreed by all parties. This seems to follow necessarily from the personal nature of the dialogue, from the principle of the interpretative equality of all parties and by the textual commitment in the letters to resolving technical differences. In this sense, technical consensus must be constructed by means of a textual merger of separately produced, personal texts. This is what I mean by suggesting that, in the letters, technical consensus is supposed to be accomplished intertextually. As we have seen, this is very difficult to achieve owing to scientists' heavy reliance on the empiricist mode of discourse. We might say, then, that the discourse of technical debate through informal letters is internally flawed and, for this reason, difficult to bring to a satisfactory completion.

In contrast, in the research literature, the dominant form of impersonal monologue avoids any need for participants to produce personally agreed technical formulations. In the first place, the conventions of these formal texts prevent the individual author from appearing as a significant textual agent. In the formal literature, the major textual agents are impersonal factors, such as experimental protocols, data, evidence, measurements, techniques of inference, and so on. It is on the whole these impersonal agents which, textually, furnish claims about the natural world (Knorr-Cetina, 1981). In the research literature the textual voice tends to remain constant although the particular author changes. This voice is that of the experimental findings/natural world. Such a continuity of textual voice tends to hide potential differences between authors. Each translates his personal textual products into a common, impersonal form of discourse. In personal letters, this community of voice is much more difficult to sustain.

The individual authors of research papers can, of course, claim some credit for having made an accurate observation, discovered a natural regularity, and so on. However, what they report about the natural world is not presented as a personal view, but as part of an independent factual realm. Moreover, the conclusions of research reports are not addressed to any particular persons. Consequently, unlike informal letters, they do not need to be acknowledged, approved or accepted by other scientists. It is in this sense that technical consensus is accomplished textually, rather than intertextually, in the formal literature. Each text is organized to convey certain facts about the natural world to anyone who is interested. Technical consensus is typically taken for granted in the very nature of each specific text. Any response by other persons is treated, textually, as irrelevant to its findings.

This does not mean, of course, that scientists simply accept all the claims furnished in the research literature. What it does mean, however, is that they are not obliged to furnish explicit textual assent or criticism. Although open, personalized debate is occasionally allowed into the formal literature, this is exceptional. Strong criticisms of particular scientists' experimental procedures tend to be excluded from the research literature and to circulate informally, largely by word of mouth. The dominant practice is for scientists to re-interpret others' formal texts in accordance with the requirements of their own personal corpus of textual work, without ever stating explicitly in the formal literature what is and what is not agreed. Individual readings and assessments of others' experimental papers are built into one's own formal texts, but at the same time they are transformed into the apparently impersonal formulation of one's experimental protocol or some other aspect of one's work which can be handled within the impersonal conventions of the research report. Thus critical comment on others' interpretative work is not necessarily absent from the formal literature, but it is on the whole dealt with implicitly. Similarly, it seems likely that concessions can be made to others' claims by means of gradual modification of one's formal texts, without one's having to acknowledge one's interpretative subordination to a particular scientist or to abandon, textually, the postulate of author correctness.

It appears, then, that the impersonal monologue written by and addressed to no one in particular is peculiarly suited to the empiricist mode of discourse. Whereas personal dialogue, *when combined with empiricist discourse*, generates direct intellectual confrontation and accomplishes consensus, if at all, through explicit textual sub/superordination, the impersonal monologue combined with empiricist discourse allows for gradual textual transformation, with each text appearing to exemplify an implicit textual consensus. Removal of the personal element from the authorship and audience of the formal literature enables each contributor to maintain his own assumption of interpretative privilege without having to persuade those making contrary claims to abandon the same assumption, and it makes it possible for each text to give an impression of factuality without ever requiring the producers of different texts explicitly to agree.

If these speculations about the organization of formal and

informal scientific discourse are along the right lines, not only have we begun to understand why scientists experience difficulties with one kind of informal debate (Yearley, 1982a), but we have also perhaps begun to understand why the research literature takes the form that it does.

A Concluding Dialogue

Textual Commentator   Dear Analyst, I see that you are about to put away your pen and paper. I have refrained from intervening in your text for many pages, as a result of our earlier difference of opinion. But I see that, if I do not act now, all chance will be lost of resolving that difference and coming to an amicable agreement. I apologize for having appeared to criticize you earlier. I did not really mean to suggest that your analysis in this paper is untenable. I simply want to understand the nature of your text and its relationship to the discourse of Marks and Spencer. For example, my initial impression was that you were simply trying to describe the organized interplay of signifiers within these scientists' texts. However, in your analysis, you seem to have taken over some of these signifiers and used them as resources in your own interpretative work. This is particularly clear when you write about the 'success' and 'failure' of the letters and of the effectiveness of the research literature. Surely 'success' and 'failure' are participants' conceptions; your job, as analyst, is to treat them as topics for investigation, not as resources for making assertions about the social world of science.

Analyst   You are right in saying that I have taken over participants' notion of success/failure and that I do not treat it simply as a topic for analysis. One reason for this is that I want to explore the possibility of carrying out an analysis which may be of some practical interest to participants. There are indications that some scientists are interested in trying to understand the success/failure of informal debates such as the stoichiometry debate. One of my aims, therefore, has been to construct an analysis which begins by trying to describe how the letters work, but ends by using its conclusions to say something of possible practical import for scientists. I have been aware from the outset that, in order to do this, it is necessary at some point to modify one's analytical discourse so that it starts to merge with participants' practical discourse; in the course of which signifiers like 'success/failure' are used relatively unreflexively and projected upon the world.

Textual Commentator   But this projection of meaning upon the world is not confined to your use of participants' everyday terms. It's very much a feature of your *analytical* practice, as I pointed out earlier. It seems to me that, in your own text, you constantly deny the textuality of your own claims. You continually tell us what's happening in your biochemists' letters: and in your text that 'happening' is often treated as independent of your own selective and artful use of language. Are you not, even in your purely analytical work, faced with a dilemma similar to that which you attribute to the stoichiometry letters, that is, does not your analysis combine a universally interpretative view of textual production with a practice which regularly appears to deny or hide its own textuality?

Analyst Yes, I accept what you say. But I want to emphasize that a simultaneous analytical recognition of and practical denial of textuality is necessarily implicit in what I understand by 'textuality'. I take textuality to mean that we construct the meaning of the world, we construct what we take that world to be, through our organized use of words and other symbolic resources. Now the very formulation I have just given of 'textuality' relies on two opposed concepts, namely, 'the world' and 'the word'. One cannot even begin to talk about textuality without using some basic semantic contrast between textuality (the word) and that beyond textuality (the world). If we restrict ourselves to only one part of this dichotomy, we can say nothing of interest. For example, we can say only that by use of the 'word' we formulate the 'word'.

I want to suggest that all discourse depends on and is made possible by such basic dichotomies. We have seen many of them at work in our scientists' texts as well as in my own. The most fundamental of these dichotomies, for our present purposes, is that between the word and the world; between language and that constituted through language. Unless we commit ourselves to acting upon this distinction, we can generate no further discourse. In using the word to speak about the world, we necessarily treat the word as referring beyond itself. Unless we project the word in some way, we can have nothing more to say.

Similarly, the notion of textuality, if it is to be used as part of an analytical practice, cannot itself be treated as no more than textuality. If 'textuality' is regarded as nothing other than an arrangement of signifiers, it does not refer beyond itself and has no implications for analytical practice. Thus, dear Commentator, your persistent concern with the self-reference of textual analysis must end somewhere along the line. Indeed, in raising these questions about *my* text, you have necessarily projected your own discourse on to that text, for example, in pointing out its denial of its own assumptions. Thus you too, in the act of speaking, have had to ignore your own textuality.

Textual Commentator I take your point. But what does it imply for your own analytical practice? It seems to me that you are close to recommending an unquestioning adoption of the uniformly empiricist discourse which, as you point out above, natural scientists seem to use so successfully in their research literature. If analytical discourse necessarily involves us in a denial of textuality somewhere along the line, and if recognition of our own textuality makes analysis difficult to accomplish successfully, why not go the whole hog and simply adopt a form of analytical discourse which does not allow consideration of its own textual production?

Analyst Well, of course, this is just what most social scientists do; even those concerned with language. But, actually, I am not advocating that solution, for the following reason. As I said in the first chapter, empiricist discourse implies an interpretative dominance over your subject of study. This is easy to maintain when writing about mitochondria. We work on the assumption that mitochondria themselves are not textual producers; even when they appear as the dominant textual agents in a research paper. Thus they enter the world of textuality with no voice of their own and, in this sense, firmly under our textual control. They do not, and cannot, challenge our assumption of interpretative privilege. But clearly that assumption is inappropriate when we are studying human beings and, in particular, when we are studying how human beings create meaning. We *have* to recognize that our analysis of participants' language-use is just one more kind of textual product; moreover, it is a second or third level textual product which depends on, makes use of, overlaps with and sometimes competes with the interpretative work embedded in participants' texts. To deny one's own textuality, therefore, when engaged in this kind of analysis is, in effect, to deny one's interpretative dependence on these texts, to claim interpretative privilege from the outset over other participants' texts, and to assert that there is one class of texts, namely, one's own, which are to be treated as beyond textuality. Thus, if our project is the study of textual production in all its forms, we can hardly refuse, by analytical fiat, to include our own texts within the scope of that project.[3]

Textual Commentator Although I think that I understand what you are saying, I have to confess that I am utterly confused. On the one hand you argue that, in order to say anything at all, we have to deny textuality. Yet, on the other hand, you state that in the analysis of textual production we must accept textuality. This seems paradoxical. Perhaps I have misunderstood.

Analyst No. You *have* understood. What I want to propose is that, in the study of textual production, we have to devise new forms of discourse which allow us both to assert and to deny textuality within the same text. In other words, we have to abandon the notion, which is fundamental to the conception of analysis borrowed from natural science, that analysis must adopt a monologic, univocal form. I propose that we begin to construct analytical texts containing multiple textual agents which can operate, to some extent, independently and thereby deal with different aspects of textuality. If we do this, we may be able to use a given text to address its own textuality as well as that of other texts. One voice or textual agent would have to ignore his own textuality in the act of analysing other texts. But the other voice could deal, to some degree, with the textuality of the analysis.

Textual Commentator   Ah, now I see why you have invited me to take part in your text and allowed me to comment on your textual practice. I also think that I begin to see why you are interested in the success and failure of scientists' attempts at interpretative dialogue.

Analyst   Yes, I think that is probably becoming clear as we talk. As analysts of textual production we are necessarily involved in making practical judgements about the effectiveness of our own forms of discourse which are similar to those made by Marks, Spencer, and their colleagues. One reason why I am interested in their attempted dialogue is because I want to explore the effectiveness of direct, personal dialogue as an analytical device in my own texts. My examination of the Spencer–Marks debate was particularly helpful in suggesting to me that personal dialogue, as a form of discourse, is somehow especially appropriate to explicit interpretative work and difficult to sustain when it relies heavily on the empiricist repertoire. Thus the combination of monologic analysis with dialogic commentary, in the same analytical text, could be a first step towards developing new forms of text suited to the dual character of textual analysis. By introducing a dialogic component, one might be able to place the typical analytical monologue in a new interpretative framework. One might be able to use dialogue to bring into the open some of the interpretative work hidden behind the unavoidable empiricist aspects of one's analysis.

Textual Commentator   Well, I realize, of course, that dialogic forms of analytical texts have been used in the past. I suppose the Platonic dialogues are the most well known. But, in moving in that direction, are you not merely resuscitating out of date forms and withdrawing into the past?

Analyst   I don't think so. I have no intention of rewriting Plato. In reintroducing the dialogic form, one is in no way obliged to repeat old arguments. My view is that use of that form encourages and perhaps enables you to say things which would not otherwise be said. Moreover, as soon as you begin to think of employing dialogic form, several new possibilities immediately come to mind. For example, why not create an analysis in the form of a dialogue with one, or more, actual participants? This kind of analysis, as far as I know, has not been tried before. It would be a stringent test of one's analysis to offer it for close scrutiny and comment to those responsible for the original texts; particularly in the case of such skilled symbol-manipulators as scientists. In the course of such an analysis, one could not be continually concerned with one's own textuality. There would be no alternative to projecting one's claims upon participants' own textual products. However, one's analysis would then become a text available to participants for deconstruction and textual analysis. In this way, by abandoning the analyst's usual assumption of interpretative privilege, one could enlist participants' help in revealing one's own textuality, whilst at the same time digging more deeply into their interpretative capacities and your own.

Textual Commentator   This sounds very attractive, assuming that you can find a participant with enough enthusiasm and time to spare. But would it actually be analytically productive? If, for example, you were to offer an analysis of the stoichiometry letters to Spencer and, because you had something to say about their failure, he examined them carefully and replied in detail, would you not have merely another set of letters about the original set of letters? If you then analysed the second set of letters, in order to see what could be gleaned from them, and repeated the process, you would be heading for an infinite regress; as well as provoking Spencer beyond endurance. Quite apart from the practical problems, how would you be able to say: 'This text states what is known about the forms of discourse used in the stoichiometry letters'?

Analyst   I think you are working with a false conception of what constitutes knowledge. You are treating it as some kind of final text which sums up the facts of the matter; a coherent set of unchanging propositions. But actually, there is no such thing as a final text in this sense. All texts are used as the starting point for some new textual production. Even the strings of symbols of Euclidean geometry were and are continually reinterpreted and re-created within new contexts and occasions of discourse (Bloor, 1976).

I suggest that we replace the notion of knowledge as a set of constant propositions with a conception of knowledge as that which contributes to a continuing process of textual production. Each new contribution has to be interpreted by its readers afresh at each and every reading and then used as a resource in their own, potentially diverse, textual productions. Thus, in so far as Spencer were to respond to the claims contained in my analytical letters and to use those claims, for example, in talking to other scientists about informal communication, those letters would be said to have furnished him with knowledge. This would be so, even if Spencer were flatly to reject all my assertions. For Spencer would then know, through my text and through his own re-telling of that text, that certain assertions were incorrect. If Spencer were to respond directly to me with approval, comment, criticism, textual decon-struction, and so on, we could treat the combined set of letters as embodying a joint, dialogic analysis; an analysis which might, through its duality of voice, go some way towards meeting your request for greater textual reflexivity. The fact that the analysis was embedded in one or more exchanges between two authors of personal letters would in no way prevent readers from treating the texts of those letters as furnishing knowledge about the original stoichiometry letters; nor would it prevent them from extracting from the analytical letters whatever resources they needed for the construction of their own subsequent spoken or written texts.

Textual Commentator Well, I'm not sure that I am persuaded by your arguments. It seems a strange analysis, to me, that can take the form of a letter to and a response from one of the men being studied. But I can see that you have given some thought to the issue of self-reference in relation to textual analysis and that your approach does encourage us to explore new forms of analytical text. Who knows what might come of it? You'll be writing plays and fairy stories next (see Latour, 1980).

Analyst I can tell from that playful remark that you are worn down, but not convinced, and are simply too tired to continue. I think perhaps its time for us, and the Reader too, to break for tea. Would you like some muffins?

Textual Commentator Splendid![4]

Notes to Chapter 1

1 Previous analyses of related material can be found in Gilbert and Mulkay (1984).
2 The idea of the Textual Commentator is taken from a paper by Anna Wynne (1983). Wynne distinguishes between comment and original text by changing the typography, as I have done above in 'Intro-ductions'.
3 Neither the Analyst nor the Commentator seem to realize that this argument is just as applicable to natural scientists' discourse as it is to social scientists' discourse. The Analyst constructs his case here by drawing a contrast between social scientists' concern with textual agents and natural scientists' concern with non-textual agents. This distinc-tion, however, depends on the Analyst's accepting natural scientists'

impersonal formal texts at face value. In such texts, scientists *appear* to be dealing exclusively with an impersonal, objective, non-textual natural world. But we, and indeed the Analyst, know that this is merely a conventional format. In view of the content of this chapter, along with that of numerous other studies (see Latour and Woolgar, 1979), one could reasonably maintain that natural scientists are not concerned with the natural world as such, but with that world in so far as 'it' is depicted in their own and in other scientists' discourse. This certainly seems a more accurate description of the Marks–Spencer debate. If we adopt this interpretative view of natural scientists' discourse, the Analyst's advocacy of 'a form of discourse which recognizes its own textuality' seems to apply across the board and not just to the social sciences. The meaning of the natural world, as well as that of the social world, is created through human textuality and this needs to be recognized in the texts in question. It seems to me that it is precisely this denial of one's own textuality which lies behind the difficulties experienced by Marks and Spencer. [The Meta-author]

4 I have decided to dispense with the services of the Textual Commentator for a while. In Chapter 2, I will use a conventional analytical monologue to confirm (ironically) the need for dialogue. In subsequent chapters, other forms of dialogue and textual commentary will be explored.

2
Conversations and Texts: Structural Sources of Dialogic Failure

In the previous chapter, I made passing reference to the importance of understanding the similarities and differences which are characteristic of the interpretative practices employed in scientists' letters and those employed in their spoken dialogue. In this chapter, I intend to explore these similarities and differences in a little more detail. Ideally, one might wish to proceed by comparing the stiochiometry letters examined above with recordings of conversations in which their authors discussed the same range of technical issues. But such an approach is impossible for various reasons; not the least of which is the fact that the letters exist precisely because the two authors were unable to talk face-to-face about the stoichiometry issue.

An alternative strategy is therefore needed. The one I shall adopt here is made possible by the availability of a considerable body of analysis of natural conversations. In this analysis certain basic features of naturally occurring spoken dialogue have been identified. Accordingly, my procedure will be to select some of these features from the literature of conversation analysis and then to examine how far they can be used to describe the organization of the stoichiometry letters and how far they need to be supplemented with additional analytical conceptions. This approach is consistent with Atkinson's recent suggestion 'that an adequate understanding of how texts are produced and responded to may remain elusive so long as the issue is pursued without making close comparative reference to how talk works' (1983, p. 230; see also Levinson, 1983, chap. 6).

Natural Conversation and Turn-Taking

Let me begin by listing five basic features of naturally occurring conversations (Sacks, Schegloff and Jefferson, 1974; Schegloff and Sacks, 1974):

(1) At least one party and no more than one party speaks at a time.
(2) Speaker-change recurs, that is, participants take it in turns to speak.
(3) Each speaker orients to prior utterances in the conversation.
(4) Special mechanisms are required to open and close conversations.
(5) Contributions are relatively brief and the close articulation of different speakers' utterances operates at the level of fine detail.

It is proposed by Schegloff and Sacks that the mechanisms of turn-taking (points 1–3 above) are the 'fundamental generating feature of conversation' (1974, p. 237). In other words, conversations are generated out of and organized sequentially around a closely ordered exchange of turns. Speakers maintain the turn-taking sequence in such a way that each utterance appears to 'fit naturally' with what has gone before (ibid., p. 243). Thus a crucial characteristic of natural conversations is that the minute detail of their structure is a joint interpretative accomplishment. The starting point for any understanding of conversational organization must be the detailed interlocking of different participants' contributions.

It is important to recognize that features such as 1–4 above are 'descriptions of the orientations of conversationalists in producing proper conversation' (ibid., p. 236). This means that not only should we, as analysts, be able to observe that such features are pervasive in ordinary conversations, but also that they are features to which participants themselves attend. Thus, when they are absent, their absence is noticed and dealt with by conversationalists. For example, it is not uncommon for speakers' contributions to overlap briefly, thus 'violating' point 1. But it is very unusual for two parties to *continue* to speak at the same time. Normally, one or other party will quickly give way. Similarly, silences do occur in the course of conversations (points 1 and 2). But the absence of speech is normally a noticeable matter and is dealt with in various ways (Sacks, Schegloff and Jefferson, 1974, p. 715). As a final example, there are occasions when conversations are not brought to a close in the manner specified by Schegloff and Sacks (point 4).

However, as these authors point out, failure to abide by the usual procedures for closing a conversation 'becomes a distinct sort of activity, expressing anger, brusqueness, and the like, and available to such a use by contrast with' the customary practices (Schegloff and Sacks, 1974, p. 241).

There are, then, two ways of establishing the importance of the kinds of features identified by conversation analysts: one is by observing regular patterns of discourse; the other is by observing what happens when recurrent patterns are disrupted or altered. With this in mind, we can return to the stoichiometry letters, with the aim of discerning how far the basic features of conversation appear in these written texts. I will concentrate initially on the existence of turn-taking and the close articulation of turns.

Parallels and Differences

One observable similarity between conversations and the stoichiometry letters is that both are made up of a series of distinct, ordered turns. In the letters, the sequence Spencer–Marks–Spencer–Marks continues from start to finish. In this basic respect, conversation and the kind of epistolary sequence examined above are both organized around the mechanism of turn-taking. Of course, such ordered sequences of turns do not always occur smoothly, without exception, in either conversations or letters. For example, in the stoichiometry letters, Spencer dispatches his second letter before Marks's reply to his first letter has been delivered. Occasional disruptions of this kind are particularly revealing, however, because, when they occur in letters or conversations, participants typically treat them as departures from the normal, proper course of events and they tend to provide some explanation and/or justification of why they are deviating from the expected pattern. This can be seen in the opening lines of S2, which are quoted below. Spencer begins S2 by mentioning the possibility that Marks has not received the prior letter. The implication seems to be that, if it is possible that S1 was never received, S2 is not 'out of turn' and no impropriety is involved in Spencer's trying to start the sequence again. The opening words of S2 seem indirectly to draw this implication to Marks's attention. Spencer then follows with the words 'At all events, I thought you would like to know . . .', which serve to justify his writing S2, even if S1 *has* actually been delivered. For they convey that what Spencer now has to say will be of interest to Marks 'at all events', that is, whether or not the latter has received Spencer's previous communication. Thus the opening of S2 attends to the possibility that it could be deemed to be 'out of turn' and is designed to deflect any charge that the latter has improperly departed from the proper sequence of turns.

The sequential organization of the stoichiometry letters, then, can be seen partly from the fact that the letters tend to occur in an obvious sequence and partly from the fact that departure from the sequence is noticed and justified by participants themselves. In these respects, there are clear similarities between letters and conversations. However, there are also differences. In particular, the exchange of letters cannot be remotely as continuous as the exchange of conversational utterances. In the latter case, a silence of a second or so can become a noticeable departure from the regular exchange of turns. But for two authors exchanging missives across the Atlantic, there can be no such detailed articulation of utterances. There is bound to be a comparatively long gap between turns. Nevertheless, despite the slow pace at which written contributions are exchanged, authors clearly treat each letter as creating an obligation to respond within a 'reasonable period'. This is evident in the concern which is repeatedly expressed in the letters about the issue of 'lateness', that is, about the regularity with which written turns should be taken.

M2   Thanks very much for your good letter. I am sorry, however, that my reply is so tardy; I have had to be away on several occasions since September.   (a gap of six weeks)

S2   I wonder if you received my letter of 30 September. At all events, I thought you would like to know . . .
                                                      (a gap of seven weeks)

M2   Thanks very much for your letter of November 17. I am sorry to be so tardy in replying, but I have been away for much of the time since.   (a gap of one month)

S3   Thanks for your letter of 17 December with enclosed manuscripts. I did not reply immediately to your letter of 12 November, because this crossed mine of 17 November in the post.   (a gap of two weeks)

S5   It is my turn to apologize for being so slow to reply to your helpful letter of 3 May. I have been rather snowed under with other matters and so have only now been able to give it the attention it deserves.   (a gap of one month)

M5   Thanks very much for your letter. It arrived just as I was about to write to you and send you a manuscript . . .
                                                      (a gap of eighteen days)

We can see from these 'openings' that six of the nine (available) letters in the sequence begin with a direct reference to the issue of lateness and/or turn-taking. Of the other three letters, one is the first in the sequence, one is a draft concentrating on technical issues, and one is *entirely* concerned with explaining in advance why there will be some delay before the debate is continued (S4). Thus it seems that a remarkably high proportion of letters attend explicitly to their proper location in an ordered series of exchanges. The regular expression of 'thanks' for the preceding letter is itself a conventional recognition of the interpretative exchange in which participants are involved. It is a formal acknowledgement of the prior 'turn' to which the writer is responding. In addition, in their references to and particularly in their justifications of lateness, both authors seem to be taking note of an implicit expectation that each recipient should respond before 'too long'.

In this respect, authors' textual concern with lateness corresponds to speakers' orientation to silence. Both indicate that participants construct their contributions as parts of an orderly sequence in which each turn follows 'directly' from the last. Of course, a 'direct' response to a letter cannot be as immediate as a 'direct' response to another's utterance when face-to-face. But authors regularly state why it is that their reply is slower than might have been expected. To refer to 'being away' or 'being snowed under by other things' serves to remove the 'lateness' textually from the writer's control. It establishes that, although the reply may seem to be slow by normal standards, it is as direct as was possible in the circumstances and, therefore, that no culpable violation of the expectation of regular turn-taking has occurred.

Another observable characteristic of the references to lateness and turn-taking in these letters is that they always come at the very beginning of the letter in which they occur. Our two authors refer explicitly to their participation in the orderly sequence of turns as a way of setting in motion their specific contributions to that sequence. It should be noticed, however, that our authors comment only on their own lateness; never on that of their partner. Thus admissions of and justifications of lateness have no interactional consequences, at least as far as the written texts are concerned. 'Lateness' is never treated as a topic for joint discussion. It is, rather, employed by each contributor as a formalized means of re-entry into a common textual enterprise.

It appears, then, that personal letters, like conversations, are organized around and generated in accordance with similar basic principles of turn-taking. However, participants' concern with 'lateness' in the letters, as opposed to 'silence' in conversation, reveals a critical difference in the time-scale of the turn-taking

sequences involved. Whereas conversations are organized in minute
detail at the level of micro-seconds, the exchange of the
stoichiometry letters operates over weeks and even months. The
relative slowness of the process of turn-taking in letters has one
obvious consequence; namely, much more interpretative work
must be accomplished during each turn. In the course of
conversations, each participant can be observed to build up an
overall contribution through a series of responses which are finely
co-ordinated with the responses of the other participant(s). Each
speaker's contribution is fitted piece by piece to other participants'
utterances as they occur. In this sense, turn-taking is *the* generative
mechanism of conversational structure. In correspondence, however, turn-taking is likely to be much less *directly* responsible for
the detailed organization of contributors' relatively extended texts.
Because it would be impossibly slow and cumbersome if participants were to construct their correspondence utterance-by-
utterance, the text of each letter tends to be relatively long, to be
less directly constrained by the nature of the other author's last
turn, and therefore to be, to a much greater extent, internally
generated. Our next question, therefore, must be: is there another
critical generative mechanism, as well as that of turn-taking, which
is observable in the textual organization of letters; and, if so, what
is it, how does it work, and how is it combined with the procedures
of turn-taking? In seeking answers, we must look for a mechanism
which is especially characteristic of extended passages of discourse,
yet which can be analysed in a similar structural manner to the
analysis of turn-taking.

Contrast Structures

The most obvious interpretative mechanism used by the authors of
the stoichiometry letters to generate and organize their extended
texts is that of the semantic opposition or two-part contrast
structure (see Yearley, 1982b and Potter, 1983). A focused, yet
generative, process analogous to the organized movement of
conversation is sustained in the letters by the use of these
dichotomous contrasts. One way in which authors are able to
generate extended textual sequences, in the absence of conversational response and comment, is by constructing them around basic
semantic contrasts which can only be resolved by means of further
interpretative work to be carried out in common.

The binary oppositions or contrast structures given below are not
sets of categories employed by the analyst to summarize segments
of participants' discourse. They are, rather, the actual terms used

by participants themselves. The following list presents in order the contrasts used by Spencer and Marks, and shows how frequently such contrasts appear in the stoichiometry letters.

S1	Glad	Sorry
	Facts	Opinions
	Derived coefficients	Unprocessed values
M1	Pleased	Sorry
	Fact	Fiction
	Fact	Meaning
	Observed value	True value
	Primary H^+ pumping process	Other ion movements
	Electrogenic antiport	Electrogenic uniport
	Observed value	True value
	$2H^+$	More than $2H^+$
	Letters	Papers
S2	Facts	Opinions
	Correct	Wrong
	Frivolous	Serious
	No	Yes
	Uncontrolled	Easy to control
	Simple	Complex
	Before the pulse	After the pulse
	Final value	Initial value
	Passion	Good will
M2	Quite a few years ago	Today
	Short report	Extensive papers
S3	Interpretation	Observation
	Super-stoichiometry	Actual stoichiometry
	Interpretation	Observation
	Plastic vessels	Glass vessels
	Raw data	Interpretations
M3	Glass vessels	Plastic vessels
	Data	Observations and conclusions
	Trivial points	Substantive responses
S4		Nil
M4		Missing
S5	Raw data	Interpretation
M5	Observations	Interpretations

In this list, I have included only items where an explicit distinction is made in the text between two contrasted terms or short phrases. There are, in addition, numerous occasions where one term is used, for example, 'observed value' or 'fact' or 'interpretation', from a previously mentioned two-part contrast. Once a contrast pair has been clearly stated in a particular letter, either part of that structure can be used later in that letter or subsequently without necessarily re-stating the contrast in full. These 'partial contrasts' or 'implicit contrasts' have not been included in the list. This is one reason why the number of contrast pairs used in each letter appears to decline as the sequence develops. Thus Marks, in M2, ends the technical section of his letter with these words: 'we have concluded that the true H^+/site ratio of the primary proton pumping mechanism is certainly at least 3·0 and may be as high at 4·0'. This statement, in which his central scientific conclusion is summarized, makes no explicit use of contrast structures. Nevertheless, it draws upon three contrast pairs which had already been clearly stated in M1, namely, 'observed value/true value', 'primary H^+ pumping process/other ion movements' and '$2H^+$/more than $2H^+$'.

In order to help clarify how such contrast structures work, it is worth asking whether Marks could have concluded with exactly the words quoted above, even if the three contrast pairs had not previously been employed. It seems to me that he could, in fact, have used exactly the same formulation, because that formulation itself implies the interpretative availability of the unstated items. In the first place, to propose that a certain figure is the 'true' ratio, seems necessarily to imply that other figures are possible, but that they fall into some category other than 'true'. This other category is variously described elsewhere in the letters as 'observed values', 'apparent values' or 'actual unprocessed values'. Similarly, it is necessary specifically to state that one's value applies to the *primary* pumping mechanism only if there are other, secondary pumping mechanisms (or ion movements) with which it could be confused. Finally, to stress that the true value is 'at least 3·0, only makes sense if some special significance is attached to values less than 3·0.

If this is correct, it follows that contrast structures can be implied without ever being stated explicitly in the discourse under study. In other words, implicit contrasts can draw on broader realms of intertextuality (see Culler, 1981 for discussion of intertextuality and literary texts). For instance, as I mentioned in the previous chapter, Spencer regularly refers to Marks's claims regarding the central technical issue as 'contentions'. Clearly, this term is selected from a considerable number of possible alternatives, including 'claims', 'propositions', 'findings', and so on. That the word 'contentions' is regularly chosen implies that these other terms are not quite right and that there is something about 'contentions' which is not captured by these apparent alternatives.

Thus the repeated use of a certain term seems to imply a contrast with a whole class of other, unselected terms, without ever making that contrast explicit in the sequence of letters.

This line of reasoning, of course, brings us close to Saussure's statement that 'in language there are only differences' (1974, p. 120). If language consists of a system of elements whose functioning depends on the differences between those elements, then participants' repeated use of a particular term involves not only a positive characterization, but also a denial of all those different terms which have not been employed. In the case of the stoichiometry letters, Spencer's use of 'contention' to describe his partner's claims may well imply a denial of their scientific validity. In other words, the implied contrast pair may be 'contention/valid assertion'.

However, one difficulty with this kind of analytical inference is that it is, by definition, difficult to document in any direct manner. Although implicit contrasts may be an important interpretative resource in the stoichiometry letters, it is unavoidably difficult for the analyst to provide firm evidence of their use. Whereas in studying conversations, the analyst is often able to support her claims about the way in which particular linguistic formulations are being put to use by reference to the immediate response of the addressee, in letters this is not usually possible and is of no use in identifying participants' use of implicit contrasts. Consequently, I shall for the moment disregard implicit contrasts and concentrate solely on clearly explicit contrast structures.

Generation and Completion

Let me set this section in motion by introducing an *analytical* contrast structure, namely, that between generation and completion or, more fully, between setting interpretative work in motion and closing it down. I suggested in the previous section that contrast structures can be used to generate or set in motion extended passages of interpretative work. Previous study of contrasts in non-conversational discourse has, however, tended to show what appears to be the exact opposite; that is, it has demonstrated that contrast structures are regularly employed to bring extended passages of discourse to completion. Before we proceed any further, we must examine how contrasts are used to bring about interpretative completion. We will find that previous studies of contrast structures and interpretative completion will help us to understand with greater precision how contrasts can generate discourse.

The research to which I referred in the last paragraph has been carried out, mostly on political speeches, by Atkinson (1983). On the one hand, political speeches resemble the stoichiometry letters in that both require extended passages of self-generated discourse. On the other hand, the relationship between speaker and audience is very different from that between two letter-writers. I will return to the significance of this difference in due course. For the moment, let us simply accept that the interpretative task facing political speakers bears some resemblance to that facing scientific correspondents.

Atkinson's research has shown, firstly, that two-part contrasts are far and away the most commonly used interpretative form by means of which politicians bring to an end their speeches or particular segments within those speeches (1983, p. 211). Secondly, he has shown that audiences are able to anticipate, probably by reference to speakers' use of contrast structures, when such a completion point is about to be reached. Let us look briefly at two examples to see how this operates.

Example A

CALLAGHAN: I can say to you Mister Chairman that in this election I don't intend to make the most promises, I intend that the next Labour government shall KEEP the most promises.
AUDIENCE: Applause

Example B

HEATH: Now the Labour prime minister and his colleagues are boasting in this election campaign that they have brought inflation down from the disastrous level of twenty-six per cent. But we are entitled to inquire who put it *up* to twenty-six per cent?
AUDIENCE: Applause

These two examples illustrate how explicit contrast structures are used to bring passages of political discourse to a, in these cases temporary, completion which is marked by audience applause. Atkinson comments that completion and applause 'recurrently occur after *self-directed* statements of praise or boasts, and *opponent-directed* criticisms or insults' (1983, p. 205). This is an important observation. But in order to appreciate its analytical implications, we need to reformulate it in more general terms. One implication of Atkinson's statement may be that each of the contrast structures to which he is referring is composed of what we can call, following Pomerantz (1984), a preferred category and a dispreferred category. Let me suggest that this is always the case, not only in Atkinson's data but also in my material on scientists. (I will return later to this issue of how to recognize preferred and dispreferred contrast categories. For the moment, I will treat them as being fairly obvious.) Accordingly, what Atkinson describes as 'boasts' can be seen to occur when speakers use a contrast pair in a way which emphasizes that the preferred category is self-referential. Alternatively, contrast structures can be used to construct what he calls 'criticisms' or 'insults' by emphasizing that the dispreferred category applies to some other actor or textual agent (such as a political party).

If we look back at the two examples, we can see that we have one of each kind. In example A, we have the contrast pair 'make the most promises/KEEP the most promises'. If we accept that the second category is the preferred one, we have an example of interpretative completion being accomplished by means of a 'preferred-category self-referential contrast structure'. In example B, we have the pair 'brought inflation down from twenty-six per cent/put it *up* to twenty-six per cent'. In this case the contrast structure emphasizes the dispreferred second item, which is likely to be heard as applying to the only textual agent mentioned in this passage, namely, the 'Labour prime minister and his colleagues'. Thus, we seem to have here an example of completion being brought about by means of a 'dispreferred other-referential contrast structure'. Every example of interpretative completion given in Atkinson's paper is brought about by one or other of these two types of contrast structure.

All that I have done so far is to re-state Atkinson's conclusions about contrasts and completions in more general terms. However, we are now able to ask some questions which were previously hidden from us, namely: do dispreferred self-referential or preferred other-referential contrasts ever occur? And if they do, to what interpretative uses are they put? Given the content of previous sections, I am implying, of course, that these latter kinds of contrast structure are used to *generate* interpretative work rather than to close it down. Atkinson's discussion of the way in which completions work can help us to understand why this may be so.

He points out that the first part of the contrast structures used in completions often sets up an interpretative puzzle, which is then resolved in the second part of the structure. The puzzle, in my terms, depends critically on the application of preferred and dispreferred categories to self and other. Thus, in example A, the first part of the contrast structure, that is, 'I don't intend to make the most promises', can clearly be heard, before the appearance of the second part, as a rather puzzling self-denigration. In other words, the first part taken alone sounds like a self-referential dispreferred category *and thereby demands resolution*. As Atkinson suggests, such puzzling formulations are likely to set up an expectation that a satisfactory resolution will be forthcoming, in this way often enabling the audience to begin to applaud whilst the second part of the contrast structure is still being constructed. To put this another way, participants regularly anticipate that formulations which employ potentially dispreferred self-references are the first part of a contrast structure which will, on completion, turn out to propose some kind of preferred self-reference (or dispreferred other-reference). In other words, we can account for audiences' anticipatory applause in response to dispreferred self-referential contrasts on the supposition that such contrasts are, and are recognized to be, unstable structures which are usually transformed immediately into self-preferential contrasts. Thus audiences can furnish applause slightly in advance of completion, before they know exactly what is about to be said, because they are responding, not to the detailed content of the speaker's talk, but to the structure of his discourse.

In example A, then, what initially seems to be a potentially negative admission by the speaker about not making promises, turns out itself to be a promise to KEEP the most promises. In the course of this artful transformation, the negative connotations of making more promises than you can keep are displaced, by implication, on to some other party. The puzzle or interpretative problem created by the first part of the contrast structure is quickly and predictably eliminated. The same argument applies, with minor modifications due to its different form, to example B. The interpretative puzzle is created by what looks like the application of a preferred category to another textual agent. In the first part of the structure, the speaker applies to the other party what appears to be a preferred category. To stop at this point, during a political party conference, is virtually inconceivable. Further interpretative work has to be accomplished and it is accomplished in a manner which is predictable in general form, that is, a positive other-reference is transformed by means of a contrast structure into a negative other-reference. In this case, the evaluative import of bringing inflation down is radically altered by being combined and contrasted with pushing it up in the first place.

In the light of this discussion, I am going to pursue the idea that dispreferred self-references and dispreferred self-referential contrast structures tend to generate interpretative work, rather than to close it down. As we saw in example A, negative self-reference can create an interpretative puzzle. In situations where negative self-reference is not the first part of the contrast pair, to be immediately transformed and resolved by the second part, but is itself the main interpretative outcome of a contrast structure, then such a contrast structure is likely to generate an opportunity for further interpretative work. Let us see how this is true of the stoichiometry letters.

Opening Up a Debate

Consider once again the two opening paragraphs of the first letter in the sequence of written exchanges about stoichiometry.

> May I say how glad I was to see you again, after so long, at the meeting at Fasano. So I was all the more sorry that you were offended by my remarks about the need to distinguish between facts and opinions in the matter of the $\rightarrow H^+/O$ or $\rightarrow H^+/2e^-$ stoichiometry of respiratory chain systems and the $\rightarrow H^+/P$ stoichiometry of ATPase systems. Certainly, no offence was meant, especially since, having dabbled in theoretical matters a good deal, it may be suggested with some force that I myself may be especially susceptible to the trouble that comes from mistaking opinions for facts!
>
> The purpose of this letter is twofold: first to say again that I am sincerely sorry that I gave offence; and second to try to identify, and possibly resolve, what appears to be a difference of opinion between us.

As we noted above, Spencer proceeds later in the letter to invite its recipient to join him in a debate about the stoichiometry issue and this debate, despite Marks's apparent initial reluctance, lasts for ten months and generates ten letters. These opening paragraphs, therefore, sucessfully initiate an extended sequence of textual production in which a 'turn' can vary from one page to seven single-spaced typed pages. What is it about this opening which sets in motion such a prolonged interpretative sequence and how is this sequence sustained?

It is clear that these paragraphs are organized around two contrast structures: glad/sorry and fact/opinion. The first pair is unambiguously self-referential: 'I was glad' and 'I was all the more sorry'. The contrast between 'glad' and 'sorry' is presented in a way which emphasizes the unfortunate state of affairs which followed from events at the Fasano meeting. The contrast is used to draw attention to and to stress the extent of the author's sorrow.

It seems, perhaps, self-evident that 'glad' is likely to be a preferred category and 'sorry' a dispreferred category. But this is not necessarily so: everything depends on how such terms are used in the text. In this case, however, 'sorry' is used in a straightforward way to refer to a state which the author intends to remedy. Thus, Spencer's sorrow is described as being due to his having offended Marks at Fasano and Spencer proceeds immediately to apologize for this offence as well as to assert that no offence was meant and that there are good reasons why no offence *could* have been meant. In other words, Spencer's attribution of sorrow to himself is followed directly by textual work to make that category no longer applicable. Spencer devotes most of the two opening paragraphs of S1 to removing the offence and, thereby, to restoring the textual priority of the preferred category 'glad'. It is precisely through this remedial work that we can recognize unequivocally that 'sorry' is being treated here as a dispreferred category. At the same time, it is Spencer's application to himself of a category which is semantically dispreferred and which turns out to be textually dispreferred that enables him to generate further interpretative work as a 'natural outcome' of his opening statement. Thus, in the first two paragraphs of S1, the stoichiometry debate is set in motion by Spencer's application to himself of a dispreferred-category contrast structure and by the further textual work which this makes possible. (There is an obvious tautology in identifying preferred and dispreferred categories by the textual work which they make possible. But this does not seem to me to be an analytically vicious tautology.)

But clearly there are limits to the amount of interpretative work which this particular contrast can generate. Indeed, this opening contrast structure seems to operate primarily as a device for linking Spencer's letter 'naturally' to preceding discourse (see Schegloff and Sacks, 1974, p. 243). In this sense, the initial contrast structure works as part of an extended turn-taking sequence. The glad/sorry contrast has the effect of depicting the previous discussion at Fasano as incomplete. It enables Spencer to report that, unknown to Marks, the previous conversation contained a misunderstanding which has to be resolved and which can now only be resolved through correspondence. However, if Spencer's letter was merely designed to clear up this disagreement, it would amount to no more than a 'proper completion' of the previous conversation. Consequently, once the first self-referential contrast structure has been resolved, that is, by the middle of the second paragraph, discourse can continue only if some new interpretative topic is 'naturally' produced.

In S1, this new topic is made available in an elegant way by placing a second contrast structure within the first; that is, the offence which was responsible for the glad/sorry contrast is itself traced back in the course of its formulation to a more basic misunderstanding about the distinction between facts and opinions in the stoichiometry matter. Consequently, in paragraph two, as soon as the topic of Spencer's 'offence' is finally terminated by an explicit apology, the text can switch immediately to the as yet unexplored task of dealing with the distinction between fact and opinion.

Given that the opening contrast in S1 between 'glad' and 'sorry' serves as a turn-taking device and that it is treated textually as deriving from an underlying contrast between 'fact' and 'opinion', we can take the latter contrast as primary and as specifying the 'first topic' of the stoichiometry letters that is available for extended development. This form of organization of initial topics closely resembles what frequently occurs in conversational openings.

> There is, for example, a position in a single conversation for 'first topic'. We intend to mark by this term not the simple serial fact that some topic gets talked about temporally prior to others, for some temporally prior topics such as, for example, ones prefaced by 'First, I just want to say. . . .' or topics that are minor developments by the receiver of the conversational opening of 'how are you' inquiries, are not heard or treated as 'first topics'. Rather, we want to note that to make of a topic a 'first topic' is to accord it a certain special status in the conversation. Thus, for example, to take a topic as 'first topic' may provide for its analysability (by co-participants) as 'the reason for the conversation'. (Scheloff and Sacks, 1974, pp. 242–3)

The contrast fact/opinion does come to occupy a special status in the stoichiometry letters, in that it provides a recurrent and critical focus for subsequent interpretative work. As we can see from the list of contrasts provided above, it appears, often in relexicalized form as, for example, fact/fiction, fact/meaning, observation/interpretation, in seven of the nine letters and often several times within a specific letter. As we saw in Chapter 1, the text of virtually every letter is addressed, in one way or another, to this contrast. It clearly operates, therefore, as a remarkably generative contrast structure. Let us examine it a little more closely.

Once again, as with glad/sorry, it appears that we have a self-dispreferential contrast. In the first place, it is clear that the category 'opinion' is dispreferred. For instance, taking something as a 'fact' when it is really an 'opinion' is treated in S1 as a mistake. This seems to imply that a fact has certain positive, creditable aspects which an opinion lacks. It seems to imply that Spencer and others would *prefer* to know the facts instead of 'merely' holding opinions. Moreover, opinions are depicted as being potential sources of trouble; at least, this is so when one mistakes them for facts. In contrast, no suggestion is made in S1 that knowledge of the facts can lead to trouble. Finally, the difference of *opinion* between the two parties is treated as something to be eliminated in the course of the proposed correspondence. It seems to be suggested that at least one of their sets of opinions is mistaken and that further debate is necessary in order to establish which set can be credited with factual status. Towards the end of S1, the goal of the letters is re-stated, not, this time, as that of resolving their differences of opinion about stoichiometries, but as simply finding out what those stoichiometries are: 'As I understand it, we have to resolve the question: what are the proton-translocation stoichiometries of respiratory chain systems?' In other words, the point of the correspondence is to establish whose views are no more than opinions and whose are really facts.

It is also clear that the dispreferred category 'opinion' is used self-referentially in the text of S1. For instance, the author is displayed in paragraph one as someone who 'dabbles in theoretical matters' and who is, therefore, especially likely to mistake opinions for facts. Moreover, it is made clear textually that he may well have made this mistake with respect to the stoichiometry matter. If Spencer is not understood as making this specific admission, his apology to Marks for appearing to have claimed factual status for his own views simply ceases to be an apology. Spencer's 'offence' consisted in appearing to treat Marks's views as opinions and his own views as facts. Thus, the apology necessarily involves Spencer in applying to his own views on stoichiometry the pejorative label of 'opinions'. Finally, in the last sentence of paragraph two, both participants are described as holding *opinions* on the stoichiometry issue and, indeed, the invitation to debate this issue must be textually premised on the assumption that, at the outset, no one set of views can be given factual status. If the whole point of the letters, as presented in S1, is to find out which set of views is factual, then neither set can be presumed to have that status at the beginning of the correspondence.

If the remarks above are accepted as broadly correct, we appear to have a case where the self-referential use of the contrast structure fact/opinion generates and pervades an extended series of written exchanges. All the remaining interpretative work in S1 as well as much of that in subsequent letters centres, as we have seen, around this basic contrast. However, in order to understand how this contrast generates and sustains not just a brief exchange of views but an extended sequence of letters, it is necessary to appreciate that it is applied by Spencer, not only to himself, but also to his discourse partner.

In this respect, the organization of the stoichiometry letters is quite unlike that of the political speeches studied by Atkinson. In the case of the latter, the main textual agents, for example, the prime minister and the leader of the opposition, do not engage in direct interpretative exchange. In other words, whereas political speeches are very close to being monologues, scientific debates by letter are much closer *in form* to being dialogues; at least in the sense that both parties make major contributions to the substantive interpretative work. Consequently, whereas political speakers can create interpretative puzzles through the use of contrast structures and then immediately resolve them to their own textual advantage and to the approval of their audience, neither Spencer nor Marks can bring their discourse to completion without textual endorsement by the other party. Spencer sets the stoichiometry debate in motion by applying the dispreferred part of fact/opinion to himself and to Marks, thereby providing them both with the opportunity of generating interpretative work which will bring that contrast to a satisfactory completion. However, although each participant in every subsequent letter furnishes a text in which the preferred category of 'fact' is applied to 'self' and the dispreferred category 'opinion' is applied to 'other', thereby furnishing individually stable resolutions of the initial contrast, these re-applications of the contrast structure are, of course, mutually incompatible. Thus, the debate over stoichiometries is very difficult, perhaps impossible, to resolve because a common reinterpretation of the initial contrast structure is virtually unattainable.

These difficulties, then, are not due exclusively to the organization of contrast structures. They occur because participants are engaged in a sequence of exchanges. Let us, therefore, examine how the indefinite extension of the debate is also promoted by the procedures of turn-taking and by the normal mechanisms for closing down a turn-taking sequence.

Striving for Completion

Let me begin this section by drawing attention to a strong parallel between natural conversations, as described by Sacks, Schegloff and Jefferson, and the stoichiometry letters. The following statement refers to conversations:

> Turns display gross organizational features that reflect their occurrence in a series. They regularly have a three part structure: one which addresses the relation of a turn to a prior, one involved with what is occupying the turn, and one which addresses the relation of the turn to a succeeding one. These

parts regularly occur in that order, an obviously rational ordering for an organization that latches a turn to the turns on either side of it. (1974, p. 722)

All the stoichiometry letters display a similar three-part or sandwich structure. We have already noted how each letter begins with a reference to its placement in a turn-taking sequence. If we now examine the other two layers of the sandwich, we will be able to see how turn-taking and contrast structures work together to sustain the continuation of the series as a whole.

As the quotation above suggests, the middle section of each letter deals with 'what is occupying the turn'. In the letters, this middle section focuses on the technical issues. The detailed content of each middle section varies, of course, from one letter to the next. However, every technical discussion of stoichiometries is linked by participants to the initial contrast between 'facts and opinions' or to some closely analogous contrast. One central feature of these middle sections is that, without exception, they enable the author to characterize the other party's view in terms of such clearly dispreferred categories as 'fiction', 'super-stoichiometry', 'inter- pretation', 'uncontrolled', 'complex' and 'wrong'; whilst the writer's views are deemed to be 'fact', 'actual stoichiometry', 'data', 'controlled', 'simple', and 'correct'. In short, the technical substance of each turn is organized so that the fact-opinion contrast or some parallel contrast operates as a self-referential preferred- category contrast structure. This observation has been documented in detail in the previous chapter.

Each letter, then, moves towards interpretative closure, in that in every text the initial, generative contrast is self-preferentially resolved. However, because the letters are dialogic, and not monologic, in form, neither writer can bring the sequence to a close without eliciting interpretative agreement from the other. Comple- tion can only be jointly accomplished. Yet, whilst each author continues to apply the basic contrast structure self-preferentially, this is impossible. And indeed, in the third and final layer of each letter, the authors appear to take for granted that the other party will not accept their own application of the basic contrast structure, that further interpretative work will have to be carried out by both parties and that the correspondence cannot, yet, be brought to a symmetrical completion. In other words, the middle section of each letter is organized to display the factuality of the author's claims. As in political speeches, the basic contrast is always resolved self- preferentially in these middle sections. However, unlike political speakers, these authors are engaged in a turn-taking sequence. Consequently, after constructing a textual resolution of the basic contrast, each author concludes his turn with a third section in which responsibility for continuing or closing the debate is passed to the other party, who in due course passes it back again. We can gain a fuller understanding of why turns are passed back and forth in this way, instead of being brought to a close, if we refer to the analysis by Sacks and Schegloff of how conversations are terminated.

Sacks and Schegloff propose that the completion of a conversation typically involves two distinct, yet closely related sections. The simplest example would be as follows:

A. OK } pre-closing exchange
B. OK }

A. Bye } closing exchange
B. Bye }

In the pre-closing exchange, the first party takes a turn where no new topics for discussion are introduced, which thereby prepares for a cessation of talk, but which allows for the possible introduction of new topics by the second party. Thus pre-closings may frequently be initiated during a conversation by either party, only to be declined by the other party's choosing to introduce something previously not considered in that conversation. For example, the first part of the pre-closing given above, 'OK', can always properly be met with 'Well, I think that . . .' or some similar asymmetrical response. The central point, then, is that conversationalists normally have to produce a symmetrical pre-closing exchange before a conversation can enter the final, closing exchange.

I suggest that a similar form of organization is probably characteristic of extended sets of written exchanges. If this is so, in order to bring the stoichiometry correspondence to a satisfactory close, Spencer and Marks have to produce something analogous to a conversational pre-closing, that is, they have to carry out a symmetrical exchange in which both parties acknowledge that no further interpretative work is required. The third layer of each letter is clearly the place where such pre-closings would be located. As Sacks and Schegloff point out, utterances/written formulations operate as possible pre-closings when placed at the end of a topic (1974, p. 247).

In the letters, as I mentioned above, there is a marked break in style and content between the discussion of the technical substance of each letter and the concluding remarks. For example, looking at S2:

End of middle layer

The conclusion seems to me to be difficult to escape that the super-stoichiometry that you have so far identified may really be super-super-stoichiometry and that your $\rightarrow Ca^{2+}/2e^-$ quotients of 2·0 per 'site' still represent a super-stoichiometry by a factor, $n/(n-1)$, of 2. At all events, it seems difficult to estimate the precise $\rightarrow H^+/2e^-$ quotient from your data in the absence of a precise estimate of $n = B^1/(B^1 + C^1)$.

Third layer and possible pre-closing

I do hope that this letter does not seem to you to be unsympathetic or destructive. The object is simply to try to reach a mutually acceptable understanding of the facts and concepts in our field . . .

The concluding section of this letter, which begins with the second of these two contiguous paragraphs, is typical in that it presents no further technical material, but comments, instead, on the nature of the debate itself. These concluding sections effectively complete each individual letter by marking the end of the technical discussion and by passing the responsibility for further discourse to the other party. Several of them are also, formally, possible pre-closings for the debate as a whole. For example, the debate could have finished immediately after S2, quoted above, if Marks had simply agreed in his next letter that Spencer's formulation of the technical issues furnished 'a mutually acceptable understanding of the facts and concepts in our field'. Of course, if he had done so, it would have been Spencer's discourse, rather than his own, which thereby acquired factual status.

Overwhelmingly, however, particular letters end, not with an offer of completion, but with an explicit recognition that further interpretative work is required. Even in the passage above from S2, Spencer assumes that his arguments will be found by Marks to be far from congenial. In other words, the concluding sections of these letters, where pre-closings are structurally possible, are consistently premised on the need for further turns and on the indefinite continuation of the debate. For example:

M2   In another letter I shall respond to your analysis of the H^+/site ratios derived from the $Ca^{2+} - BOH$ measurements.

In the meantime, my best wishes to you and your family for the approaching holidays.

(last two sentences)

S3   the observed value of $2H^+$ that we have found experimentally has not yet been seriously undermined by other more reliable or relatively more extensive data.

We have often wished in my lab, that more biochemists would take an active interest . . . so it is good that your work . . . promises to liven things up . . .

(last two paragraphs)

S4   I would be especially grateful for a quick reply, so that I can get on with the homework you have set me . . .

(last paragraph)

M5   I hope that these comments may serve to clarify further the experiments described in the manuscript. As soon as we have completed it, we will send another manuscript that describes determination of the H^+/site ratio by a kinetic approach.

We look forward very much to hearing from you.

(last two paragraphs)

We can see from these passages that each letter comes to an end in a way which presupposes and generates further debate. In the concluding section of each letter, the opportunity to initiate a symmetrical pre-closing exchange is never taken up. The task of beginning the pre-closing exchange is regularly passed to the other author. I suggest that this is so because, once S1 has set the debate in motion, both authors exercise a strong textual preference for the dominant form of self-preferred contrast. After S1, there are no examples of a writer adopting a self-dispreferred contrast. Every text is constructed around a self-preferential interpretation of the basic contrast structure. Yet the effective resolution of the fact/opinion contrast structure, and thereby the completion of the debate, is structurally possible only if one participant does furnish a self-dispreferred application of that basic contrast.

Given the structure of the debate, something analogous to the following highly simplified sequence is required.

A	I see now that what I thought were facts are actually only opinions.	
B	Good. I'm glad that at last you have come to see what the true value is.	pre-closing
A	Bye.	closing
B	Bye.	exchange

However, given also participants' marked reluctance to employ self-dispreferred contrasts, such a closing sequence is very difficult to accomplish. Thus we can now see how procedures of turn-taking and closure similar to those operative in conversations combine with the contrast structure of the debate to sustain the extended sequence of written discourse about stoichiometries.

Monologue and Asymmetry

In this chapter, I have begun to explore how far the discourse of ordinary conversations resembles and differs from the discourse found in scientists' letters. I have approached this task by taking over some of the formal conclusions of such conversation analysts as Sacks, Schegloff and Jefferson about turn-taking and mechanisms of conversational closure, and by examining the stoichiometry correspondence in the light of these conclusions. There can be no doubt that certain basic features of naturally occurring conversations recur in these letters. Both in conversation and in this particular sequence of letters there appears to be a definite pattern of turn-taking, a distinct three-part turn structure and evidence that participants' texts contain interpretative work which attends to their location in a turn-taking sequence.

Although some of the procedures of conversational turn-taking are clearly discernible in the stoichiometry sequence, there are also significant differences. In particular, written turns appear to be much longer, more complex and less directly generated and constrained by the mechanisms of turn-taking. As a result of these distinguishing characteristics of written correspondence, it was necessary to try to devise a form of structural analysis which was compatible with that carried out on conversations, but which could cope with the extensive content and self-generating capacity of written texts. This was done by drawing upon Atkinson's work on the use of dichotomous contrasts in political speeches.

Comparison of Atkinson's data and analysis with the textual material of the stoichiometry letters revealed that whereas certain kinds of contrast structures are used to bring discourse to a point of completion, other sorts of contrast structure may well be used to *generate* discourse. It also became clear that participants' use of contrast structures in political (or other) monologues would differ from their use of contrast structures in the formally dialogic interchange of written correspondence.

These conclusions provided the starting point for a more formal examination of the interpretative organization of the stoichiometry letters than was provided in Chapter 1. The idea that self-dispreferential contrasts tend to be unstable and to generate further interpretative work helped to explain the structure of the first letter in the series. For this letter made use of just such a contrast to set the debate in motion. Because this dispreferred contrast structure was applied equally to both participants, further interpretative work was required by both parties. As was observed in political speeches, the self-dispreferred contrast was quickly abandoned. Once the debate was underway, both parties organized/reorganized their texts in terms of self-preferential contrasts. As in the case of political speeches, this was easily accomplished by each individual actor. But in the stoichiometry correspondence, participants' texts also formed part of a turn-taking sequence. Consequently, interpretative resolution of the initial contrast did not bring about completion but, because each author's resolution was treated as unacceptable by his partner, simply generated more turns and further debate. In formal terms, participants' persistent use of the same *self*-preferential contrast structure to organize their separate and opposing texts prevented the construction of a symmetrical pre-closing exchange and thereby removed any possibility of bringing the debate to a satisfactory conclusion.

This analysis of some of the basic structural features underlying the stoichiometry debate confirms and supplements that presented in Chapter 1. It indicates that the interpretative stalemate arose out of the combination in the letters of monologic techniques and the kind of turn-taking sequence essential to dialogue. We may speculate that, as discourse becomes removed from the basic generative mechanisms of turn-taking, it comes to rely increasingly on alternative techniques, such as contrast structures and the empiricist repertoire. These techniques make possible the formulation of extended written texts and spoken monologues. But, in so doing, they promote the interpretative dominance of the author/ speaker. They remove the producer of discourse from the restraints imposed by dialogue and they enable him increasingly to construct his discourse so that *his* facts, *his* opinions and *his* voice are paramount. In other words, the forms of monologic discourse tend to foster textual asymmetry and to make effective dialogue unattainable.

Textual asymmetry is not only evident in the discourse of scientists and politicians. It is also present in virtually all sociological analysis, including this text, in the sense that participants' discourse is treated as no more than the raw material for sociologists' interpretative work. Like Spencer and Marks, sociologists work on the assumption that only they can see the real meaning of the raw data provided by their partner (the participant). The crucial difficulty arising from sociologists' endorsement of this interpretative asymmetry is that the social world of actions, texts and other interpretative forms is thereby treated as a realm of fixed meanings which can find expression exclusively through the analyst's voice.

This seems to me to be untenable. I take it as a basic premise that the social world is open to an indefinite variety of alternative interpretations and that forms of analysis should be devised which allow us to deal with this interpretative fecundity. Our denial of analytical competence to so-called participants probably has more to do with sociologists' use of monologic forms (e.g. the contrast structure 'analyst/participant') than with the inability of a particular class of actors to do sociological analysis. Thus one possible way of modifying the customary asymmetry between analysts and participants would be to allow the latter to contribute actively to our analysis. In doing this, we could begin to move away from our normal reliance on monologic forms towards an analytical dialogue, by means of which a genuine interpretative duality could be encompassed. In such an analysis, the analyst would no longer have the sole right to speak on participants' behalf to an impersonal audience. Rather, the two (or more) 'analyst-participants' would take turns in addressing their analysis to each other, thereby recognizing, in the very form of their discourse, the 'multiple reality' of the social world and the ever-present possibility of alternative construals of that world (Schutz, 1972; Goffman, 1974). At the same time, the analyst-participants might be able to go some way towards giving a practical demonstration of an effective dialogue.

3
Talking Together: An Analytical Dialogue

In 1979, Spencer was interviewed by Gilbert and Mulkay in the course of the study published as *Opening Pandora's Box* (1984). Late in 1982, Spencer contacted Mulkay and asked whether he would be interested in attending as an observer a small meeting of bioenergeticists. The idea was that the two of them might collaborate in studying, and perhaps eventually help to improve, the processes of technical communication among research scientists. Mulkay declined this invitation. However, in December 1983 he initiated an exchange of letters with Spencer on the same topic. In the first part of this chapter, we will look at the four letters written between December 1983 and March 1984. In the latter month, the correspondents were able to meet for an afternoon of conversation. This was tape-recorded and transcribed; and provides the material for the rest of the chapter.

Ideally, one would have preferred to present the letters and the conversation in full. But this was impossible. Thus, what follows is a series of extracts from the original texts. Continuation dots are used to show where passages have been omitted. The transcript of the conversation has been 'tidied up' to avoid including material that is unnecessary for the purpose of this chapter and to make it relatively easy to read. The openings and closings of the letters have been omitted. The texts presented in the remainder of this chapter will not be analysed. In the present context, the analysis is taken to be contained in the dialogue between the two 'analyst-participants'.

The Letters

The first letter in the series is unusually long; seventeen pages in the original. It is closely based, however, on the first draft of what has become Chapter 1 above. There is, therefore, no need to repeat it here in detail.

Mulkay to Spencer, December 1983
. . . The purpose of the present letter is, if you consent, to set in motion a leisurely debate between the two of us about the pattern of communication contained in the stoichiometry letters and about scientific communication in general. . . Whilst writing this letter, I have noted what seems to be a very relevant passage in a short editorial in *Chemistry in Britain* . . . which celebrated your receiving the Nobel Prize.

> Spencer believes that this person-to-person type of communication can be much more effective than that achieved in the usual busy conferences or through the mass scientific literature, where there are strong inducements from the audience or readership to stake claims and to become involved in competitive antagonisms, rather than in sympathetic dialogue. Indeed, the very word dialogue (that is different from monologue) implies person-to-person communication, which is easier to achieve in a small private meeting than in a public arena.

I take it that this passage is a fair summary of one of the points you had made to the editor of *Chemistry in Britain*. I was particularly struck by the use of the terms 'dialogue' and 'monologue'; for I have also used these terms in carrying out a preliminary examination of the stoichiometry letters. If the passage above is accurate, you seem to have argued that personal dialogue is, in principle, a much more effective form of scientific debate than the impersonal monologue of the research literature. Let me begin our own dialogue by presenting a counter-argument: that is, I will try to show that personal dialogue, at least within the restrictions imposed by the personal letter, is incompatible with certain basic features of technical discourse, and that the latter is more suited to the impersonal monologue of the formal literature . . .

If the discussion so far is taken to be broadly correct, we can begin to see why the stoichiometry debate was unsuccessful. It seems to have failed because neither author was able to sustain the textual forms necessary for an effective dialogue. Although we find sporadic reference in the letters to the dialogic ideal of maintaining interpretative equality in pursuit of an agreed formulation, the textual practice regularly moves in a radically different direction. The ideal of interpretative equality and personal discourse is overwhelmed in the letters by reliance on textual practices close to those of the research literature. In other words, whereas dialogue requires personal discussion between interpretative equals, the textual practice of the letters becomes predominantly impersonal and asymmetrical as contributors assert their own privileged access to the realm of factual discourse and employ monologic forms which create interpretative inequality and avoid acknowledgement of personal involvement in the scientific claims advanced.

The impersonal monologue is clearly the dominant form used by scientists to write about the natural world. But when this form comes to predominate within a person-to-person exchange, it poses insurmountable interpretative problems. When two authors both use the impersonal, empiricist mode to address to each other incompatible claims about the natural world, it becomes virtually impossible to reach a resolution. Each author writes much of the time as if he were a neutral agent acting, without recourse to personal interpretation, on behalf of the natural world itself. In this kind of text, the facts of the natural world appear to speak directly through the impersonal voices employed in the text. Yet true dialogue requires authors continually to acknowledge, in their texts, their personal responsibility for the interpretative work on which their texts and their claims about the natural world depend. Only if this is done does it become possible for authors to modify or abandon their claims in direct response to others' interpretations. I suggest that person-to-person dialogue can only be sustained as long as those involved recognize in the very form of their statements the personal character of these statements.

A central problem, then, for the maintenance of dialogue in the stoichiometry letters is that they combine direct, personal address with heavy reliance on the impersonal textual forms of the research monologue. Because the letters are addressed directly to particular persons, the debate can only be properly resolved through the identification of a technical formulation which is agreed by both parties. But technical consensus is very difficult to accomplish because both parties tend to present their incompatible positions as impersonal accounts of the facts of the matter. Because both authors tend to presuppose the correctness of their own discourse as they construct their letters, it becomes impossible for either party to move towards a reconciliation of their differences. There seems to be no way in which the incompatible, impersonal formulations which each author uses to speak 'on behalf of the natural world itself' can be translated into a more personal idiom, where authors can admit mistakes, uncertainties and the possibility of different scientific conclusions.

It seems to me, therefore, that the research literature has a great advantage, as a medium of scientific debate, over informal letters.

For, in the research literature, the impersonal form of the research monologue avoids any need for participants to produce personally agreed technical formulations. The impersonal mode of technical discourse which scientists routinely employ to present their claims about the natural world is appropriately matched by the impersonal form of the research monologue. . . I offer these comments on dialogue and monologue in biochemistry for your consideration and appraisal. I would be interested to hear whether you think my remarks about the stoichiometry letters are at all accurate. I would also be interested to know how far you think that this kind of analysis could be applied to other epistolary debates. . . I would also like to know whether you think that there is any significant difference between person-to-person dialogue which relies on the written word and the kind of dialogue which is possible when those involved are face-to-face. . .

Spencer to Mulkay, December 1983
In general principle, I am delighted to respond to your suggestion that we exchange thoughts and experiences about scientific communication. But at this stage in the attempt to assimilate what you say in your letter, I am not convinced that a detailed study of the Marks/Spencer letters will lead to any helpful conclusions. . .

I am not sure that I appreciate the significance of what you describe as 'interpretative equals' or 'interpretative equality'. Do you not think that, when there are two different and mutually incompatible interpetations of a given set of scientific observations – e.g. the electron has a definite charge (Millikan), or the electron can carry fractional charges (Ehrenhaft) – and when it turns out that one interpretative view was mistaken, it follows that the interpretative capabilities of different scientists (Millikan and Ehrenhaft) are not always equally effective? Does the assumption of interpretative equality seek to deny that, in many scientific disagreements, the interpretative position of one of the parties to the disagreement is inferior to that of the other *at the commencement* of a dialogue intended to resolve the disagreement (when the two parties would actually reach interpretative identity)? Perhaps the two parties need to begin by admitting initial interpretative inequality in order to permit a discussion to lead to agreement as to what the best (correct?) interpretation may be. What do you think?

In response to your point about the alternation between formal scientific statements (or monologue) and informal statements (or dialogue) in letters about scientific matters, may I suggest that this may correspond to the need for analytic and appreciative types of communication in the transmission of scientific knowledge, particularly in the difficult process of transforming 'private' to 'public' science. I enclose a reprint of a formal lecture that may help to explain what I mean.

Extracts from Spencer's Lecture, 'Science and Humanity' . . . As Holton (1973) has pointed out, there are two related, but essentially different, kinds of activity or subject that are both described by the word science. One is the subjective or private activity, the speculative, science-in-the-making activity, perhaps largely non-verbal, with its own motivations and its own methods or, in some cases, without self-consciously examined methods. The other is the objective or public subject, science-as-an-institution, the inherited world of agreed, codified, concepts and factual information, that have become part of a scientific discipline that can be taught – no longer showing more than minor traces of the evolutionary processes by which the subjective efforts of the individual scientists created it. My object here is to focus attention on the rational and irrational aspects of the creative activity of subjective science, pursued by individual scientists or different scientific schools, and on the processes of analytic and appreciative communication that are required to enable the subjective scientific activity to be transformed into objective science. . .

It is remarkable that extremely divergent views – such as those of Kolbe and van't Hoff, or such as those of the extrinsic proton pump and vectorial metabolism schools – can be tenaciously maintained by different people or schools, for comparatively long periods of time, in the face of the same experimental evidence. This remarkable phenomenon gave rise to the well-known pessimistic dictum of Max Planck, to the effect that a new scientific idea does not triumph by convincing its opponents, but rather because its opponents eventually die . . .

. . . although objective science depends on a system of observations of reality reaching from the more complex and singular to the more general, it has to rest logically on the purely conjectural foundations below by means of the upwardly directed process of logical deduction (Popper, 1963, 1972). A change of conjectural foundation, a change of theory, is not a logical step in this scheme. It is more like a leap in the dark, the consequences of which cannot be adequately appreciated until after a good deal of analytic experimental testing and conceptual familiarisation and development has been done. Imaginative thought-experiments are, of course, a great help for the subjective scientist seeking out possible new conceptual foundations that may be an improvement on the old . . . the inhabitants of the new and old conceptual buildings may accept different views of the same facts, and may find it difficult to establish adequate contact with each other through their respective analytic communication systems. They must be prepared to overcome the Planck apprehension barrier and leap across, in order to appreciate each other's point of view. As Churchill said: 'We shape our buildings; thereafter they shape us.'

There are evidently two distinct methods, with separate sets of criteria, for deciding between alternative hypotheses or theories. One method is analytic and involves quantitative experimental or observational tests of the predictive capability of the hypotheses. It provides quantitative comparisons of World I with World III, through the analytic mechanisms of the human mind (World II). This observational method for establishing the truth or falsity of a hypothesis is ultimately very powerful, because of its objectivity. But, owing to experimental or observational imprecision, and because of the scope for selecting the experiments that seem to show what a given hypothesis predicts one should observe, the very prediction of a phenomenon or entity may temporarily give rise to its apparent observation – as, for example, with the planet Vulcan. Consequently, it may take some time to settle even such a simple scientific question as: does the hypothetical proton pump of cytochrome oxidase exist or not? The other method of deciding between hypotheses (that must, of course, adequately satisfy the criteria of the analytic observational method) is appreciative. In this case, the question is: which theory does the scientific fraternity prefer to use, which has the greater generality, and which is the most attractive and convenient? There is no final arbiter, other than the scientific fraternity. In Einstein's words: 'Everything should be made as simple as possible, but not simpler.' As van't Hoff (1878) pointed out, the scope for imagination and artistry in subjective science – and, indeed, the scope for humanity – is very great at the level of what Holton (1973) has described as its thematic origins. It is unfortunate that this has not been more widely recognised. . .

Mulkay to Spencer, January 1984
. . . Let me turn to the questions you raise about my suggestion that scientific dialogue is likely to be effective only if participants are able to maintain interpretative equality. You ask whether the assumption of interpretative equality seeks 'to deny that, in many scientific disagreements, the interpretative position of one of the parties to the disagreement is inferior to that of the other *at the commencement* of a dialogue intended to resolve the disagreement . . .'. This question focuses our attention on what can and cannot legitimately be assumed at different points in time during a scientific debate. It is clear that, after a debate has been resolved, participants can make unambiguous judgements about the interpretative standing of the parties to the debate. And these

judgements are usually applied retrospectively; that is, once scientists know the 'correct' scientific answer, they can reasonably claim to know who was interpretatively superior at the commencement of the debate. However, at the moment of commencement, although participants may reasonably assume that *one* of them is right (or more right than the other(s)), they cannot properly claim to know *which* of them is right. For if they knew this, the proposed debate would be redundant. It is in this sense that interpretative equality can be taken to be a necessary feature of effective scientific dialogue. It seems almost to be implicit in the very meaning of 'debate'. In agreeing to enter into a direct, personal debate, participants seem to be accepting that the question of interpretative superiority has yet to be decided.

Although scientists do refer in various ways to the need for interpretative equality in the course of technical debate, they do so, as I suggested in my previous letter, in a rather selective fashion. Moreover, in practice, they adopt the rather different procedure described in your second paragraph; that is, each part quickly asserts his own interpretative superiority and consistently responds to the other party's claims by defending that superiority. My impression from your second paragraph is that we broadly agree that this is how many scientific debates actually operate. Where we may not yet agree is in relation to my suggestion that participants' immediate assertion of interpretative superiority at the commencement of the debate makes a successful outcome much less likely. It seems to me that, in so far as both (all) parties to a personal dialogue deny interpretative equality in practice and pre-suppose their own interpretative superiority, whilst advancing incompatible scientific claims, they make the attainment of interpretative identity impossible. The consequence of this argumentative strategy can be seen in the Perry letters (which I've just been re-reading) as well as the Marks/Spencer letters, namely, a potentially endless sequence of contradictory claims and counter-claims.[1]

One might argue that scientists' asymmetrical strategy is nevertheless appropriate, because the question of interpretative superiority in science is decided by reference to the experimental facts. According to this view, interpretative identity will be attained in due course as all inferior interpretations are gradually abandoned in the light of the accumulating experimental evidence. This argument is presented occasionally in the Perry letters and the M/S letters. For example, you wrote in the former of the possibility 'of resolving specific scientific questions experimentally according to the marvellously peaceable notion of experimental truth' (Letter 58). This conception seems to be implicit in the distinction between fact and opinion which recurs throughout the M/S letters. However, quite contradictory views are also to be found in these letters. For instance, one of the contributors to the Perry letters writes that: 'It seems to me that everyone thinks the experimental evidence is in favor of his theory. I shall not be able to convince anyone that the evidence is in favor of [mine], so I shall leave this question aside' (Letter 60). Similarly, in the M/S letters you are led to stress several times (S1, S3 and S5), partly in response to Marks's accusation that you are ignoring his data, that the differences between you do not arise from your making or accepting experimental observations but from your placing different interpretations upon the available observations.

In the M/S letters, then, you insist, and I think correctly, that the nature of the $\rightarrow H^+/2e^-$ ratio cannot be reduced to a matter of 'mere observation'. This line of reasoning is developed further in your paper 'Science and humanity', where the meaning given to particular observations by a specific scientist is depicted as depending on that scientist's conceptual apparatus, logic, general theory and, most fundamental of all, conjectural foundations. As I understand your argument, differences in these interpretative resources, and especially in conjectural foundations, can help to explain how 'extremely divergent views . . . can be tenaciously maintained by different people or schools, for comparatively long periods of time, in the face of the same experimental evidence'. This is a nice formulation. But am I right in detecting a note of condemnation in the phrase 'tenaciously maintained'? Perhaps not. If no disapproval is implied, that is, if one comes to accept that significantly different interpretations of 'the same experimental evidence' are not only always possible, but also often reasonable, one is led to ask: what does this imply for the conduct of scientific debate?

One important implication, it seems to me, is that one should abandon the rigid distinction between fact and opinion which pervades so much scientific debate. Your radical separation between the realm of human symbols (World III) and that of the natural world (World I), with which I agree whole-heartedly, seems to me to imply that all the symbolic manipulations carried out by scientists operate within the realm of opinion, in the sense that there can never be conclusive grounds for regarding them as isomorphic with the 'real world'. In your words, 'there is no final arbiter'. If this were to be accepted in the course of scientific debate, it would seem to imply that participants should cease to claim a privileged 'factual' status for their own technical discourse, but rather seek to understand the interpretative procedures whereby each party, themselves included, comes to different interpretative conclusions, often on the basis of the same facts or observations. This is close to what I meant by 'interpretative equality' and what I take you to mean by 'appreciative communication'.

Although I did not have this conclusion in mind when I began to write this letter, it seems to me now that there may be a partial correspondence between the notions of 'interpretative equality' and 'appreciative communication'. One might suggest that interpretative equality is a potential feature of scientific debate which, if it were regularly maintained, would enable those involved to explore the interpretative basis of their divergent positions and to reach an appreciative understanding of their differences. Participants in a debate of this kind would not proceed by seeking to demonstrate from the outset their own scientific superiority; they would, rather, concentrate on the prior task of understanding how it is that they have come to differ.

In your final paragraph, you have already suggested the possibility of a correspondence between your notions of analytic and appreciative communication and my conception of monologic and dialogic exchange. I agree with the suggestion you make in that paragraph (that the alternation between formal scientific statements (or monologue) and informal statements (or dialogue) may correspond to the need for analytical and appreciative types of communication) to the extent that I think that the use of direct, personal forms of address creates an *opportunity* for appreciative communication. However, it seems to me that, at least in the M/S and Perry letters, participants fail to build upon this opportunity. Although the authors tend to begin and end each letter on a personal note, the main technical discussion in between proceeds in a manner which diverts the discussion away from balanced consideration of the interpretative work on which all parties' factual claims depend and therefore away from the appreciative understanding of divergent interpretative stances.

I hope that these comments begin to clarify what I meant by 'interpretative equality' and why its presence or absence may have significant consequences for direct, personal debate among scientists. I also hope that the parallel between your analytical dichotomy and my own has been made a little clearer to both of us. In conclusion, I would like to ask some questions which grow out of our discussion so far and out of my reading of your paper. . .

Spencer to Mulkay, March 1984
Perhaps my question about the meaning of equality in the context of interpretation is in danger of diverting our attention from more substantial aspects of our quest for better techniques for enabling people to appreciate one another's views and arguments. I think

your idea of the need for interpretative equality might have been equivalent to the idea that the parties to a dialogue may be more likely to understand each other, and come to a consensus of opinion, if they begin by assuming that their partner in the dialogue can be persuaded by reasonable arguments. Is that right? It seems inevitable that each party would appreciate the strengths of their starting position in the dialogue. Otherwise they would not have chosen to advocate that position or interpretation of the facts, rather than the position or interpretation of the facts adopted by their partner in the dialogue. Do you think that the superiority/inferiority relationship concerning the my/your interpretation of the facts adopted by each partner to the debate arises naturally (and inevitably) at the beginning of a debate because of the above historical circumstance? I agree with the implication of what you say near the bottom of page one of your letter, that the 'assertion' of this superiority by each of the participants at the commencement of a debate or dialogue may make a successful outcome less likely. But my experience suggests that this may not be so if the participants appreciate the symmetry of the position of disagreement (perhaps related to what you call interpretative equality), and so are not actually annoyed by their 'adversary' in the discussion. There is, perhaps, a difference between a civilized formal private dialogue or a civilized formal public debate, and the rowdiness that one witnesses, for example, at Prime Minister's Question Time, or the 'dumb insolence' that I suspect you may be complaining about in scientific 'contacts' through the post!

The interpretation of a considerable number of items of 'soft' data, all of which contribute to the 'facts' concerning a phenomenon that one is trying to interpret (e.g. are the protons you measure pumped from inside the membrane or do they only dissociate from the outer surface of the membrane?), is technically difficult because the weight that one attaches to each (possibly false) item of 'soft' data depends very much on the accumulation of 'relevant' experience. It may depend on assessments of the reliability of various experimentalists who have been involved in obtaining 'soft' data, as well as assessments of the reliability of the experimental set-up and equipment through which the data is obtained. Also, we should not overlook the comparatively humdrum circumstance that many (perhaps most) scientists are very busy, and the editorial policies of scientific journals require papers to be short. Many misunderstandings occur, and then persist, because the brief explanations that time or space allow are ambiguous or inadequate, or they may become rigidified in misleading terms (such as the term chemiosmosis).

May I say that one point I was trying to make in my 'Science and humanity' paper was, by implication, that the conjectural foundations may profoundly influence the weights that one gives to the various items of soft data used for interpreting the so-called facts. That would seem to be a factor in locking a given scientist into a particular 'building' and causing that scientist to be 'shaped' by it. The use of the phrase 'tenaciously maintained' was not intended to carry more or less 'condemnation' than might have been in the mind of the reader. It was simply intended to reflect the well-known position: 'I am firm, you are obstinate, he is a pig-headed fool.' Perhaps I get myself into trouble, sometimes, because my sense of humour (and perhaps of mischief in the face of authority) is stimulated by some of the more bizarre aspects of scientific activity and history.

May I please defend a strong (but I hope not excessive) distinction between fact and opinion? I wish to do this because most of the 'facts' (about World I) with which my branch of science deals are 'soft' in the sense that there is a considerable chance that they represent false data, or misreadings of the events in World I. On the other hand, strong opinions are often maintained about the veracity of some facts, as opposed to others, as indicated above. Thus, the skill of interpretation may reside partly in judging which facts are misreadings of reality. One scientist may have a much better track-record than another (interpretative inequality?) in this respect. A scientific colleague once remarked to me about a scientist of our acquaintance that 'he had been more often wrong about major scientific issues than any other scientist, living or dead'.

I hope I have not been going on with too much of a monologue in the above. I am only trying to explain what is in my mind.

I agree completely with what you say about the desirability of mutual respect between the parties to a dialogue, and the need for self-criticism and the willingness to exchange hats or places (interpretative equality, appreciative communication or what you like). But I find it difficult to appreciate how each party can hope to persuade the other party to abandon their conceptual building and come to share that which they themselves occupy, without extolling the virtues of their home base! (But see the final paragraph of this letter.) I have trouble in understanding your objection to the alternation in scientific personal correspondence between technical or analytical (monologue) descriptions of each participant's detailed experimental and interpretative position and appeals (dialogue) to the other participant to accept and come over to that position. However, I agree that this method, as actually practised, may annoy or antagonize one or other of the participants and fail to achieve any movement towards consensus. Where you say the authors fail to build on the opportunities for appreciative communication, do you think it would be fair to remark that persuasion tends to go all at once; and the after-effects of a correspondence that seemed, at the time, to achieve nothing may actually be more profound than one might have expected? I think that scientists sometimes find that a fairly radical shift of view can be prompted by the coming together of some quite small technical details (embedded in the monologic information-transfer in a letter), the key significance of which was not readily recognized without the influence of some other knowledge or imaginative stimulus from another source.

With respect to the distinction between analytic and appreciative aspects of communication, I think I meant to distinguish areas of scientific knowledge that are being filled in, following the general acceptance of the formality of the World III representation of the events of World I. One is conscious of a kind of modularity and heirarchical state of affairs in World III, and apparently also in World I. Following Popper, I accept that the conceptual framework of World III is built up by a series of mental constructions generated from World II, which retrospectively, using logical analytical methods, can be seen (via World II) to correspond satisfactorily enough (as far as the scientific fraternity can judge) to be acceptable as models of reality. Following Gerald Holton (1978), I accept that, as in the case of the influence, for example, of Ostwald and Ernst Mach in the debate between Millikan and Ehrenhaft about the charge on the electron, the interpretation of 'facts' (particularly with respect to the assessment of the extent of factual misreading) is profoundly affected by theoretical preconceptions or, in other words, by conjectural foundations. Accordingly, I think that the present controversy about the existence of the proton pump in cytochrome oxidase is strongly influenced by the fact that the majority of biochemists think of transport processes (e.g. proton pumping) in terms of a formality that has foundations in physics and physiology, while they think of the chemical transformation processes of (redox) metabolism in terms of a formality that has foundations in chemistry, which are basically separate from those of physics and physiology. The conceptual distinction between the chemical process of reduction of dioxygen by ferrocytochrome c in the catalytic site of cytochrome oxidase and the physical and physiological process of proton pumping in the respiratory chain system, which includes cytochrome oxidase, has, in my opinion, contributed substantially to the notion of the 'redox-linked' proton pump of cytochrome oxidase. Of course, this matter may be of special topical interest because we do not yet know whether the putative proton pump of cytochrome oxidase exists or not, and the views of the parties to the debate are not tainted by any retrospective adjustments. However, you may, perhaps, agree that the debate over the charge on the electron, which is somewhat analogous to that about the proton pump, has the advantage that the story is now complete, and can be viewed from a historically convenient distance.

I think your question about the relative uses of analytic and appreciative communication can probably best be answered by the analogy of alternative languages, such as Greek or English, wave or particle. Misunderstandings or mistakes can arise from faulty semantic or syntactical usages or from failures of skill or apparatus in practical experiments. Such problems can generally be resolved at the analytical level. On the other hand, disagreements can arise as a result of the use of different sets of assumptions, or different kinds of conceptual analogue for describing the same phenomena. The latter type of problem can generally be resolved at the appreciative level. In most real problems, the weight given to the items of data in the analytical scheme may be influenced by theoretical preconceptions that stem from the conjectural field; and so both analytic and appreciative communication methods may be required. I have lately been wondering about the position of problems for which it is impossible to write an algorithm. I suspect that the boundary between the analytic and appreciative fields might possibly be set by the condition of computability. What do you think?

. . . I think that the bits of 'monologue' amongst the dialogue in our letters (including this one) are inevitable because of the need to state a case or assemble evidence in a concrete form before one can usefully comment upon it. Perhaps I have misunderstood your question?

May I conclude by asking whether you think that it might be helpful, in the case of particularly intractable scientific disputes, to persuade representatives of the opposing factions to put the case of the 'opposite side'. Perhaps this is what you had in mind in your idea of 'conceptual equality' but pursued to the logical conclusion, where the two protagonists do all they can to sell the view that they oppose? It hadn't escaped me, of course, that the setting up of the position of the opposition (before showing it to be untenable) is a well-known debating technique.

The Conversation: March 1984, University of York

S What I meant to say to you was: what did you really want to do? Did you want to have a discussion about ways in which methods of communication between scientists might be technically improved? or did you want really to explore what *I* happen already to have thought about that? Because the former would be really more interesting to me. Because I've been floundering about, and the floundering has become a little bit less disorganized. I'd like to think that. It had been mostly in connection with the actual practical job of trying to achieve some sort of understanding of one's own fellow scientists. But also to try and persuade those fellow scientists to be less quarrelsome amongst themselves. . .

M Well, I was aware that your interest was primarily the former. And I think essentially that is my interest as well. I suppose one step towards that goal was simply to ask you about your experiences and your concerns. Perhaps I ought to mention a kind of *third* interest which is, I think, exclusively *my* interest in this matter. It's the sort of thing that it is very difficult to say in letters, because it seems to be going off the point. But I have this additional interest which is in the nature of communication within *social* science, which is parallel clearly to your interest in the nature of communication and debate amongst biochemists and other natural scientists. One of my beliefs is that communication and debate within the social sciences has increasingly come to be modelled on the pattern taken to operate in the natural sciences, and I think to the disadvantage of the social sciences, in many ways. So that underlying my concern with all of these issues is a concern with how I can improve the nature of communication in my realm. And one step towards achieving that goal is to understand how it operates in the natural sciences, because that does provide this model; certainly the model for the formal research literature. So I was particularly struck by *your* dissatisfaction with the formal literature as a means of communication. That's something that I haven't said before, that lies behind my concern with these issues.

S I think I have a similar, reciprocal sort of interest. But not, of course, an interest that comes through communication in the social sciences. But rather the thought that what happens in a discussion in what one assumes is a comparatively unemotive area, in science, whether what happens *there* might have some lessons for what happens in real life. So I suppose in as much as sociology is concerned with studies of human life – in fact, I really laughed at myself this morning thinking that . . . here are you and me trying to communicate with one another and not succeeding yet and the object of this is to talk about how others came to communicate with one another.

M Well, yes. But it does give us this added opportunity, doesn't it? Because we can constantly think about our own communication and learn from it.

S Yes, it depends at what level, I suppose, the critical faculty operates. There are some processes that are rather inhibited by too conscious attention. They can be more or less destroyed, such as the poetic part . . . I hope we're not going to do that to ourselves.

M Well, I think we both start from the premise that the existing patterns are not as good as they could be. Certainly I start from that premise with the social sciences. I can see certain major defects which need to be removed. So, in that kind of circumstance, I think probably we both believe that you have to start thinking about what is going on. One can't just continue to perform as one has always performed.

S No. While it's in my head, there's another specific point where I'm a little uncertain about *your* interests. This stems from your letters to me about bits of correspondence in which I happen to have been involved. In the case, for instance, of the argument about whether the proton pump of cytochrome oxidase exists or not, we may be at something of a disadvantage for the reason that the story's not finished. I think from the point of view of *your* looking at the matter, you might also be at a disadvantage if you talk to me about it, because I happen to be one of the people engaged in the debate. So it might be more difficult to interpret accurately what the situation is, because of one's direct involvement. Whereas if you look back, say, at the argument that happened years ago between Ehrenhaft, who believed in the continuity of matter . . . and Millikan . . . who believed in distinct charges. . .

M I suspect that it's impossible to work out the details of that kind of historical situation. There clearly are advantages to studying debates as they occur and there are also advantages to studying debates which are now, in a sense, finished. But both of these procedures also have great *dis*advantages. One of the disadvantages of studying events retrospectively, as Holton does with the Millikan and Ehrenhaft case, is precisely the way that we now *know* the answer, as you say in your letter, or we think we know the answer. Although, as I understand it, the question of charges has been raised again. Some people have recently argued that Ehrenhaft was, as it were, more right than Millikan.

S Oh really? That would do something very funny to cytochrome oxidase, if the electron could have a fractional charge . . . I mean, it would do very funny things to *chemistry*, if electrons really carry. . . One feels convinced that there was something wrong with his measurements.

M I'm not sure. If one's conclusions and one's measurements and the meaning one gives to them depend on conjectural foundations, I'm not clear that those conjectural foundations can ever themselves be *shown* to be correct. So it's always possible that we can get a set of consistent results which work out perfectly well within a given set of conjectural foundations, yet the conjectural foundations *could* be different, leading to different interpretations of experimental results. Perhaps the most that one might say is that *could* be the case with the electron and its charge.

S As a *general* argument, I must say that worries me a good deal. It sounds like the answer to a question, even to a well formulated and tested question, can be both yes and no. In my sort of science, we try to produce questions where the answer has got to be either 'yes' or 'no', or of course it could be 'don't know'. But it can never be 'yes *and* no'. With regard to the electron, it would be hard – but I don't know, with what you were saying, it takes a long time to think about – it would be hard to think of differences in conjectural foundations that would allow, within anything *like* the same model, an electron which still would be, where the word 'electron' would still be understood to refer to the same thing. . . Let's consider both the Millikan/Ehrenhaft problem and the proton pump/not proton pump problem, because they seem to be rather similar. What should the people – well, actually no, let me think, there is a specific respect in which it's a bit *dis*similar, and that is it wasn't very long before the majority of the scientists thought that Millikan was right and that Ehrenhaft was wrong. With respect to the proton pump, the majority of the scientists think that the proton pump exists. I'm in the Ehrenhaft position. And, well, perhaps I shouldn't be saying so. This is one of the disadvantages of my position. But I think there's a very good possibility that the majority view will turn out to have been wrong. Whereas that *didn't* happen with Millikan/Ehrenhaft.

M Yes. Though, if I were talking to Ehrenhaft now, he would presumably be saying something very similar.

S Exactly the same. So the question is, how do Ehrenhaft and I go about trying to get a faster resolution of the situation? How am I going to be persuaded that Millikan was right? How am I going to be persuaded that the view that the proton pump exists is right? I keep trying very hard to persuade myself, but I haven't succeeded. What am I to do?

M Yes. That is, it's the problem of what we mean by successful communication, isn't it? It seems to mean different things for different people. Clearly for Millikan at a particular point in time and for your opponents at a particular point in time, communication is working quite efficiently, because their view seems to be winning out. For them there's no problem.

S But can we not also say though, that from the point of view of the evolution of knowledge, I would have thought there was a good case for saying that that should affect science. That's not as altruistic as it may seem. But if we want to improve the winning of new knowledge which is true. The word 'true' might be thought to be vague, but it doesn't need to be too vague. Having got the codified knowledge, we put it to the test and we try to find out, does it work if we try to use it? Because if its untrue, it won't work. This is a very good test.

M   I'm not sure about that question, though. Many false theories have been found to work.

S   Only up to a point.

M   That's the most one can ever expect, surely, of a theory. It works up to a point. Because it's a theory, it defines reality in a rather limited and restricted fashion. Theories work with *ideal* realities, rather than the everyday world, which is full of awkward complexity. So, any idealized theory will only work to a certain extent.

S   Right. And this is completely Popperesque, isn't it? That none of them work completely, but at least they work to present satisfaction. That doesn't remove the general idea that *many* theories don't work at all on the ordinary scale. All right? So that I think we do have a fairly crucial kind of test. Let me try to put it another way: the knowledge that we're going to say is 'true' at least works to certain reasonable expectations; that's how you tell whether it's true or not, by putting it to the test. Somebody announces an experiment that gives a certain result, that something happens when they do this, that and the other thing. Now they've described it well, somebody else will find if it works. This person says, 'Yes, what that other scientist told me about getting this experiment to work must be true.' It may be there could be other detailed interpretations of the experiment, which still might not be true. But basically, I think, the good thing about science is that theories *can* be trusted, because you can discover whether they work or not.

M   Yes, though I do have reservations about that. Could I perhaps say what some of those reservations might be? If one thinks back to that discussion that you had with Marks on the issue of stoichiometry, in a sense there, both parties could repeat the other's experiments and get them to work. The debate is not about reproducibility or the accuracy of each other's experiments, but what those experiments mean.

S   Yes. But I think now we've gone back to the one experiment. I was endeavouring to generalize beyond that. . . What has troubled *me* in science is that there may be long periods of stalemate when it seems that different schools disagree and the very occurrence of the disagreement appears to inhibit the process of discovering what *is* the truth. Now I would have said that, even although that might seem very satisfactory to those whose theory is still surviving, I would have said it's not satisfactory for *science*. Because, if there's still a reasonable degree of disagreement, then the main object of the exercise is to bring consensus. So, I'm being Ehrenhaft again, I'm in a minority, I can't persuade myself that the majority is right. I want very much, in the interests of good science, to bring this matter to a successful conclusion, where we all agree whether the thing exists or not. Whatever am I going to do so that we can all come to the same view, other than simply go to the lab and do a lot more experiments? I have a feeling that may be the best answer.

M But that's what everybody is doing already, isn't it, doing experiments?

S Well, some of them are. But they often don't do the sorts of experiments that are good for possibly falsifying their own theory. That's another of the difficulties. I have the illusion that I do do experiments to falsify my theories and I don't particularly mind if my theories are wrong. I say 'illusion'. I'm not sure it's entirely an illusion. But I sometimes think it must be, because I have the feeling that some of the others also have that feeling and in *their* case I think it is an illusion [laughter from both parties].

M This is the Popper idea, isn't it? My view of that kind of rule, the Popperian rule, is that the crucial terms in Popper's rules, like 'falsification', only acquire meaning when they're interpreted in terms of the concrete experimental practices and theoretical presuppositions of acting scientists. So that the term 'falsification', even for scientists working on more or less the same problem, that term can have radically different meanings in terms of experimental practice. That's why I have a feeling that two or more scientists can both claim to be trying to falsify and neither attempt at falsification is recognized by the other party.

S Yes. But what do you do? . . . Ill will is generated by the existence of non-consensus. How can we improve the prosecution of science? We want consensus to be achieved soon, rather than late. The idea's often put forward, 'Well, in the *end*, the truth will out.' Well, I'm not so very confident. There have been cases where the truth didn't out for so long that. . . But even if you still do say, with Pangloss, 'well, OK, in the end the truth will out', that's not satisfactory. We're spending public money. Also it's a matter of the improvement of life. As scientists, we want to hasten that. . .

M . . . It does strike me that most of the experimental differences that I've looked at at all closely do seem to focus around the meaning given to the data. What seems never to be accepted, or very seldom to be accepted, is the point, which you made at the beginning of your first letter to Marks on that occasion, that one isn't arguing about crude data, one is arguing about the meaning to be given to the data. One has this small selection of words, like 'results', 'findings', 'data', 'facts', and so on, there may be one or two others, and they're often used interchangeably, but moving from one word to another frequently has important consequences for the argument being advanced. So that somebody will start off by suggesting that this is simply data, which has to be interpreted, but on another occasion the so-called data will be called 'facts' and of course 'facts' *can* be taken to mean the interpretation *given* to data. So that, without appearing to have introduced any interpretation, without appearing to depend upon pre-conceptions of any kind, the claimant ends up with a statement, 'Well, this is just the way the world is. That these *are* the figures and anybody will get them.' It strikes me that in these debates, the use of these terms is really quite important.

S Do you think that really *does* make a difference, though? I think one of the things I'm wondering about is which way you help participants in the dialogue to go on feeling friendly. Do you get the participants to go on feeling friendly on the basis that they are both allowed to feel that their view is right? Which I have a feeling is what you meant by 'interpretative equality'. Or do you help them to participate without being annoyed, by getting them to agree at the outset that *one* of them *must* be wrong, and is going to be shown to be wrong? It does seem to me that the latter comes nearer the reality of the situation. Of course, I am aware that in some cases it will turn out that neither of them are right. But if they're doing the science properly, they will and should see that there are alternative positions. I don't mind, if somebody writes to me and says these are the observations, these are the facts as I understand them. . . Therefore I believe that you are wrong . . . about the interpretation. . .

M Well, I'm sure that is frequently the way in which it is done. One would expect that on many occasions that works perfectly well. One of the things I feel is that the batches of material *I* get to look at are often exceptional.

S Well, they are, you see. I've been meaning to say that. In some of the other letters, where one or the other of us says 'I'm awfully sorry, I was all muddled up the last time I wrote to you. And that's it and you're quite all right.' But I still want a positive suggestion from you. Because it may be useful in a couple of months' time. What do I do when the scientist I mentioned before comes to visit me?

M Well, in this case, you have a situation which *is* exceptional, it's the sort of case that I will have looked at. The disagreements are marked and about important issues. It's back to the dilemma I referred to earlier: why is collaborative dialogue so frequently submerged? and why is adversarial dialogue so predominant? The reason is, perhaps, like this. If your colleague comes along and you adopt a collaborative attitude, you say basically 'Tell me where I am wrong'. That's one of the things you can say, isn't it? Instead of putting him on the defensive, you invite him to collaborate with *you* in finding out where *you* are wrong. That depends on the assumption that he will allow you the *same* right, that you can *trust* him not to take advantage of the opportunity you've given him to exercise his critical abilities in relation to *your* claims. So there's a kind of trust that he will reciprocate in a like manner. What seems to have happened at the meeting that I was unable to attend, as I understand it, is that that offer was made by your side and the other side didn't reciprocate. They simply took advantage of that offer, to make it *appear* that your case was a very poor one. And because you had collaborated in allowing them the opportunity for that critique, on that particular occasion your side was not able to re-establish its own arguments. It seems to me that's the problem for any kind of collaboration of this kind. It is premised upon the other person's agreeing to act in the same way and if the other person does not collaborate equally, you're lost, at least for the time being. It's like the prisoner's dilemma, where because one can't trust the other party, because neither of the two parties can trust the other, they both get the worst of all possible worlds. I feel that this may have something to do with the predominance of this form of argumentation in science. On any occasion, by arguing in the way that scientists so frequently do, they are *least* likely to come off badly. So it's a strategy for minimizing one's own losses, rather than a strategy for maximizing the benefit of science. That's one of the lessons, I felt, that can be drawn from the consultative meeting.

S But I think it was more a matter of *time*. I wouldn't say that we didn't have the opportunity to try to say rather briefly why we didn't believe that the evidence in favour of their point of view wasn't very sound. But only about 20 per cent of the time was spent examining this overwhelming evidence in a critical manner. So my feeling about the outcome was that it was mainly a matter of psychological reinforcement. It wasn't really to do with a level-headed assessment of the facts at all, it couldn't be. . .

M The only strategy I can see that you might adopt which would be different from the standard pattern would be to invite your colleague to collaborate in jointly identifying precisely those points in the chain of reasoning, used by both sides, where you disagree. There must be certain points in the experimental techniques and the chain of reasoning associated with them where you *do* agree. There must be certain points where you say 'I interpret it this way and the other person does not. Why?' And if it can be agreed in advance that one is going to do that with both sides of the argument, that *might* be a way of removing both parties from the usual stance of arguing *their* case. Both parties would collaborate in looking together at both cases, to see what they can find right and what wrong with them.

S Our thoughts are obviously very close on that. Because what's going on in my lab this week is to set up some experiments for him to participate with. What we're going to do is to set up some observations which are basically identical to observations made by him in order to demonstrate that there are certain things that happen which he doesn't seem to have *seen*. . .

M I think you made a very good point in your last letter about the fact that, if such discussions and correspondence *do* have effects, they may often be delayed. They don't occur whilst the correspondence is taking place or whilst people are talking. So one can't pin down the causes of peoples' changes of opinion.

S To come back though, sorry I interrupted you the first time, to this question. What are you to do where you've got this kind of situation? You feel that you want us to get away from the thing, where we write our formal construction of what it is, then we comment upon them in a more conversational way. But how otherwise can we present the formal data without this sort of monologue?

M I take that point. Again, I'm not giving you an answer to that question. But I take your point about the unavoidability of monologue and, indeed, you may well have noticed in my first letter in the sequence, there was a great deal of monologue.

S Well, you began by apologizing for putting the questions you were going to put in a formal way.

M Yes. And in a way it was intentional that there should be such a lot of monologue there. And I think you've commented on it in your last letter, that to some extent one can't get away from monologue, no matter how much one is convinced that it is through *dialogue* that one comes to understand other peoples' positions and through dialogue frequently that one changes one's own position, nevertheless monologue is an essential part of debate and discussion. So I would agree that one can't avoid it. One must try and make use of one's own monologic texts as productively as possible. One of the reasons why I'm, at the moment, unable to give a terribly helpful answer is that I don't myself understand how these different kinds of texts or different kinds of occasions of debate actually differ from each other. I think you've long been convinced that when you have people down to your lab, it's a much more effective kind of discussion that can take place under those circumstances, where you can talk freely and directly to each other, in the way that we've been doing this afternoon. I'm sure that this is the case. I feel that, for example, *our* discussion this afternoon has taught me a great deal more than we could have done simply from writing to each other over many months.

S Yes, I think so. It's a very ancient thought, isn't it? Wasn't it said of Socrates that the reason why he was so reluctant to write was because books don't answer the questions that you put to them? You may find that the very question you want to ask is not dealt with. I suppose that's the big difference.

M But what I'm not clear about, and what I think that general argument is never very clear about, is exactly what happens in these personal discussions, these face-to-face discussions, that doesn't happen in letters, even though there are many similarities between the form of letters and the form of conversations. And again what happens in letters and conversations that doesn't happen in research papers? That's been part of my definition of the problem, that one can't begin to provide good answers to these questions until one can begin to understand the differences of the structure to these different forms of discussion and debate. . . I wanted to follow up what you've just been saying. You made this point in the last letter, the dependence of scientists' interpretations of their data on things like background assumptions and judgements of other peoples' experimental skill, notions of how right they've been in the past, and that kind of thing. Now it's clear that those background assumptions are not made explicit in formal research papers, and even in letters they're seldom made terribly explicit, though perhaps they are referred to *rather* more frequently in letters. *One* of the important reasons for the benefits of this kind of direct personal communication may be that the informal nature of the communication allows you to discuss such background issues. I think, even in our talk today, we must have talked about some of our background assumptions in a way that probably wouldn't have arisen through formal correspondence. That may be an important consideration that would enable us to begin to explain why informal conversation *is* such a useful means of resolving difficulties, or perhaps a *better* means of resolving difficulties than formal research reports or even letters.

S Yes, I think it must be. I'm very prejudiced towards the view that person-to-person communication is highly efficient. I feel myself *wanting* to think that that's true. But I sometimes ask myself whether that really *is* true. Obviously, when you have face-to-face discussion, there are certain personal pleasures in the way that thoughts move, the speed with which you can make progress, and so on, the personal rapport that makes it a much more enjoyable experience. So, I sometimes wonder whether it might not be that it is much more enjoyable and therefore that's what you like to believe. But I find it difficult to convince myself that that's what happens. I really *do* think I can identify instances where, not only has it worked well at the time, but it has had an important carry over. On the other hand, I can *also* identify instances where it seems to have been peculiarly unsuccessful and disappointing. Maybe one ought to try and collect some real, hard information about it. I think I distrust it a bit. Why do *you* feel – you seem to be saying that you're convinced that person-to-person communication really does work. But why do *you* think it works so well?

M I'm not *sure* that it does. Perhaps, like you, I'm inclined to want it to work better. And I certainly feel that the other forms of communication are much more limiting in what they allow you to say and do. So that, I'm convinced that this kind of discussion is better, if only in that it allows you a much wider range of possibilities. It's possible for us this afternoon to engage in limited monologues. But I think we have to do a lot of other things, and are able to and are encouraged to do a lot of other things as well. And that might explain why some of us find this kind of thing so much more enjoyable; that the enjoyment itself is a by-product of a genuine difference in the form of discourse.

S . . . Is it possible that this is the answer to the question we're asking? That scientists who disagree ought to go to greater lengths, ought to be prepared to find money, or to travel, or perhaps to telephone. Well, telephoning is *somewhat* more friendly. But there's nothing to beat actually being in the same room. But I think further than that, that staying in the same *house* for one or two or three days does a lot more, especially if it's warm and it's pleasant, and you have nice pictures, good wine and some nice food. Maybe that sounds awfully elitist. But the fact is I think it actually works. I don't really see why it shouldn't. But I must admit I'm slightly worried by it.

M I think that what one might *expect* is that the sorts of things that people are able to say to each other changes over the course of several days under those circumstances (It does, yes). And as what we're centrally concerned with is what people say or communicate to each other, it seems to make sense that it could have that effect.

S Perhaps we should persuade politicians, instead of going to great banquets, to quietly meet in pairs somewhere.

M It's interesting that they often do several things. They debate with each other at these various levels, don't they? (Yes) I'm not sure about politicians. I feel that politicians are locked even more within their own mansion than research scientists.

S So maybe the solution with my colleague's visit, I'm sorry, I'm being a bit selfish (It's looming up, isn't it). It had already occurred to me that I might preface the occasion by saying, 'Come, but I hope this is only the beginning of a series of visits and maybe the later ones won't be so short.' In the hope that if experimental information comes out while he's staying, if it doesn't come out to his liking, then he won't feel impelled to go off and not come back.

M I imagine that if he's actually there while the experiment is being carried out, and if as you say he doesn't like the results that you obtain, it *should* be possible for you both to go through those results and to begin to specify exactly where it is that your interpretations differ. That ought to be quite critical. Whichever way it came, whichever of you wasn't happy, the task then would be to find out why.

S Yes. But it's funny, you know. I'm almost completely convinced that it won't come out his way. But I suppose *he* must be almost completely convinced as well.

M Well, as you said earlier about critical experiments, there are very, very few such experiments and the way one operates is by making sense of a whole range of experiments, none of which are really critical. I suppose it's another statement of your notion of the data being soft.

S . . . Can we move to another dimension, the size of meeting? Maybe there's something very special about the meeting between only two people.

M Well, I had it in my notes that we, in our discussion so far, had tended, largely because of the way I defined some of the issues, to think in terms of two parties. Perhaps that's inappropriate for science, because it may be the *third* party that's critical in changing scientific views and bringing about a new consensus. It's the arguments that can persuade the third party, if there *are* uncommitted third parties, it's those arguments which are the critical ones. I'm not sure about cytochrome oxidase, whether there is such a thing as an uncommitted third party.

S There *are* third parties around. I've been trying to consort with some of the third parties, in order to get feedback from what seem to be uncommitted minds. But this is a very dangerous activity in a way, because the definition of 'uncommitted' seems to be the ones who don't know which side they're on at the moment. It doesn't necessarily mean that they don't have a bias, because there isn't, as it were, a neutral force operating between the two points of view. So, I think the thing of using uncommitted parties is a bit tricky. . .

M Yes, I was just thinking that all these people who were centrally involved will not be third parties. And all the people who are not centrally involved will feel themselves not quite able to judge the evidence.

S One feels the only really potent method is to bring the people who represent the extreme points of view, to bring those people together. . .

M . . . My feeling is that the bitterness that scientists experience, arising from these differences of opinion over technical issues, is possibly related to that pattern of accounting for error that's described in the *Pandora* book. If one attributes disagreement to the non-scientific attitudes and characteristics of other people, if that pattern is at all widespread, then it would account to some extent for the bitterness that people experience.

S We do our science for personal reasons. I suppose that could be one of the things that influences the difference of attitude when you're closeted with another scientist, compared with what happens if you're writing a letter or giving a formal paper. The process is somewhat depersonalized. Whether you have ambitious motives or motives that are strictly the sympathy you have for your fellow scientists, maybe they get stronger at big gatherings. People often try to make a special impression.

M Yes. At the moment, one doesn't know enough about what happens to people's arguments and the way in which these arguments are presented at gatherings of that kind, compared with what happens in ordinary conversations. Certainly as you imply, it changes its form. But these changes could operate independently of people's motives. I'm always worried about talking of people's motives. One knows from one's own experience that one's motives are remarkably complex and that whatever it is that moves you to do things is not open to simple description in terms of isolated impulses. One knows that motives are always complex and can be described at various levels of detail and sophistication. And that the account you give of your *own* motives very much depends upon the context in which you're talking about them. It may be quite independent of motives, whatever it is that leads people to act and talk the way they do at big meetings.

S I suppose it's almost completely accidental, isn't it, how scientists manage their communal affairs, in being more generous or less generous in the intercourse between scientists? It may alter. But we don't seem to have any mechanism for trying to adjust that process if it doesn't seem to be proceeding satisfactorily. Perhaps that's unfortunate.

M Yes. It goes back to something you were saying earlier about the, I'm not quite sure of the terms that you used, but what you might describe as the beliefs that scientists have about their own rationality. I *think* it's fair to say that widespread in science is a conception of science as very much an empirical practice. It's a practice for revealing a whole set of facts about the natural world. If that *is* the dominant conception of science, and I think it's the one which is reflected in the form of the research literature, one can understand what you might call this complacency, the notion that the truth *will* out (Yes) and therefore that there's no need for any special mechanisms, that if scientists simply get on with the straightforward practical job of doing their experiments properly nothing else needs to be touched.

S I don't know to what extent you have this problem in sociology, but there has been at times anyway a strong discipline actually in the laboratory, where attention has been directed to making up solutions carefully, attending to proper standards of measurement, calibration of spectroscopes and this kind of thing, and one is constrained to use the right techniques of measurement, everything must be well defined. When you come to the conceptual side, all sorts of different words are used to mean the same thing and the constructions are often very awkward indeed. . . Things like this, I think, are frightfully neglected. If you become interested in them, as I have tended to do, quite a lot of scientists say you're playing with words, this is sort of semantics. I don't agree with that, I think that we should perhaps pay *more* attention, not just to the nomenclature, but to a systematic way of developing whole sets of thoughts which have a reasonably good one–one relationship to the phenomena which we *think* are operating in World I. It must be even more difficult in sociology, mustn't it?

M Yes, I think it is. I think it's made even more complex by the fact that you're studying subjects who themselves are users of words. My increasing concern has been to try to understand how the people I'm studying use words. And that is regarded as, a bit like the reaction to your concerns, by other sociologists, that is regarded as mere semantics. But it's through the use of words that people create the world around them, give meaning to it. And so there is a kind of parallel there. What happens in sociology, I think, is that sociologists take over their own terminology from the native speakers that they're studying and then, to some extent, try to give these terms a special technical meaning. But the words are so much embedded in the talk of the native speakers that this is very difficult and leads to endless confusion. I find there's also a tradition in sociology, and perhaps in all the social sciences, a tradition of resistance against new technical terminology. The belief is, to some extent, that all the words we need are already there. They're provided by native speakers. So one is in a double bind, really. I suppose there's nothing in sociology which corresponds at all closely to the formalisms, the sets of technically defined formalisms of physics and chemistry and perhaps even bio-chemistry. The use of language is much closer to the use of language of native speakers, ordinary language. But, in a sense, masquerading as a special kind of technical expertise.

S   You have an awful lot of one-off events in sociology. So, I suppose, it must be particularly difficult to handle. . . I was wondering whether one-off things may be intrinsically of very special interest. But I find it a little difficult to understand what to do about them. They must have special properties. . .

M   Yes, I suppose there are certain areas where the one-offness, the uniqueness of events and products is almost the defining criterion, like painting, some forms of music, and so on, where if you decide that it is *not* unique, then it no longer counts.

S   I was thinking of *living*. Getting up in the morning and doing what you do is the most one-off business that you could possibly imagine really. . . We need some special way of analysing one-off events that enables us to recognize somehow their importance, without destroying it.

M   Yes. I suppose the way I would instinctively approach the study of one-offness would be to treat it not as a feature of events as such, but as a feature which people could attribute to events. So the interesting thing would be under what circumstances, and how, would people come to treat a certain event, or a product, as a one-off. So that, for example, a young man and a young woman meeting may be well inclined to treat *their* meeting, their relationship, as a very unique event. Though you or I, looking at it from the outside, might say this is just a repetition of something that has gone on from time immemorial. [Long pause]

S   Well, I don't know about you, but I think I'm exhausted. [M laughs] It's a beautiful evening.

M   Yes. You've had quite a busy day.

Note to Chapter 3

1   'The Perry letters' is a set of 80 letters initiated by a scientist to whom I have given the pseudonym 'Perry'. Spencer was centrally involved in this correspondence which exhibits many of the features to be found in the M/S letters, but which is too complex to be examined here.

PART 2

Replications

4

Don Quixote's Double: a Self-Exemplifying Text

There can be no doubt that 'replication', in ordinary language, has something to do with the 'sameness' of or 'close similarity' between two or more events or objects. Likewise, 'experimental replication' in science seems to refer to attempts to 'copy closely' a prior set of experimental procedures and to obtain 'the same results'. Replication in science is usually taken to contribute to the process whereby experimental claims are validated. Valid claims are supposed to be 'reproducible' by other competent experimenters and it is often assumed that experimental observations come to be accepted only after thay have been successfully replicated, that is, repeated exactly, by numerous independent observers (see the discussion in Zuckerman, 1977).

Described in this way, experimental replication appears to be fairly simple and straightforward. But recent work by several sociologists has begun to show that the process is much more complex than may at first appear (see Collins, 1975; Travis, 1981; Pinch, 1981; Harvey, 1981; Pickering, 1981). The following quotation is taken from Collins's recent article on scientific replication in the *Dictionary of the History of Science*:

Werner Heisenberg (1901–76) has written: 'We can finally agree about their [physicists'] results because we have learned that experiments carried out under precisely the same conditions do actually lead to the same results.' The view that replicability is essential in science is widespread. This view has only recently been examined in detail, the major problem being the meaning of 'the same conditions'. Since no two events are identical a set of *relevant* conditions must be specified. But ideas of relevance will rest on an understanding of the [scientific] phenomenon in question and this will be incomplete where the very existence of the phenomenon itself is in doubt. (1982a, 372)

In this passage, Collins makes problematic our initial, straight-forward account of experimental replication. He does this by emphasizing the literal impossibility of *exact* experimental replication. He points out that no two experiments can ever be exactly the same. For if they were exactly the same, we could speak only of one experiment and not of two. Collins suggests, therefore, that when scientists treat two or more experiments as the same or as different, their judgements of similarity depend on criteria of relevance which do not inhere in the experiments themselves but are formulated and applied by the scientists involved.

Collins's final point in this quotation is that scientists' criteria for judging experimental sameness/difference often derive from, or at least vary with, their views about the scientific phenomena under investigation. Consequently, it seems to follow that experimental replication is not an invariant criterion for establishing the validity of new experimental results. Rather, the very meaning of 'replication', in any particular instance, is bound up with and dependent on scientists' potentially divergent scientific views about the very phenomena whose existence and character are to be established by means of experimental replication.

Making the 'Same' Experiments 'Different'

Collins's central points, then, are that the sameness/difference attributed to two or more experiments depends on interpretative work carried out by the scientists concerned; that the sameness/difference actually attributed will vary in accordance with other aspects of scientists' interpretative work, for example, in accordance with the scientific viewpoints they profess; and, consequently, that judgements of experimental replication can be highly variable (see Collins, 1981a, b, c). Let me illustrate this variability by means of a set of quotations from interviews with biochemists, in which each of the speakers is referring ostensibly to the 'same' series of experiments. These are the 'stoichiometry experiments' and they include the experiments by Spencer and Marks discussed in Chapter 1. The names given at the end of these quotations are pseudonyms of biochemists working in the same field as Marks and Spencer. The number following these names are the relevant pages of the interview transcripts. Each 'sentence' has been numbered for ease of reference. For further details, see Gilbert and Mulkay, 1984.

(A)   1. Then we verified that the number through the ATPase was two in intact mitochondria. 2. There is still an argument about that because one is somewhat bugged by the porter systems. 3. The ATP has got to get in and the ADP has got to get out. 4. The Pi has got to go through. . . 5. There's a controversy at the moment as to whether Pi can also get in by another route. 6. Because we think we have identified a calcium phosphate porter. 7. And almost without exception everyone else at the present time says it doesn't exist. 8. But none of these people who say it doesn't exist have really repeated our experiments in detail. 9. Our feeling is that if they do, they will – well I think it may turn out that it does exist. 10. So that there is a little doubt about the ATPase stoichiometry. (Spencer, 43–4)

(B)   1. We repeated all [Spencer's stoichiometry] experiments. 2. We can get the same answers that he did. 3. There's no question of not believing his data. 4. It's not a question of that at all. 5. We reported this and we showed that with our experiment and everything we get exactly the same answers. 6. That's all recorded in our papers. 7. But what was wrong was. . . (Marks, 13)

(C)   1. These proton stoichiometries, now there you have a series of discrepancies. 2. But if you look, no two people have done exactly the same experiment. 3. So this is part of the reason why I am somewhat cynical about the whole business. (Pope, 35)

(D)   *Interviewer*   1. Is there in fact any disgreement about actual observations?
Respondent   2. Nothing major. 3. There *are* some disagreements, but they're not very important ones by and large. 4. Not between the position that Spencer holds and the position that Marks and I have held, or are holding. . . 5. We can do the same experiments and get the same results. (Crane, 24)

(E)   1. Crane and Spencer disagree on one particular issue. 2. On others they merely disagree on their own interpretation. 3. On one they seem to disagree on fact. 4. They have not actually done the same experiment twice. 5. But they have done two different experiments that should be the same. 6. Spencer says that if you reduce the temperature, to reduce the rate of the phosphate porter to such an extent that you can see the phosphate going in and you can see the rate that it is going in and you can see that you are *not* missing protons. 7. Crane says that if you slow the phosphate porter, you can see the slowing of the phosphate porter going in, but the stoichiometry rises to three and not two. (Read, 29)

(F)   1. I really don't know what the battle is all about. 2. But [Spencer] seems very adamant in sticking to his numbers of two. 3. I could not care less, if I was him. 4. Whether it is two or four, it makes no difference. . . 5. The fact as to whether it's two or four is irrelevant. 6. Basically, it supports [Spencer]. (Peck, 30–1)

In passage A, Spencer notes that there is some controversy in relation to the stoichiometry experiments (A2, 7, 10). He mentions his basic experimental finding that two protons cross the membrane for every ATP formed and he draws particular attention to experiments in which he claims to have identified a 'porter' which carries phosphate across the membrane (A5–7). The existence of this porter is said to be denied by most other scientists in the field. But Spencer suggests that this is partly because they have not done the same experiments as he has (A8). Despite some hesitation at the end of the passage, Spencer seems to imply that if other scientists were to repeat his experiments in detail, they would reach the same scientific conclusion.

In passage B we have Marks, who is regularly described in our interviews as Spencer's main opponent on the issue of stoichiometry. Marks maintains that he has repeated all Spencer's stoichiometry experiments and has published his results (B1, 5). furthermore, although he does not mention here any specific experiments of Spencer's, he stresses that there is no question of not believing Spencer's data (B3–4). Thus Marks seems to be saying that he has repeated many, perhaps all, of the relevant experiments, that he is able to obtain the same results as Spencer, and that if there are experiments which he has not repeated, he does not doubt that they are repeatable. However, whereas Spencer proposes in passage A that repetition of his experiments by others would help to convince them of the validity of his scientific interpretations, Marks maintains that his scientific viewpoint has been unaffected by this experimental replication. Immediately after this passage he explains why Spencer's conclusions are wrong despite their reproducibility.

In passage C, we have a speaker who forcefully denies that there has been *any* experimental replication at all in this area, thereby clearly contradicting Marks's claim to have repeated Spencer's results (C2). In passage D, however, we have another participant maintaining that at least Spencer's major experiments can be, and have been, repeated by Marks and himself (D2–5).

The speaker in passage E, Read, returns to the specific experiment on the phosphate porter mentioned by Spencer in passage A and compares it with the wider debate about stoichiometries. Read claims that most of the disagreement about stoichiometries between Crane (the speaker in passage D) and

Spencer is merely a matter of divergent interpretations (E2). Given the way in which Read uses terms in this passage, this seems to imply that, in relation to the stoichiometry debate in general, Crane and Spencer have not carried out identical experiments. In relation to the phosphate porter, however, they are said to differ over a matter of fact (E3). Even here, they are not described as performing *exactly* the same experiments (E4). Nevertheless, their different experiments are treated by Read as being scientifically equivalent; so much so that their observing different numbers of protons is treated as being a simple observational discrepancy which is not to be explained as due to variations in experimental procedure (E4–5).

The treatment of experimental sameness/difference in passage E is, in one respect, more complex than in the previous passages. Unlike the previous speakers, who treat sameness/difference in these quotations simply as observable features of experiments (e.g. 'no two people have done exactly the same experiment'), Read maintains that two experiments which are undeniably different in detail may be taken to be indistinguishable for certain interpretative purposes. Thus, for Read, it is possible for two given experiments to be both different and the same. In this respect, passage E resembles passage F, where all the stoichiometry experiments, no matter what their detailed findings, are treated as much the same. The final speaker, Peck, a vocal opponent of Spencer's chemiosmotic theory, is able to treat any experiments which purport to show that protons contribute significantly to the production of ATP as scientifically equivalent. In passage F, all the fine distinctions provided by previous speakers are obliterated. In this passage, all the stoichiometry experiments are basically the same. They are equally Spencerian and equally misconceived.

These quotations illustrate how a specific set of experiments can be variably depicted by different speakers as the same, as different and as different yet the same. This supports Collins's suggestion that participants' statements about experimental sameness/difference, and therefore their statements about experimental replication, depend on complex, and potentially variable, interpretative work. Thus in order to understand scientists' claims about experimental replication, we must understand how attributions of sameness/difference are linked to other aspects of their interpretative work. This implies that we should try to understand how attributions of experimental sameness/difference operate within scientists' discourse. Accordingly, our central questions become: what do scientists accomplish interpretatively by means of such attributions? What further claims, portrayals, evaluations, and so on are made possible through specific attributions of experimental sameness/difference? The underlying assumption here is that, because the sameness/difference of any set of experiments can always in principle be depicted in varying ways depending on the kind of interpretative work which is being carried out, we can gain some insight into the nature of such attributions by examining how they contribute to the discourse in which they are embedded.

Experimental Differences as a Means of Validation

Our customary view of scientific replication leads us to expect that scientists regularly claim support for their own and others' experiments through assertions that the same experiments have been repeated by other researchers and the same results obtained. This view is epitomized in the statement by Heisenberg quoted above. In my material, however, claims of this kind occur infrequently. Much more frequent are claims that given experimental findings have been and should be validated, not by the *same* experiment, but by something experimentally different. Consider the following example.

(G) 1. Whether or not any scientific statement is true, I mean, is very – I mean there isn't really any great deal of argument about it as a general rule because, 2. although nobody – well people very seldom test precisely the same experiment, 3. if it is of any significance it leads to predictions which other people will use in their own experiments 4. and either it stands or falls according to the results other people get. 5. So I think the experimental thing is a test which enables all these scientists who are just like anybody else, just as bigotted and prejudiced and emotionally involved as anybody else would be, 6. I mean it actually enables people to be objective – because there is an alternative criterion. (Bamber, 23)

In this passage, the speaker is talking in general terms about the validation of scientific statements (G1–2). He suggests that, on the whole, the validation process operates without a great deal of argument (G1). However, he then rejects the view that such validation depends on scientists' performing precisely the same experiments (G2). He appears to begin to say that *nobody* ever does exact replications, but changes this in mid-sentence to the more moderate claim that testing precisely the same experiment occurs very seldom. The speaker then tells us how scientific validation normally operates. He does this by contrasting the customary account of exact replication with an alternative account which portrays scientists as exploring the validity of others' important statements by investigating how far predictions derived from those statements are confirmed by the results of 'their own experiments' (G3). Thus the speaker's alternative account depicts researchers as being able to test any specific scientific claim by carrying out new experiments which, despite their differences from the original experiment, can have clear implications for the original claim (G3–4). The speaker makes no attempt to explain, either in the quoted passage or subsequently, how these new experiments can have such unequivocal consequences for the validity of the original claim. Rather, he achieves interpretative closure by treating the scientific meaning of these new experiments as entirely unproblematic; even although his initial interpretative task was that of showing how scientific claims, *in general*, are validated.

This speaker's presentation of an apparently 'objective criterion' for assessing the validity of scientific claims is accomplished by his first identifying all scientific claims and experiments as problematic and, in principle, in need of validation; and then by his introducing a sub-set of 'new, different experiments' which can in some unexplicated way, despite their being themselves implicit members of the initial problematic set, be used to check the adequacy of the original experimental conclusions. When re-described in this way, after detailed re-examination, Bamber's account of the process of experimental replication seems weak and unconvincing. During the interview, however, it went unchallenged. The interviewers seem to have accepted it as an entirely plausible account of experimental replication. Thus the speaker in passage D furnished an interpretatively successful account of the process of scientific validation which denies the importance of exact replication or close experimental copying and stresses instead scientists' reliance on experimental variation.

It is clear that validation of scientific claims in general can be discursively accomplished by emphasizing experimental differences. The same pattern can also be found in the next two passages.

(H) 1. . . . many times you have an observation, interesting, that relates only indirectly to something I'm doing. 2. And I will take that observation and extend it. 3. That's what in fact is much more common [than exact replication]. 4. An extended observation into your normal area of research. 5. And does it work, here, in these particular conditions? (Shaw, 62)

(I) 1. If [an experiment] is really important you will end up doing something. 2. Maybe not repeating that experiment exactly. 3. But you will repeat some variant or some other thing to show the same thing. 4. Yes, I think it is important that more than one lab do the experiments, if they are important experiments, or do experiments bearing on the same point. (Fasham, 13)

The speaker in passage H begins by referring to his own practice. Much of his own work, he says, consists of taking up observations made by other scientists which appear to relate in some indirect fashion to his experimental concerns (H1–2). In sentence three, he can be read as widening his frame of reference and as talking about biochemists in general. But this is uncertain. He may still be talking only about his own work.

At this point the speaker, Shaw, proposes that taking somebody else's observation and extending it is much more common than some form of action which he does not specify at this point, but which he takes as being obvious to his audience (H2–3). It is clear from the full interview transcript that he is speaking here of the act of doing 'exactly the same experiment' which he had referred to previously. Thus, like Bamber in passage G, Shaw also explicitly denies the importance of exact replication in scientific practice and emphasizes the role of experimental variation. Furthermore, once again like Bamber, Shaw seems to treat experimental variation as having some kind of validating effect. The point of extending somebody else's observation into your own area of research is said to be to find out whether it 'works' under these new conditions (H4–5).

The account given so far by our respondents of the process of experimental testing does not depend on different researchers being able to agree that their experiments were conducted under exactly the same conditions. Their version emphasizes that validation is achieved, rather, when another researcher's observation works under distinctly *different* conditions. Nevertheless, speakers like Shaw cannot claim to be checking somebody else's experiment, that is, finding out whether it works, without asserting *some* degree of 'sameness' for the two experiments. Thus in passage H there is an unspecified something which is treated as common to both experiments and which is taken to be open to validation through its re-appearance in the second experiment, despite the variation in experimental conditions (H5).

This combination of 'scientific sameness despite experimental differences' is repeated in passage I. Like our two previous respondents, Fasham tends to minimize the role of close experimental copying (I2) and to stress the importance of doing something different in order to check other scientists' important experiments (I3–4). But, in his words, 'you will repeat some variant or some other thing *to show the same thing*' or 'bearing on the same point'.

This formulation of the process of scientific validation seems to imply that the scientific statements which are being tested are more general than those embodied in the observations furnished by any particular experimental set-up (Mulkay and Gilbert, 1984). Only if this is assumed is it possible for speakers to maintain that there is some element of scientific knowledge which persists across varying experiments and which can be verified, validated or replicated by means of various experiments, each with different experimental conditions. This recurrent discursive form, then, avoids the participant's interpretative problem identified above by Collins, namely, that of how to decide whether or not two experiments have exactly the same experimental conditions; for differences in conditions are treated as an essential part of the validation process. Nevertheless, its users are able to sustain the claim that they are engaged in experimental replication by assuming that experiments which differ in detail can have the same scientific meaning at a higher interpretative level.

The Prevalance of Triangulation Accounts

Accounts in which scientists assert validation of given experimental results by reference to other different experiments, I will call 'triangulation' accounts, because the need for *three* different experiments is so frequently mentioned (see Marks in Chapter 1). I will provide no further examples of triangulation accounts here. This pattern has been documented in detail elsewhere (Mulkay and Gilbert, 1984). The point I wish to emphasize is that triangulation accounts occur much more frequently in my interview material than that of validation by reference to exact replication or to close experimental copying. In this material, the ratio is about two to one in favour of triangulation accounts. In addition, references to validation through exact replication tend to be noticeably weaker, that is, more tentative and qualified, than references to triangulation. Compare, for example, Spencer's formulation in passage A with that of Bamber in passage D.

> *Spencer* But none of these people . . . have really repeated our experiments in detail. Our feeling is that if they do, they will – well I think it may turn out that it does exist.

> *Bamber* . . . if it is of any significance it leads to predictions

which other people will use in their own experiments and either it stands or falls according to the results other people get.

Such differences in the interpretative strength of the two forms are typical. There may, of course, be many reasons for the relative strength and prevalence of triangulation accounting. However, one possibility is that such an interpretative form becomes dominant, within certain kinds of interpretative context, because it facilitates other types of important interpretative work. I suggest that one recurrent concern in scientists' discourse, and perhaps particularly in their interview talk, is that of scientific originality. Thus the specific possibility which I will investigate is that triangulation accounting enables scientists to accomplish validation whilst at the same time helping them to make certain sorts of originality claim. I will begin to pursue this idea in the next section by means of a short digression into the realm of literature.

Borges, Cervantes, Menard

In a story entitled 'Pierre Menard, author of the *Quixote*', Jorge Luis Borges (1970) explores the problem of how to reconcile exact literary replication with literary originality. Borges's story concerns a (presumably fictional) little-known author, Pierre Menard, who, writing during the period 1899–1934, is said by Borges to have included within his *oeuvre* 'the ninth and thirty-eighth chapters of the first part of *Don Quixote* and a fragment of chapter twenty-two'. Borges recognizes that 'such an affirmation seems an absurdity'. Nevertheless, he tells us, 'to justify this "absurdity" is the primordial object of this note'. By including these fragments of *Don Quixote* within the list of Menard's writings, Borges depicts himself as rectifying a previous incomplete catalogue of Menard's work from which they had been omitted. Thus Borges's text implies that the prior catalogue had, incorrectly, treated these fragments as not a genuine part of Menard's original writings. Borges's aim is to convince us that these fragments are not mere copies of parts of a prior work of genius, but original contributions to world literature.

According to Borges, Menard dedicated much of his life to the remarkable objective of writing *Don Quixote*. Menard 'did not want [merely] to compose another *Quixote* – which is easy – but *the Quixote itself*. Needless to say, he never contemplated a mechanical transcription of the original; he did not propose to copy it. His admirable intention was to produce a few pages which would coincide – word for word and line for line – with those of Miguel de Cervantes.' Thus, in so far as Menard succeeded in his task, we have two identical texts each with a separate author. Borges claims, however, that Menard's text is much more original than that of Cervantes and massively superior to it in terms of literary merit. The way in which Borges establishes Menard's literary originality, despite the textual identity, is evident in the following quotations.

> To compose the *Quixote* at the beginning of the seventeenth century was a reasonable undertaking, necessary and perhaps even unavoidable; at the beginning of the twentieth, it is almost impossible. It is not in vain that three hundred years have gone by, filled with exceedingly complex events. Among them, to mention only one, is the *Quixote* itself.
>
> In spite of these . . . obstacles, Menard's fragmentary *Quixote* is more subtle than Cervantes'. The latter, in a clumsy fashion, opposes to the fictions of chivalry the tawdry provincial reality of his country; Menard selects as his 'reality' the land of Carmen during the century of Lepanto and Lope de Vega. What a series of espagnolades that selection would have suggested to Maurice Barres or Dr Rodriguez Larreta! Menard eludes them with complete naturalness. In his work there are no gipsy flourishes or conquistadors or mystics or Philip the Seconds or autos da fe. He neglects or eliminates local colour. This disdain points to a new conception of the historical novel. This disdain condemns Salammbo, with no possibility of appeal.
>
> Cervantes' text and Menard's are verbally identical, but the second is almost infinitely richer. (More ambiguous, his detractors will say, but ambiguity is richness.) It is a revelation to compare Menard's *Don Quixote* with Cervantes'. The latter, for example, wrote (part one, chapter nine):
> '. . . . truth, whose mother is history, rival of time, depository of deeds, witness of the past, exemplar and adviser to the present, and the future's counsellor.'
> Written in the seventeenth century, written by the 'lay genius' Cervantes, this enumeration is a mere rhetorical praise of history. Menard, on the other [hand], writes:
> '. . . truth, whose mother is history, rival of time, depository of deeds, witness of the past, examplar and adviser to the present, and the future's counsellor.'
> History, the *mother* of truth: the idea is astounding. Menard, a contemporary of William James. . .

What Borges does in such passages is to make Menard's verbally identical text *different* from Cervantes's at the level of literary meaning by linking it to its differing historical, literary and intellectual context. Whereas Cervantes's literary aims are described as reasonable and appropriate for their time, Menard's undertaking is said to have been almost impossible some three hundred years later. Borges's emphasis on the differing contexts of the two texts enables him to attribute radically different meanings to shared stylistic features and to identical verbal sequences. For instance, whereas the avoidance of 'espagnolades' can be treated as a routine feature of Cervantes's text, for Menard, aware of nineteenth-century popular writing about Spanish life, it can become a praiseworthy accomplishment of stylistic restraint. Similarly Menard's conception of history can be treated as truly remarkable for a man writing at the same time as William James.

In short, we can see that Borges creates for himself an artificial situation in which, initially, the literary originality of the supposed author appears particularly doubtful owing to the identity of his text with that of Cervantes. However, the subject's originality is established by Borges's use of various interpretative techniques which enable Borges to treat Menard's text as different from that of his predecessor and to attribute new and remarkable meanings to the content of the second text. It is clear that without a display of interpretative differences between Menard's and Cervantes's *Don Quixotes*, Menard's originality cannot be sustained. Thus Borges's story helps us to see how claims for originality depend on the recognition of differences; and also how differences can always be created at a higher level of meaning, even in situations where there is in some sense undeniable identity.

Borges's accomplishment in this story has clear implications for our understanding of scientists' routine emphasis on experimental differences in their talk about replication. Like Borges, scientists are, at least partly, referring to similarities and differences among texts. For Borges the texts are literary products; for scientists they are research reports. Like Borges's texts, scientific reports can always, as we have seen, be construed as the same, as different or as both different and the same. Some element of sameness between texts is a necessary component of any claim for experimental validation in science. Exact duplication of literary texts, in contrast, appears to be a very unusual occurrence. Borges introduces this element artificially into his narrative as a way of making the interpretative production of originality particularly difficult to achieve. He then accomplishes originality by establishing differences between the texts in question. In the next section we will examine how scientists accomplish originality in a manner analogous to that used by Borges, that is, in their case, by using the attributions of difference which are characteristic of triangulation accounts as a basis for claiming scientific originality.

Originality and Difference

It has been suggested elsewhere that, when scientists talk about their research to outsiders, each speaker typically claims and/or assumes that his view of the scientific phenomena under investigation is, at least basically, correct. It also seems likely that most speakers take for granted that they have made some kind of original experimental contribution to the understanding of these phenomena (Gilbert and Mulkay, 1984). The interpretative accomplishment of validation and originality are, in fact, closely connected in much of scientists' informal reports about their own and others' experimental activities. Scientists employ forms of talk which enable them to accomplish both self-validation and the attribution of originality. More specifically, by linking experimental validation to differences as well as to sameness, speakers create interpretative space in which to establish their own and others' originality without thereby jeopardizing their own claim to be advancing experimentally validated conclusions. In other words, the element of difference enables them to attribute originality and the element of sameness enables them to attribute validity.

Consider the following exchanges between interviewer and respondent.

(J)*Respondent* 1. If something has been published, a phenomenon, and it has been explained in a certain way, and you believe the phenomenon but you don't believe the explanation; 2. then you are necessarily obliged, I think, or practically so, to repeat the phenomenon, 3. but now you'll need to take samples here and there and go and measure what *you* think is causing the effect. 4. Everybody does this, constantly. 5. It's perhaps one of the commonest ways in which progress is made, I would say. . .

Interviewer 6. So you're seldom in a situation where you are repeating very closely and trying to reproduce exactly the work which you find in research papers.

Respondent 7. No, I wouldn't say very seldom. 8. It really can be quite frequent if one is going up a different path. 9. Do you see what I mean?

Interviewer 10. Yes. So you're seldom interested in pursuing *exactly* the same path.

Respondent 11. This, as far as it goes, may be right. 12. It's both boring, uninteresting and unpublishable, *just* to repeat it. 13. It's really only if you can add something. 14. If you can find out *why* something has happened, instead of just saying 'this happened'. (Howe, 26–7)

The speaker in passage J begins by identifying the kind of situation in which he would engage in replication. He describes this as a situation in which he believes the phenomenon reported in a research paper, but did not believe the explanation (J1). As he talks, it gradually becomes clear that he is assuming that the reported phenomenon or the experimental effect is reproducible in principle and that he will be able to repeat it (J2–3). Thus the goal of his own experimental work is not depicted as that of experimental repetition, but as that of providing a new, and scientifically more satisfactory, interpretation for this reproducible effect (J3).

The reproducibility in principle of most published findings is widely taken for granted in biochemists' talk about replication (Mulkay and Gilbert, 1984). Hence, they regularly describe themselves as making special attempts to replicate others' work specifically in situations where, like Howe, they have identified some interpretative defect in that work. Accordingly, although they portray their actions as in part a repetition of another's previous experimental work, this is always accompanied, as in passage J, by an emphasis on their own additional and different contributions (J3–5).

In passage J, the interviewer attempts to clarify how far Howe is claiming to repeat other scientists' actions very closely (J6). Howe's reply is subtle and difficult to grasp; a point which the speaker himself seems to recognize, when he asks; 'Do you see what I mean?' Whatever the exact meaning of J7, Howe seems to be proposing that he quite frequently does repeat others' experiments closely, but also that he combines such repetition with 'going up a different path'. Thus Howe maintains a careful balance between experimental sameness and experimental difference. In J10, the interviewer reformulates the issue of sameness. He is so emphatic this time about the high degree of similarity that he has in mind that Howe is led to deny that his work is ever *quite* that repetitious and to make it clear that, if his work added *nothing* different, it would necessarily be 'boring, uninteresting and unpublishable' (J12–14). In other words, the series of exchanges between interviewer and respondent leads the latter to express explicitly the interpretative difficulty of reconciling close experimental repetition with the attribution of scientific originality.

The following quotation has a very similar structure to the previous passage.

(K) *Interviewer* 1. In fact, do you repeat, replicate, other people's experiments quite often?
Respondent 2. Never for the sake of it, no. 3. I never go into the

library and say: 'So and so's seen this. I will also see if I can see it.' 4. The way I would do it would be: 'So and so's seen *this*, and using *my* set of prejudices, they ought to be able therefore to show that like *that*.' 5. So I'd set their experiment up and first of all demonstrate to myself that I can repeat it, 6. and then try and show that and that as a test of my hypothesis or a test of my theory, that they're working on the wrong hypothesis. 7. This, therefore, makes all their assertions fit in with my hypothesis. 8. Something like that. 9. I do *know* people who will do experiments just to repeat them, to see if they can do other people's experiments. 10. But that strikes me as a futile way of behaving. (Crane, 46)

The speaker in this passage claims at the outset never to repeat others' experiments 'for the sake of it' (K1–2). He does not seem to mean by this that he never repeats their experiments at all. For he states clearly in K5 that he does, on occasion, set up other people's experiments and demonstrate to himself that he can, in some sense, do the same experiment. However, he seems to be suggesting that when he does repeat others' experiments it is never 'mere repetition'; that when he repeats other's work, something more is involved than simply making sure that he can observe the same phenomenon (K2–6).

Like Howe in passage J, Crane seems to assume that he will engage in replication only when he has some kind of doubt about somebody else's claim (K6), but, also like Howe, that he *will* be able to reproduce the other researcher's observations (K5–6). Thus the goal behind Crane's concern with replication is depicted as that of adding new and different observations to the initial findings in such a way that he can re-interpret that finding in accordance with his own scientific viewpoint (K6–7). Hence it follows for Crane, as it does for Howe, that 'just to repeat' others' experiments, that is, to make no original contribution, is scientifically futile (K9–10).

Both Crane and Howe portray their attempts to check the validity of others' claims as involving a necessary element of experimental sameness or experimental repetition. These speakers' assumption of sameness follows from their taking (most of) their colleagues' observational claims to be reproducible in principle. But the similarities between their and other people's experiments (texts) are treated as relatively uninteresting and scientifically unimportant. Experimental copying, like literary copying, is deemed to be trivial and both scientists deny that they ever engage in such a boring and futile activity. Both speakers also stress that the process of validation depends on their doing something different from other scientists; and both emphasize that the correct scientific meaning of others' observations can only be established through new and original experimental contributions. In this way, by making the process of validation appear to depend more heavily on experimental variation than on experimental repetition, Howe and Crane are able to depict themselves as engaged in validation, and even in replication, whilst simultaneously depicting themselves as making original contributions to scientific knowledge.

In the two examples examined so far in this section, speakers have treated replication as essentially a negative procedure, that is, as a way of checking doubtful claims. But replication can be treated in a more positive fashion. For instance, when scientists talk about replications of their own work, they usually maintain that other people have repeated, and thereby confirmed, their findings. Even in such cases, however, some degree of experimental variation is routinely identified and used to display the originality of the replicators.

(L) *Interviewer* 1. Can I ask if anybody has replicated *this* paper, or done what you might call a replication?
Respondent 2. Yes. There's a lab in Amsterdam that has done some of this work. 3. I mean, not all the way through. 4. They've used some of the tricks that we've used here, yes. 5. If they'd just done *straight* replication, they probably wouldn't even write a paper. 6. But they've used the ideas and the methods for their own particular problems. 7. And also two labs in the States as well have also taken this thing further on. 8. Again, with different objectives. (Peck, 25)

In passage L, three replications of the speaker's paper are mentioned (L2, 7). But it is stressed that these are not *straight* replications. As in the two previous passages, the idea that competent researchers would 'just repeat' (L5, K9, J12) somebody else's experiment is treated as most unlikely. The speaker makes it clear that replication has occurred as other researchers have used the content of his paper to solve their own particular problems and to attain their different objectives (L3–8).

No indication is given in passage L, however, that the three replicating labs were in any way involved in *re*-interpreting the original findings. In this respect, passage L differs from the two previous quotations. Although the speaker makes no explicit claim that these replications confirmed his results, it seems to be presumed that the methods and ideas contained in his paper were deemed to be adequate by these other researchers. In this passage, then, a standard triangulation account is used to validate the speaker's own experimental findings whilst attributing scientific originality to those carrying out the replication.

Sameness and Lack of Originality

In the same way that attributions of difference can be used to display the originality of the speaker and of other reseachers, attributions of sameness can be used to deny scientific originality. There are no examples in my material where such denials are self-referential. In other words, all the denials of originality in my data are applied by a given speaker to other people. As I suggested above, speakers' originality, as well as the validity of their scientific views, is routinely taken for granted and continually reproduced through their discourse.

> (M)   *Interviewer*   1. If I could go back to that question of replication. 2. You wouldn't say that you never replicate other people's work or would you?
> *Respondent*   3. You might try to on your own system, if somebody had shown something on mitochondria. 4. Surely you would go into the lab: 'I wonder if *bacteria* do that?' and try it. 5. Yes, of course you'd do that. 6. But you would hardly go in and repeat the same experiments on mitochondria. 7. I have never done that. 8. Other people have, particularly with Spencer's proton-pulse experiment. 9. They have gone and tried this experiment. 10. Potter and Travis is an example of work there. 11. And many other people have repeated these experiments and improved them or found out new things about them. 12. They've gone on to do that. 13. Not just repeated them and stopped there and said: 'That's nice, they do work, he's right you know.' (Jay, 26)

In passage M, the interviewer begins by returning to a previous statement by the respondent that he did not try 'to repeat much of other people's work'. The interviewer's question is organized in a way which encourages the respondent to say that he does sometimes replicate other scientists' experiments: 'You wouldn't say that you never replicate, would you?' Not surprisingly, this question elicits the kind of response that it appears to take for granted. The researcher replies that he may well sometimes try out other people's results on his own system (M3–5). Nevertheless, he consistently adopts the standard triangulation account of experimental replication when talking about his own actions and he strongly rejects any implication that he might ever repeat another scientist's experiment exactly (M6–7).

At this point, the respondent extends the original question and applies it to other people. He appears, quite clearly, to claim that some other scientists *have* carried out exact replications or very close experimental copies. He seems to be saying that these scientists have 'repeated the same experiments as other people on mitochondria' (M6–8). 'I have never done that', he continues, but 'other people have' (M7–8). As he proceeds, however, the conception of replication which is being applied to these other scientists seems to be revised. In M11, these third parties are credited for the first time with having improved upon the prior experiment and with having 'found out new things'. Thus, whereas the speaker had previously contrasted the mere repetition carried out by these scientists with his own strategy of experimental variation (M7–8), he now seems to be acknowledging that these scientists have also done something different and that they have thereby achieved some degree of scientific originality.

In the final sentence we find, as in previous quotations, the implicit comparison between 'just repeating' somebody else's experiment and doing something new. The speaker seems here to be unambiguously retracting what he had previously implied, namely, that these other scientists had made no original scientific contribution. By the end of the passage, therefore, the speaker has rescued these other scientists from the charge of 'mere replication', by reformulating their actions in such a way that they can now be seen to have been involved all along in experimental work which combined an element of repetition with a scientific component which was different and original. Passage M, then, appears to be an instance where the difficulty of reconciling sameness with originality is dealt with in the text by the withdrawal of the attribution of sameness and by the introduction of differentiating features which are used as the basis for attributions of originality.

The following passage has a somewhat similar structure. In this case, however, the denial of originality is the main interpretative accomplishment and the accusation of experimental sameness is not withdrawn.

(N)   *Interviewer*   1. How often do you actually check out in your own laboratory the kinds of results that you are finding in other people's papers?
       Respondent   2. We don't make *any* effort to repeat what somebody else does. 3. We have so many problems unexplored that result from our own initiative, that we would never think of going back to repeat something that

Joe Blow does. 4. It's interesting, there is a laboratory that I've never visited and which shall remain nameless, but I have a colleague who has visited and he says that when you go there the Professor says, 'Well, here is Mr So-and-So, he's working on the Marks phenomenon. Here's Mr So-and-So, he's working on the Perry stuff.' 5. They actually take pride in the fact that they are checking papers that have been published by others, with the result that a great deal of confirmatory work precludes their truly innovative contribution to the literature. (Long, 15–16)

This passage begins with the interviewer asking how often the respondent checks other scientists' experiments. Long provides an emphatically negative response (N2). He then goes on to provide a justification for not repeating other people's work (N3). The justificatory effect of this sentence depends on the assumption that experimental repetition as such is less valuable scientifically than the exploration of his own original contributions. The relative triviality of repetition is not stated explicitly here, but is implied by the dismissive turns of phrase, for example, 'we don't make *any* attempt', 'we would never think of', 'something that Joe Blow does'. In this respect, Long's discourse resembles previous speakers' references to the triviality of 'just repeating' others' experiments.

The invidious comparison between repetition and original research is developed further in the rest of the passage by means of an implicit condemnation of a laboratory which is supposed to specialize in replication. In N4, the speaker decides not to reveal the name of the laboratory. The only other situation in which respondents insisted on the need for other scientists' anonymity was when they were making allegations about fraud. Thus, in this passage, the act of simply repeating others' experiments seems to be treated as improper; more specifically, as infringing taken-for-granted norms requiring scientists to make original contributions to knowledge (N5). In addition, because the members of the nameless laboratory are depicted as pursuing goals which are, scientifically, largely irrelevant, the speaker treats their actions as puzzling. 'They actually take pride' in replication, when they should obviously be doing what Long does, namely, making truly original contributions to the research literature (N5). In short, the contrast between experimental sameness and scientific originality provides the interpretative basis in this passage for the condemnation of other scientists' actions.

Analytical Self-Reference

In this chapter, I have used Borges's story, along with my own sociological data, to show that resemblances between texts (or between actions) can be, and regularly are, constructed and reconstructed by participants in diverse ways. At the start of this chapter, I illustrated how participants can variably construe the degree of similarity among a set of scientific experiments. Once we recognize the existence of this kind of interpretative variability among scientists' attributions of experimental sameness, it becomes difficult to pursue any form of sociological analysis which treats replication as a stable feature of scientists' experiments in themselves, rather than as a contingent feature of scientists' interpretative work.

In this text, therefore, I have tried to identify some of the interpretative outcomes which scientists routinely accomplish through their variable attributions of experimental sameness/difference. I have tried to show some of the things that scientists do with similarity attributions. Specifically, I have maintained that attributions of experimental difference enable scientists to display their own and others' scientific originality; and that attributions of sameness can be employed to condemn others for lack of originality. I have also suggested that respondents use a standard triangulation account, combining the attribution of sameness at one level with the attribution of differences at another level, which enables them interpretatively to accomplish scientific validation along with the allocation of originality.

Although I have emphasized above the import which Borges's story has for *participants*' interpretative work, I must accept that it has similar implications for the composition of the present text. Like Borges, and like my biochemists, I have constructed this chapter by identifying, compiling and using a series of similarities/differences. For example, I have presented various passages from different interview transcripts in which are to be found different combinations of words. Yet I have claimed that some of these passages exhibit 'the same interpretative structure'. Although these similarity claims always have some basis in the original texts, the identification of 'the same features in different texts' depends on and exists through the interpretative work I have carried out on those texts; in the same way that the sameness/difference of Cervantes's/Menard's texts is accomplished in a particular way through Borges's interpretative work. The similarities which I have identified above could, by means of different textual work, be interpretatively deconstructed.

This 'admission' may appear to imply an inadequacy in the

present text. For, it may be argued, if the sameness/difference of texts is always interpretatively accomplished, there is no compelling reason to accept the analyst's attributions of sameness/difference in this text. However, this criticism, in turn, can be said to adopt 'the same position' as that proposed in this chapter; that is, although it rejects the particular readings of sameness/difference advanced above, it accomplishes this rejection by assuming that sameness/difference is interpretatively accomplished. Thus, it seems to be possible to read this criticism as both a rejection and a confirmation of this chapter's central conclusion; or, to put it in the terms used above, as a replication through difference.

Another view of the present text can be obtained by addressing my own analytical question to it: namely, what does it accomplish through its attributions of sameness/difference? (see Ashmore, 1983). One of the things it can be said to accomplish is a replication of the sociological claim about replication which is contained in the papers by Collins and others cited above. In other words, it can be taken to be one more study confirming 'the potential local interpretative flexibility of science' and further establishing the 'socially negotiated character of experimental replication' (Collins, 1981b, p. 4).

Although the present text has certain distinctive features, this need not affect its being treated as primarily a repetition of prior work. For example, Collins treats a paper by Travis (1981) on 'a new area of science' as, 'in the main, a replication of earlier work on replication!' (1981b, p. 4). Thus, the fact that the present text also contains new empirical data need not necessarily prevent it from being deemed to be the same as, a straightforward replication of, previous sociological research. At the same time, however, the present paper can be read, like that of Travis, as having a certain degree of distinctiveness and, thereby, of originality. For instance, it is the first replication study which uses data obtained from bioenergeticists; it is, possibly, the first such study to compare the attribution of scientific originality with that of literary originality; and it is, perhaps, the first replication study to emphasize the interpretative connection between replication and originality.

I can, therefore, easily link the present text to certain predecessors by means of a standard triangulation account. I can provide textual evidence to show that it reaches basically the same conclusion as these predecessors, but that it does so by an analysis which differs from previous studies in various ways. Accordingly, we might conclude that the present study serves to validate the prior conclusion; whilst making an original contribution of its own.

Possible readings of the sameness/difference of the present chapter do not stop here, however. For this text can also be read as radically different from those of Collins and as fundamentally incompatible with Collins's main conclusions. There are various ways of doing this, one of which is as follows. In this concluding section of the present chapter, I am extending conclusions which I have derived from data on natural scientists to the realm of sociological analysis. My argument, in this sense, depends on an assumption of sameness between the two realms of intellectual endeavour. Collins, however, denies this sameness in several of his texts (especially 1981c). In these texts, Collins prescribes that we should 'treat the social world as real, and as something about which we can have sound data, whereas we should treat the natural world as something problematic – a social construct rather than something real' (1981c, p. 217). In other words, whereas I am trying to explore the self-referential implications of my own analysis, Collins rejects this degree of analytical reflexivity because it is taken to lead to 'paralysing difficulties'.

In so far as I take my concern in this part of the chapter to be with the way in which we, as sociologists, interpretatively construe the social world, my conclusions seem to be diametrically opposed to those of Collins. Whereas Collins proposes that we should only treat the 'natural world' as interpretatively accomplished, whilst treating the attributes of the social world (such as the sameness/ difference of texts and actions) as 'real', my conclusion is that both social and natural worlds are variably constructed through participants' discourse. It appears, then, that not only can the present chapter be read as the same as Collins or as the same but also different; it can just as easily be read as fundamentally incompatible with Collins's claims.

All of these readings of sameness/difference can be textually legitimated and strongly defended. I do not, therefore, wish to insist on the validity of any one. They are all viable readings. The final reading above, however, is particularly interesting for it depicts Collins as basing his claims about the social world upon a privileged form of 'realist' discourse available only to the sociologist. Scientists, in contrast, are denied access to such privileged discourse. From this analytical position, participants' discourse is to be deconstructed through the supposedly superior discourse of the analyst. This arbitrary interpretative asymmetry seems to me to be untenable, even though I have myself, like most other sociologists, taken it for granted in previous work. It is for this reason that I have tried to emphasize in this final section that the analysis presented in this chapter is self-referential and self-exemplifying. The textuality that I have tried to display in participants' discourse is an inescapable feature of my own discourse. I suggest that the self-referential character of the sociological analysis of discourse is not something to be rejected or hidden, but rather to be welcomed and celebrated as in the chapter which follows.

5

The Scientist Talks Back: a One-Act Play

Programme Notes

This chapter takes the form of a text for a one-act play. The play is focused around the topic of experimental replication in science. One reason for choosing this topic is that both scientists and sociologists draw upon the notion of 'replication' in characterizing their own actions. Consequently, a discussion of replication in science can lead quickly to an examination of replication in sociology and, thereby, to the more general topic of reflexivity (Ashmore, 1983). As discourse about replication becomes self-referential, it creates interpretative difficulties. The essential problem is that self-referential discourse on the topic of replication tends to generate paradoxes, to become self-contradictory or self-refuting.

It may well be that this is a very general feature of self-referential discourse. For example, Hofstadter (1979) has shown how self-reference generates interpretative difficulties (as well as creative opportunities) in musical, pictorial and mathematical discourses and how it produces what he calls 'strange loops', that is, potentially endless sequences of discourse which constantly invert and undermine initial assumptions, yet which can return unexpectedly to the original point of departure and set the whole sequence going again. Accordingly, the discourse below has been organized in the form of a 'strange loop'. In this way, through the use of a strange loop and a dramatic format, I have tried to devise a manner of sociological presentation which can do justice to the interdependent and self-referential character of participants' and analysts' discourse about social action in science; yet which is not itself undermined by its acceptance of reflexivity. Woolgar (1982, p. 489) captures the principle behind this chapter when he writes that 'We need to explore forms of literary expression whereby the monster [reflexivity] can be simultaneously kept at bay and allowed a position at the heart of our enterprise.' My aim is to show that it may be possible, through a creative approach to our own discourse, to devise ways of accepting, learning from, even enjoying, reflexivity.

The dialogue of the play has been constructed in the following way. All the statements made by sociologists are taken from research papers written recently by sociologists of science. I have frequently combined statements from several papers by the same author in a single conversational turn. But each sociologist in the play consistently draws upon the writings of one actual contributor to the sociological literature. Only minor changes are made to his/her actual words, apart from the addition of linking phrases like 'I'm afraid you don't understand' or 'I agree with that'. The statements of 'The Scientist' are based directly on material obtained by G. Nigel Gilbert and myself in the course of interviews with a set of biochemists (Gilbert and Mulkay, 1984). Most of the Scientist's statements are direct quotes from these interviews. Thus the context in which the words were originally uttered, that is, a situation where a scientist was discussing science with two sociologists in his own lab, is similar to that recreated in the play.

I have intervened more directly in the interview material used to construct the Scientist's dialogue than I have in formulating the sociologists' statements. I have combined statements by different scientists in one conversational turn. I have also sometimes paraphrased segments of interview transcript in order to make them fit the imaginary situation of the play and I have occasionally put into the Scientist's mouth my own summary versions of statements made in different ways by several biochemists, as well as, at the end, some inventions of my own which seem to 'grow naturally' out of the preceding dialogue. Details of the original sources can be found in Mulkay (1984a), on which the text below is based.

Stage Directions

The curtain rises to show the cafeteria of a famous American enzyme laboratory late on an autumn afternoon. Casually dressed research students slump untidily at scattered tables, sipping Coca Cola or ersatz coffee softly from plastic cups and staring out, morose and unblinking, through the upper floor window over the highway network below. The rumble of the traffic furnishes a constant background noise.

At a table placed centre-front stage sit three persons. One is a

male biochemist of mature years. He is Head of the Enzyme Lab
and author of more than a hundred research papers. He has been
interviewed twice today by two different sociologists. He was
surprised to find how dissimilar were the two sets of questions. It
had originally seemed convenient to arrange these interviews for
the same day, but he has found the experience remarkably tiring.
He is still courteous, however, and in this relaxed, informal setting,
he is still trying to help the sociologists get it right.

The other two people at the table are the sociologists. They are
both younger than the Scientist. Sociologist 1 is a smartly dressed
American woman. She will be moving on that evening to interview
another eminent scientist tomorrow at another laboratory and in a
different field. Sociologist 2 is English. He is staying at the Enzyme
Lab for another day in order to talk to some rank and file scientists
working in the Scientist's area of research. As we join them, the
Scientist is just clarifying for his two listeners a fundamental truth
about science.

THE SCIENTIST   Reproducibility of results is a key element in
   biochemistry and in science generally. To have experimental
   control gives you an understanding of the mechanisms at work,
   the precise nature of things. Exact replication shows that you are
   studying something real.
SOCIOLOGIST 1   Yes, this is the starting point for the sociological
   analysis of science. The institutionalized requirement that new
   contributions be reproducible is the cornerstone of the scientific
   community's system of social control. The requirement of
   reproducibility serves not only to deter departures from cognitive
   and moral norms but also makes for the detection of error and
   deviance.
SOCIOLOGIST 2   I'm sorry, but you are both being philosophically and sociologically naive. You are adopting an algorithmic
   model of social action in science which assumes that knowledge
   is reducible to something like the programme of a digital
   computer. You are implying that there is a finite series of
   unambiguous instructions which can be formulated, transferred,
   and when correctly followed will enable a scientist to copy
   another's experiment exactly. But this simply isn't the case.
   Scientists are never able to specify exactly how they produce
   their experimental results. There is always room for doubt,
   therefore, as to whether two or more experiments are the same.
   Thus replication is not a firm criterion in relation to which
   scientists' actions and knowledge-claims are assessed and regulated. What scientists call 'replication' is the uncertain outcome
   of processes of social negotiation.

THE SCIENTIST   Well, I would like to see the evidence for these claims. I suspect that you and those sociologists who take a similar view must have concentrated on areas marginal to science or on controversial fields. Things may be as you say in such areas. But I can assure you that in the harder sciences and in normal circumstances experimental procedures are sufficiently explicit to allow any competent scientist to repeat others' observations as a matter of routine. It is probably true that the researcher cannot state in each short research paper *everything* on which his results depend. But he will cite methods papers where the basic procedures are set out more fully. And in those few cases where somebody finds it difficult to repeat an experiment, a short discussion over the 'phone will usually solve the problem. It seems to me that, by focusing on controversial areas, where almost by definition unusual experimental difficulties exist, you may have obtained a false impression of science as a whole.

SOCIOLOGIST 1   I agree. We do have to accept, of course, that all scientific contributions are not equally reproducible. The potential for true replication varies greatly among the sciences according to their cognitive texture. For instance, it has been shown that virtually no replications seem to be published in the major psychology journals. But this extreme situation is in contrast to the case for such sciences as physics, biochemistry and genetics, where replication appears to be far more frequent, especially when the original findings presented are theoretically anomalous or important or both.

THE SCIENTIST   Thank you for your support. However, there is one small point on which I have to correct you. You imply that there is probably less replication in psychology than in other disciplines because psychologists don't publish replications. But neither do we biochemists. A straightforward 'exact replication' is simply not publishable. It makes no useful contribution to scientific knowledge. In order to publish, you must produce original results, say something new.

[At this point another sociologist joins the group at centre stage. The lab seems to be full of them. This sociologist, however, is not a mere migrant. She is not passing through in order to tape-record what scientists *say* about science. This intrepid woman has learned to live among the natives. She has observed them at close quarters and she knows what really goes on in the lab. She takes up the last remark, speaking with a slight European accent.]

SOCIOLOGIST 3   That is correct! Scientists do not strive for repetition, they aim for distinctiveness. Scientists are not interested in checking others' results in order to establish whether or not these results correspond with reality. When looking at actual laboratory practice, it becomes clear that the stakes are not defined in terms of the correspondence-theory of truth. Each scientist is oriented to making others' results work for himself within a 'reality' which is highly artificial and essentially self-created out of local resources. Thus the results each researcher produces are idiosyncratic, reflecting choices and interpretations that are crystallizations of order in a local contingency space. Scientific 'facts' are the hybrids constructed by means of those choices. Their *originality* and their *distinctive value* derive from the idiosyncracies which mark their production. Only by recognizing that the process of scientific production operates in this localized manner can we account for the fact that scientific products are anarchic and variable and the fact that most published results cannot easily be re-generated or validated. Furthermore, I want to stress that these conclusions have been confirmed by my studies in *this* laboratory as well as by anthropologists observing elsewhere. These findings apply generally in science and not to a few abnormal or controversial areas.

SOCIOLOGIST 1　I can't accept that! I'm afraid I have to accuse you and your colleagues of anthropological myopia. You've made the fundamental error of confusing what happens in particular labs with what happens in the community as a whole. We must not forget to distinguish between the private and the public phases of scientific work. When scientists' findings enter the public domain, they become subject to rigorous policing, to a degree perhaps unparalleled in any other field of human activity. I take the point that simple replications are seldom, if ever, published. But this does not mean that the reproducibility of results is not constantly checked and, in the great majority of cases, confirmed. In the process of research, even long accepted contributions periodically come under renewed scrutiny, not necessarily by design but as a by-product of using them for further work. Error and deception can thus be uncovered, even without individual intent, through the social mechanism of replication which is institutionalized within the research *community*.[1]

THE SCIENTIST　Yes, I think that's coming close to the way replication works out in practice. And, in fact, the claims you two are making [looking at Sociologists 1 and 3] are quite compatible. Exact replication occurs very infrequently. Probably you would try to repeat an experiment precisely only if it was important for your own research and if you had doubts about it. And even then you might just ignore it. Usually what's done is, people don't even try to repeat the identical experiment, but they repeat some experiment that's germane to the same idea. I think as a philosophical point, it is always better to do many different experiments on the same point than to keep repeating the same experiment over and over again. Because if you do many different experiments, often something new will come out of it that you would not get from the one experiment. In so far as people in different labs use their own resources and personal skills to produce some variant of the original experiment which *shows the same thing*, the scientific result can be taken to be independent of the idiosyncratic circumstances attending each experimental production. So it is true that scientists strive for distinctiveness and that exact repetitions of others' work are neither easy to produce nor frequently sought. However, it is precisely *through* this diversity of experimental procedures that conclusions are generated which are independent of their context of production. Scientific knowledge is that which persists *despite* the heterogeneity of scientists' practices.

SOCIOLOGIST 3   That is an elegant argument, but I'm afraid it won't hold water. For it depends on the unsatisfactory distinction between private and public phases of research introduced by Sociologist 1. If we look at the process of knowledge-production in sufficient detail, we find that production and validation are inseparable. Scientists constantly devise their experimental practices and their interpretations of their results in accordance with the expected responses of their colleagues/competitors in other labs. Claims are based on what is 'hot' and what is 'out', and they are linked to a whole range of other social considerations. Similarly, whether a proposed knowledge-claim is judged plausible or implausible, interesting, unbelievable or nonsensical may depend on *who* proposed the result, *where* the work was done, and *how* it was accomplished. In other words, scientists virtually *identify* results with the circumstances of their generation. Thus, where do we find the process of validation if not *in* the laboratory itself? What *is* the process of acceptance if not one of selective incorporation of previous results into the ongoing process of research production? Consequently, we are simply unable to identify a body of invariant knowledge which is separate from the multifarious and idiosyncratic practices of specific scientists constructing their unique 'realities' within their own laboratories.

SOCIOLOGIST 2   It seems to me that the Scientist is actually close to accepting the kind of sociological view of replication which Sociologist 3 and I have proposed. He is agreeing that as the scientists in a research network produce their unique cultural products, they engage in social negotiation about what is to count as a competent experiment, that is, they negotiate which set of experimental accomplishments is to be treated as scientifically equivalent. We are certainly agreed that scientists are not normally concerned to create a batch of isomorphous experiments. There are many possible ways of explaining this, but a convincing interpretation is that in the absence of general agreement of what is to count as a 'working experiment', secondary experiments which do not show the same results as the original experiments may still be seen as 'competent' so there is no special impetus to copy the original experiment. Scientists' actions may thus be seen as negotiations about which set of experiments in a field should be counted as *the* set of competent experiments. In deciding this issue, they are deciding the character of the natural phenomena under study.

THE SCIENTIST   I accept much of what you and Sociologist 3 have said. I particularly like your recognition that 'there are many different ways of explaining scientists' actions'. You seem here to be making a point which we biochemists often stress when talking about replication, namely, that theoretical conclusions are never fully determined by empirical observations. As a friend of mine put it to me recently: 'I am primarily an experimentalist and I love clean experiments. I don't give a damn whether the models are right or wrong. The only thing I really defend are my numbers. The interpretation – well, biological systems are usually so damn complicated that to get the right interpretation you have to be very lucky.' Now I think that's right; and you change your interpretation in the light of other people's findings which are closely related to yours. In this way, you get confirmation of concepts and data without any attempt at exact replication. You take for granted that, if you did exactly what other experimenters did, you'd get the same results. When I read the literature I'm much more impressed by two or more ways of showing the same thing. In this way, you limit the range of possible interpretations. So, your central aim as a scientist is to establish the most reasonable deductions from a set of similar, but not identical, observations which relate to a specific scientific issue or phenomenon. If this is what you mean by 'social negotiation', I have no reason to deny that that's how science works. But I feel that for you and Sociologist 3, this phrase has implications of which I'm not fully aware.

SOCIOLOGIST 3   Your concession that scientific theories are logically underdetermined by the data is a crucial one. As we know, scientists do regularly come to theoretical conclusions, even though these conclusions are never logically entailed. Thus it follows that some kinds of non-logical factors must play a role in theory-choice. I and others have shown in a growing corpus of empirical studies that these non-logical factors include participants' argumentative skills, the prestige or other symbolic and material resources which scientists mobilize to convince each other, the political saliency of the findings, the support proponents can attract and so on.

SOCIOLOGIST 2   Yes, if I could sum up the central conclusion established by these detailed case studies of knowledge-production in science, it is that scientists' interpretations could always have been otherwise. Scientific knowledge is socially contingent. Thus, scientific truth becomes conceivable only as a socially organized upshot of contingent courses of linguistic, conceptual and social behaviour. However, let me stress that the influence of these contingent factors is not 'disreputable' but inevitable. It does not constitute the intrusion of 'external factors' into science, but constitutes the inescapable social process of scientific method.

THE SCIENTIST   Well, I accept, of course, that scientific knowledge is uncertain. It is, as you say, a human accomplishment and can never achieve ultimate certainty. But it seems to me that the observations and conclusions of science are less affected by these local and contingent factors than you maintain and, indeed, less affected by them than any other area of human endeavour. Although each individual scientist is undoubtedly prejudiced and affected by his social situation, his knowledge-claims only come to be accepted if they can be freed from their particular origins by leading to predictions which other people can use successfully in their experiments and in *their* local circumstances. Scientists' experimental or theoretical claims stand or fall according to the results other people get. Exact experimental replication plays a part in this process of evaluation, but its contribution is largely negative. It is certainly not an unequivocal criterion of scientific validity.

SOCIOLOGIST 2   Your reference to 'exact replication' depends on the assumption that recognizing an exact copy of the experiment to be replicated can be unproblematic. You still seem to believe that *genuine results* evidence themselves by their repeatability (whether or not scientists actually do repeat them) and that the criterion of replicability distinguishes the unique set of genuine results from the set of false ones. But my colleagues and I have shown that it is precisely through contingent 'negotiations' over the replicability of phenomena that one result rather than another is 'discovered'.

THE SCIENTIST   No, I am not saying that experimental replication is ever unproblematic. There can always be a hundred reasons why two experiments may differ, despite every attempt to replicate exactly. Nor am I saying that genuine results 'evidence themselves by their repeatability'. For instance, it is obvious that experimental artefacts are often as reproducible as valid results; although of course a lot of artefacts are not replicable. So reproducibility is not a distinctive feature of genuine results and I can hardly imagine any experienced researcher making such a claim. In traditional philosphical terms, replicability is a necessary but not a sufficient condition of validity. That's what I meant when I said that its contribution to scientific practice is largely negative. Let me give you an example: a scientist I know produced a set of coherent observations which had major theoretical implications in my field. I tried to repeat his experiments as closely as I could, but I didn't get the same results. So I went to his lab and did one of his experiments there with him on my bacteria to see whether it worked. It worked in his lab, but I couldn't get it to work in mine. Back in my own lab I tried once again to do an exact replication. He said he shook the reaction mixture, while I'd stirred it. He said shake not stir. So I tried to copy all the apparently trivial details like that. But it still didn't work. So I gave it up and I have continued to treat his experimental claims as doubtful. People in other labs have done very similar experiments to his and have also failed to get the same results. Consequently, his claims have been disregarded. It doesn't matter that these other scientists have not attempted 'exact replications' in the way that I did. The expectation would be that, if it's a real effect, you could repeat it just by following the same *general* recipe. It really shouldn't matter what piece of machinery you use, so it's only if it fails that you start to wonder about that. It's in this sense that failure to replicate across a variety of local conditions acts as a powerful negative criterion.

Now what would have happened if I *had* been able to reproduce these results in my lab after close consultation with the original author? It certainly wouldn't have meant that his claim to have identified certain basic phenomena occurring naturally in bacteria would have been substantiated, nor the supposed implication that the existing theory of energy production was wrong. Once I had achieved regular reproducibility, my next step would have been to try to understand exactly *how* this set of experimental procedures generated these results. Was the phenomenon biologically important or was this just some trivial effect that has no bearing on energy production, but just depends on some minor variations in the way the system is treated experimentally? For instance, the experimenter in this case said that you had to put one reagent in the fridge before it worked. But he didn't examine that reagent to see what changes might have taken place. It may be that the procedure produced a breakdown compound which was catalysing his reaction without his knowing it and leading him to misinterpret as well as misleadingly describe his results.

I'm sorry to have gone on at such length. I just wanted to show how replicability can operate as a fairly strong negative criterion, but as only a weak positive criterion. We biochemists assume that the great majority of published experiments accurately report their authors' procedures and results. Our task, then, is that of assessing their scientific meaning. This necessarily involves a close reading of the methods sections of experimental reports. The point of methods sections is not primarily to enable other readers to duplicate published results, but to let them know how the results were produced and, accordingly, to enable them to interpret their scientific meaning, mainly through extending and building upon these results in their own researches.

SOCIOLOGIST 2   Your example is an interesting illustration of the informal interaction through which what is to count as a replication is negotiated. But let me repeat the main findings of our studies which show that, because the outcome of scientific controversies depends on the establishment of what counts as a competent or successful experiment, it follows that the results of experiments themselves do not determine the outcome. Thus, scientific outcomes depend on the relative 'power' and status of the opposed parties, and their skill in rhetoric and the other components of 'social negotiations'. Consequently, replicability should be seen as part of the 'rhetoric of scientific persuasion' – a means of *accomplishing* objectivity, rather than demonstrating it.

THE SCIENTIST   But you don't seem to have understood my argument at all, nor the point of the example. I thought I had made it quite clear that establishing the competence, that is, the reproducibility, of an experiment in no way determines what you call the 'scientific outcome'. Meaningful reproducibility as I have previously described it, that is, not necessarily exact replication but some kind of equivalent observation, is a prerequisite for taking a claim seriously. But this is merely the first step towards establishing its scientific meaning. You have to think of the process as a sequence over time. Typically what happens is that somebody discovers a big effect. This means that anybody can see this effect. Remember that in much of biochemistry, when you add a reagent you don't get a mere 1,000 counts, you get nearer 20,000. Now whether it turns out to be 15,000 or 10,000 or even 5,000, it doesn't make a lot of difference. The phenomenon is still there. You add the reagent and you get a *huge* increase in activity. Once this has been established through various different, yet overlapping, research procedures, then you start getting involved in: well, why was it only half the size today than yesterday? Why is it regularly greater in his lab than mine? Thus the subtle variations may not be initially reproducible. But it's through exploring these details that you begin to understand the phenomenon in question. Now I have no reason to think that this is greatly influenced by the kind of personal and social factors that you have mentioned. The crucial factor is experimental success. Of course that's never unambiguous. Each researcher has to develop his own feel for how good experimental data are and you hope that's adequate. But the fact that scientific judgement is always uncertain does not imply that it's non-logical or that the scientific assessment of experimental evidence is mere rhetoric. You have assumed that because replication doesn't operate as a clear-cut criterion of valid knowledge (although scientists sometimes seem to say that it does operate that way), it follows that scientists' references to reproducibility are empty and that they act as a cover for non-logical, social elements. However, I have shown that your definition of the problem is misconceived and that the algorithmic version of replication which you claim to have replaced is totally irrelevant. I have also provided a plausible alternative account in which these hidden social factors play no significant part. You admitted earlier that the story can be told in several ways. Why not tell it my way?

SOCIOLOGIST 2 I think that you are taking our sociological arguments as an attack upon science, but this is not so. You are assuming that the invasion of the heartland of science by sociological thought entails a prescription for scientific anarchy. This, however, is far from the case. There is no need for you to be defensive. Our analysis makes the basis of scientific authority more clear rather than less. We have shown that scientific authority is not based on scientists' ability to devise replicable experiments; for different groups of scientists are able to claim that the same set of experiments demonstrates radically different things. Thus the meaning that scientists give to experimental results and, therefore, the ultimate basis of their authority is socially negotiated and socially sanctioned. In this respect it is like moral and legal authority. Scientists are experts on the natural world in the same way as lawyers are experts on the law. In both cases the most valuable opinions are to be had from, respectively, scientists and lawyers. But neither lawyers nor scientists are immune from criticism from their colleagues by virtue of their access to some extra-social realm of pure reason or pure fact.

[Participants have by this time become rather heated. Faces are red and all of those involved seem rather irritated by the other parties' refusal to make concessions. There is a brief lapse in the conversation. This allows a tall, grey-haired man seated at an adjoining table, where he seems to have been recording the debate to which we have been listening, to lean across and offer the following comments in a quiet, soothing tone.]

ANONYMOUS SPEAKER   Perhaps you all tell the story of science and of replication in many different ways. Maybe there is no single, coherent story. You, Scientist, began with an apparently much stronger account of replication than you have provided subsequently. Similarly, I know that Sociologist 3 has written that she does not deny that scientific findings are replicable, despite her emphasis on the idiosyncratic, local production of scientific facts. Maybe we all speak with forked tongues about the social world. Why not accept that 'replication' has multiple meanings? Why not relax and accept that none of us is engaged in describing *the* social world? We are creators of meanings appropriate to the occasion, like dramatists, novelists and ordinary speakers.

[The anonymous speaker leans back and checks that his tape-recorder is still working. He plays no further part in the discussion. But his brief intervention seems to have encouraged the Scientist to change from defence to attack. He addresses himself to Sociologist 2.]

THE SCIENTIST   Well, I've noticed several times that, although you said that the story could be told in different ways, both you and Sociologist 3 have insisted that your interpretation of replication in science is based firmly upon the empirical evidence provided by numerous sociological studies. You seem to regard these studies as replicating, and thereby confirming your central point.

SOCIOLOGIST 2   Oh yes! There are numerous studies confirming that the potential local interpretative flexibility of science prevents experiment, by itself, from being decisive. In particular, the socially negotiated character of experimental replication is well replicated. One of the most well-replicated outcomes of this work is that concerning the social negotiation of reproducibility.

THE SCIENTIST   If I understand you correctly, you are claiming to have validated, through replication, the finding that replication itself is a contingent social accomplishment, and the finding that the attempt to treat replication as an unproblematic source of validation is merely a part of the rhetoric of persuasion. Does this not involve you in a paradox?

SOCIOLOGIST 2   Not at all. You are trying to force me to be unnecessarily reflexive. Undue reflexivity can be a hindrance and lead to paralysing difficulties. It seems to me that the question of whether the patterns of explanation applied by sociologists *to science* are equally applicable *to sociology* is not a question to be answered by those sociologists who are engaged in the sociology of science. It seems more sensible for the sociologist of scientific knowledge not to worry about this sort of problem but rather to assume that the things that he or she finds out about scientific knowledge are 'objective' – that is, he or she should go about finding out things about the social world of the scientist in the same spirit as the scientist goes about finding out things about the natural world. I have come to realize that this is an unusual view – some even find it shocking. Not only does it deny the importance of (currently fashionable) reflexivity, but it reverses the accepted wisdom about where certainty and reality are to be found. My prescription is to treat the social world as real, and as something about which we can have sound data, whereas we should treat the natural world as something problematic – a social construct rather than something real. This seems to me to be an entirely natural view for a social scientist.

THE SCIENTIST   I must say that your sudden change of perspective has taken me by surprise. It seems to imply that my 'natural attitude' to the physical world is entirely justified, indeed inescapable, as is your parallel attitude to the social world. It also seems to imply that our apparently conflicting accounts of science do not actually clash; they merely coexist as the divergent versions of science produced by speakers engaged in different kinds of socially located discourse. From your perspective, we both seem obliged to defend our own research practice in 'the spirit of the natural sciences', that is, in 'realist' terms, and to treat our own replications as socially unproblematic; yet at the same time, we are both able to offer alternative, contingent, sociological accounts of the other's practice. (I'm beginning to talk like a sociologist!) I'm not sure whether either of us can accept this implication. Indeed, although it does seem to follow from your argument, it seems at the same time to contradict your own view of the simple facticity of the social world. I, and many of my colleagues, reject your conclusions. Science does not look like that to us. This seems to suggest that the 'facts' about the social world of science are far from self-evident and will have to be socially negotiated – exactly as you say facts about the natural world are negotiated. I suppose that you might decide to disregard our views and treat them as the blinkered opinions of mere participants. But even if you eliminate us arbitrarily from your professional debate, it is clear from what Sociologist 1 said earlier that not every sociologist who looks closely at science replicates your finding. In order to substantiate your claims about replication in science, therefore, you will have to enter into social negotiation with other sociologists about what is to count as a competent sociological replication. Thus, in treating sociological data and sociological replication as unproblematic, you seem to me to be acting in a way which is both philosophically and sociologically naive. You are adopting an algorithmic model of social action in social science which assumes that knowledge is reducible to something like the programme of a digital computer. You are implying that there is a finite series of unambiguous instructions which can be formulated, transferred, and when correctly followed will enable a sociologist to copy another's study exactly. But this simply isn't the case. Sociologists are never able to specify exactly how they produce their observational results. There is always room for doubt, therefore, as to whether two or more sets of sociological observations are the same. Thus replication is not a firm criterion in relation to which sociologists' actions and knowledge-claims are assessed and regulated. What sociologists call 'replication' is the uncertain outcome of processes of social negotiation.

SOCIOLOGIST 2 I doubt if you have much evidence to support these assertions. I can assure you that in normal circumstances observational procedures are sufficiently clear to allow any competent sociologist/anthropologist to repeat others' observations as a matter of routine. . . [The discourse has now completed the first of a potentially endless sequence of strange loops. The dialogue begins to repeat itself, but with the major protagonists having changed places. The debate proceeds as before, with only minor alterations, for a period of time sufficient to enable the audience clearly to perceive that it will go on indefinitely with each speaker changing direction as he/she veers from defence to attack and back again. The talking continues unabated as, gradually, the lights dim and the curtain slowly falls.]

Note to Chapter 5

1 It has been pointed out that any actress playing Sociologist 1 would be distinctly miffed by the fact that she is never allowed to speak again. However, it seems that there are precedents for such a prolonged

silence. In *A Winter's Tale*, Florizel and Perdita hardly speak at all in the last scene. Moreover, it can be argued that this silence makes a dramatic point, namely, that Florizel and Perdita are completely submerged by their new environment. Does Sociologist 1's silence fulfil a similar function? Does the sudden termination of her discourse imply that her views are currently unfashionable among sociologists of science? Unfortunately, I don't know the answer. I can, however, suggest another equally relevant question, namely: why is she there in the first place? Can it be that she makes a critical contribution to the unfolding of the plot, and to other participants' assertions, even though she sits there in silence? As with all the *difficult* questions about this text, the Author doesn't even try to help. [The Meta-author]

PART 3

Discoveries

6
Genius and Culture: Folk Theories of Discovery

You may be surprised that the discussion of discovery should occur at this late stage in the book. After all, does discovery not come before dialogue and replication, and should it not, therefore, have provided our point of departure? My reason for placing the analysis of this topic here is that the apparent temporal priority of discovery is something of an illusion. It is an illusion in the sense that discovery is socially accomplished over time, sometimes over surprisingly long periods of time, and is interpretatively projected backwards upon earlier events. Specific events, actions or texts are revealed to *be* discoveries by the routine interpretative work embedded in informal dialogue, debate over replicability, and so on. The social construction of discovery is a facet of scientists' continuing discourse; and discovery is best seen, not as something which sets scientific discourse in motion, but as an interpretative outcome of that discourse.

Our understanding of the social construction of scientific discovery has been transformed in recent years by the work of Brannigan (1981) and Woolgar (1976; 1980). My intention in this chapter is to build upon and extend that work by examining some textual material dealing with the 'discovery of chemiosmosis'.[1] A central point made by both these authors is that, for the purposes of sociological analysis, discoveries are not to be treated as naturally occurring events open to explanation in terms of some combination of prior causal processes. Rather, both analysts focus on describing the interpretative practices by means of which certain 'events' are made out to be or not to be discoveries. It is argued that discoveries should not be treated 'naturalistically' by the analyst, because they are events whose status *as* discoveries is variable, context-bound and dependent on the contingent interpretative work carried out by participants. From this perspective, 'discovery' is not to be treated by the analyst as a distinctive kind of action or product, but as a *method* whereby a particular interpretative status is attributed to specific actions and/or textual products by those involved.

I begin from this position in the present chapter. My aim will be to investigate some of the details of how scientists use their interpretative resources to accomplish 'discovery'. This concern follows directly from Brannigan's analysis:

> The present study has paid more attention to the fact *that* social understandings are central to the status of scientific discoveries; this emphasis has been derived from the need to break the grip of a naturalistic sense of discovery prominent in other writings. Consequently we have become vividly aware *that* discoveries are methods, at the expense of understanding *how* such methods have operated. (1981, p. 164)

Folk Theories of Discovery

Although discoveries are to be treated analytically as contingent interpretative accomplishments, both Brannigan and Woolgar stress that participants themselves routinely treat discoveries as 'real, obdurate, natural and unavoidable social facts' (Brannigan, 1981, p. 142). Thus, for the analyst, this apparent externality of discoveries is regarded as something accomplished through participants' interpretative work (Woolgar, 1980). The obdurate 'out-there-ness' of discoveries is taken to be an aspect of or a by-product of the organization of members' discovery accounts (either spoken or written). The process is directly analogous to that whereby the possible contingency of factual claims about the *physical* world is progressively hidden from view by scientists' adoption of increasingly empiricist formulations of their knowledge-claims (Latour and Woolgar, 1979; Knorr-Cetina, 1981).

Brannigan takes this idea of the textual 'objectification' of scientific discoveries in an empirically specific direction by identifying certain 'folk theories of discovery' regularly employed by scientists. Brannigan employs this phrase to refer to participants' theories 'about the processes by which discoveries are made' (1981, p. 143). Although these conceptions about the nature of discovery are described as 'theories', this does not imply that they are articulated in any elaborate or systematic manner. They are, rather, used in an apparently *ad hoc* fashion, after the event, to explain *why* a discovery of a particular kind occurred at a specific juncture in scientific development. By making a discovery understandable and 'only to be expected', folk theories contribute to the sense that a particular scientific contribution was indisputably a discovery. Thus folk theories also form part of the interpretative *method* whereby discoveries are socially constituted. Brannigan suggests that there are two main theories employed by scientists in their discovery accounts. One of these is a social or lay-sociological 'theory' of cultural maturation. The other is an individualistic 'theory' of genius.

Brannigan offers a general explanation of why scientists make use of these folk theories. They are necessary, he suggests, in order to enable scientists to make sense of discoveries in a way which preserves 'the mundane assumption of the reciprocity of perspectives' (1981, p. 156) on the natural world. Both theories furnish an account of why the discoverer's perspective on the world should have been different from, yet ultimately consistent with, other peoples' perspectives on the one, knowable-in-common world. The theory of cultural maturation treats each discovery as an inevitable outcome of a self-generating accumulation of objective knowledge. The particular discoverer is treated as being largely irrelevant. He is merely the person who was at the right place at the right time to add a particular segment to the growing body of knowledge. In contrast, the theory of genius emphasizes the creative role of the individual. By 'assuming that the mental prowess of certain scientists is awesome, the occurrence of the discovery is made highly accountable. That scientific laws have been uncovered is to be *expected*, given the profound mental abilities of successful, scientific researchers' (1981, p. 156).

Brannigan stresses that these theories embody 'folk reasoning' in the sense that participants take them for granted in the act of accounting for discovery. For example, the only evidence normally furnished for the discoverer's genius or his being in the right place at the right time is the very discovery which genius or cultural maturation are supposed to explain. If one were to query whether the discoverer really was a genius (or in the right place at the right time), the answer would tend to take the form: 'He *must* have been a genius (right place/time) to make that discovery.' In this sense, the two folk theories seem to be applicable whenever and wherever they are needed. Yet, if this is so, it is worth asking why there should be two such general-purpose theories and not just one. If the theories both serve the same function of sustaining the reciprocity of perspectives equally well and if they can both be applied to any and every case, the existence of two theories is slightly puzzling.

Let us bear this question in mind, therefore, as we examine three discovery accounts in some detail and observe both theories in operation. Our guiding questions will be: do Brannigan's two folk theories play a significant part in these accounts? What interpretative work is being carried out in these accounts? What contribution to this interpretative work is made by the folk theories of genius and cultural maturation?

Genius and Uniqueness

During the 1970s, Spencer was awarded a Nobel Prize for his chemiosmotic theory. This led to a crop of articles in which Spencer's contribution to bioenergetics was explained and celebrated, and its historical origin and development briefly described. Although all of these articles imply that Spencer must have been an exceptionally able scientist, only one actually uses the term 'genius'. This is a five-paragraph appreciation by a scientist called Cunningham. Let us look at the organization of this text.

The first paragraph of Cunningham's article is as follows:

> The award of the Nobel Prize to Dr. Spencer recognises the unique character of his chemiosmotic hypothesis, and its enormous importance to our understanding of the mechanism whereby living cells trap and conserve radiant and redox energy, and transduce it into their chemical energy currency in the form, principally, of adenosine triphosphate (ATP).

In these opening words, the text endorses the correctness of the Nobel Committee's judgement. The award of the Nobel Prize is treated as 'recognizing' in ceremonial form what the author, and presumably others, already know to be the case. What the author already knows is, first, that the chemiosmotic hypothesis in some sense belongs to Spencer (it is *his* hypothesis), secondly that this hypothesis is 'unique', and thirdly that it is of 'enormous importance to our understanding' of the biological processes of energy-production. We will see, in due course, that this way of characterizing Spencer's work is by no means as straightforward as it appears to be in this text. For the moment, however, I will do no more than describe what is asserted or taken for granted in the text under consideration.

The second paragraph of Cunningham's article depicts the historical context in which Spencer's contribution to bioenergetics appeared. It is assumed that, in order to appreciate Spencer's contribution to science, we must understand how it fits into the temporal development of scientific thought. Cunningham begins with the 1950s, which is described as a period when 'rapid advances in biochemical knowledge' were being made. The 'dramatic birth and development of molecular biology' is mentioned as one such advance and reference is made to Crick and Watson. There then follows a brief summary of how biochemists thought of the processes of metabolism at that time.

Metabolism was conceived of as a series of linked reactions, catalysed by enzymes and taking place in solution within the cell cytoplasm; it was spatially directionless, or, to use Spencer's own terminology, scalar.

This scalar or directionless conception of the processes of metabolism, which is said to be based on Lipmann's concepts of group potential and group transfer, is portrayed as having been successful in various ways, but as leaving certain important problems unresolved.

There remained, however, major areas of mystery in respect of, for example, the mechanisms of photo- and oxidative phosphorylation and the transport of ions and nutrients across cellular membranes.

Paragraph two, then, in summarizing the complex developments in biochemistry during the 1950s, focuses our attention on the fact that, although rapid advances were being made in many areas, the study of metabolism was still faced with the two major mysteries of oxidative phosphorylation and membrane transport; and that those working in metabolism thought of the chemical reactions involved as being directionless. This provides a context in which the central element in Spencer's work, as portrayed here by Cunningham, can be readily understood and its scientific significance appreciated. The second paragraph makes clear, even for those with little knowledge of biochemistry, that Spencer's contribution will have to do with the directionality of metabolic reactions, with membrane transport, with solving the two mysteries, and thereby with setting in motion the kind of rapid advance which had already occurred in other areas of biochemistry. And indeed, what we find in the third paragraph is a textual rearrangement of elements mentioned earlier, accompanied by the introduction of 'Spencer's genius' as an explanatory device.

It was Spencer's genius which, at a single stroke, added an extra dimension to Lipmann's group potential, and so laid the foundation for an intellectual and experimental development in cell biology parallel to that given by Jacob, Monod and Lwoff to molecular biology. Spencer argued that, at the molecular level, metabolic reactions are not scalar. This is most readily demonstrable when an enzyme is situated within a membrane, as such a situation allows for vectorial [i.e. directional] metabolism and group translocation across that membrane. This concept was, therefore, first applied to the coupling of cell metabolism to membrane transport.

Spencer further developed this concept and proposed in 1961 his chemiosmotic hypothesis in which energy conservation [necessary for the production of ATP] is achieved through the flow of protons across the transducing membrane. . .

The notion of 'genius' operates here as an appropriate explanatory factor because it neatly accounts for the development of research into metabolism *as it is depicted in this text*. In the first place, the notion of 'genius' seems appropriate because, according to Cunningham, it was Spencer and Spencer alone who was able to solve problems which, for others, remained a mystery. Furthermore, not only did he resolve the mystery of photo- and oxidative phosphorylation, but also the other major outstanding problem, that of ion transport across membranes. Secondly, these mysteries were dissipated 'at a stroke'. This seems to imply that Spencer's intellectual capacity was truly remarkable. It also seems to imply that Spencer had no significant intellectual forebears or helpers. His resolution of these long-standing problems is depicted as having been achieved by means of a radical, personal reconceptualization of the scientific issues. Thirdly, it has been assumed from the outset that Spencer's solution is correct. Thus, Spencer did not simply provide *a* solution, but *the* solution. In addition, Spencer's contribution was fundamental in that he overturned one of the basic assumptions of research into metabolism. Unlike other researchers, Spencer was able to recognize the limitations of the conception of scalar reactions and to replace it with an alternative and more experimentally productive conception. Accordingly, Spencer's contribution can be portrayed as being similar in kind to those of the other particularly illustrious figures in the development of modern biology who are mentioned in the article. Like these other members of the biological pantheon, Spencer has defined and set in motion a whole new area of research which, without his remarkable work, would simply not have existed.

The fourth paragraph of Cunningham's article consists almost entirely of a summary of the four postulates of Spencer's chemiosmotic hypothesis. The article then concludes as follows:

These four postulates which were originally proposed on purely theoretical grounds, have now been experimentally verified many times over in laboratories throughout the world. Difficulties remain over details of certain of the molecular mechanisms involved, but the broad outline of the hypothesis and its essential components of vectorial metabolism, group translocation and the proton current remain inviolate. It is these components and their integration in the chemiosmotic hypothesis that have revolution-ised our understanding of cellular metabolism, its energetics, integration and control, and have earned for Spencer the Nobel Prize.

The final paragraph returns us to the celebratory point of the article. It confirms that Spencer's revolutionary ideas were not only highly original, but also correct. Moreover, the essential compon-ents of the theory are depicted as having remained constant over the ensuing period of seventeen years. The essential discovery was made by Spencer alone in 1961; what has happened in the field since then has been no more than experimental confirmation of that original event. In much the same way that Spencer is depicted as having no intellectual forebears or contemporaries who contributed to his reconceptualization of bioenergetics, it is made clear in this final paragraph that there have been no subsequent modifications to or revisions of his theoretical contribution which deserve mention.

Through this manner of presentation, the discovery of the chemiosmotic theory is, in Brannigan's terms, objectified and associated indissolubly with Spencer's name; it is made to appear that a unique discovery by Spencer actually occurred in 1961, even though few participants recognized it at that time for what it was. In this way, Spencer's original and unprecedented discovery is made to appear as a 'natural fact' in the historical development of biochemistry. Cunningham's text makes it evident that, even though we could not be sure that chemiosmosis was a genuine discovery until after the experimental work carried out in the 1960s and 1970s, we now know that it was a discovery all along. Accordingly, he concludes that, now that we do recognize the unprecedented, revolutionary and unique character of Spencer's achievement, it is only proper that we make that recognition public by conferring on him the most prestigious of scientific awards.

One of Brannigan's central points in his discussion of the 'folk theory' of scientific genius is that it is analytically vacuous; it adds nothing new to our understanding of how a discovery came about. We can see that this is true in the present text, in the sense that all the implications of Spencer's supposed genius are already present in other components of the text. If we accept Cunningham's descriptions of the development of biochemistry, the status of Spencer's hypothesis, and so on, as literal descriptions, then Spencer's 'genius' is self-evident. In other words, any man who, single-handed, brings about at a stroke a successful and experimentally productive reconceptualization of major scientific mysteries which ranks with the highest contributions made by other eminent scientists is, by definition, a genius. This is what 'scientific genius' means.

It appears, then, that Cunningham's attribution of 'genius' to Spencer is a terminological condensation of some of the major features of the story he is telling about the 'discovery of chemiosmosis'. In this sense, it adds nothing to our understanding of the discovery. If we were to eliminate 'genius' from the beginning of paragraph three and make it read: 'Spencer's great contribution was to add an extra dimension . . .', it seems unlikely that our understanding of the discovery would be discernibly altered. Given all the surrounding interpretative work embodied in Cunningham's text, 'Spencer's genius' and 'Spencer's great contribution' are closely equivalent.

However, Cunningham's reference to 'genius' does introduce a new textual agent which is essential if he is to furnish a complete discovery account. Although the notion of 'genius' is implicit in the remainder of the article, the article provides no explicit explanation of the discovery until 'genius' is identified textually as the responsible agent. To refer to Spencer's unique and unprecedented contribution, and so on, certainly implies his remarkable mental capacity. But until the notion of 'genius' or some similar active agent is introduced into the text, it contains no statement which has the form of an explicit explanation of the unprecedented character of that contribution. Consequently, in the actual text it is not Spencer, but Spencer's *genius* which adds the new dimension to bioenergetics. Thus, as far as the organization of Cunningham's text is concerned, the use of the term 'genius' is not vacuous. It is precisely through his use of this term that the author provides an explicit discovery account, that is, in attributing the discovery to Spencer's genius he explicitly identifies what it is about Spencer that purports to explain the discovery and to provide an understandable genesis for the whole remarkable course of events.

An analyst, such as Brannigan, can correctly point out that participants' attribution of 'genius' contributes nothing substantial to the surrounding text. But it is precisely through the organization of the text in a particularly appropriate way that participants make the attribution of 'genius' appear convincing and, for everyday practical purposes, explanatory. The notion of 'genius' is 'explanatory' precisely because it sums up much of what is implicit in a particular kind of discovery account (see Woolgar, 1980).

In his analysis of discovery, Brannigan showed that events are socially constituted as discoveries in so far as participants are successful in construing them as meeting certain interpretative criteria; and in particular, the criteria of appropriate motivation, originality and validity. Actions which are deemed to meet these criteria can be treated as discoveries, whether or not the term 'discovery' is used on any particular occasion, because these criteria define what members mean by 'discovery'. My conclusions, so far, about 'genius' are very similar. I suggest that a discovery can be deemed to be a product of genius if it is taken to meet the following criteria: it is conceived by one particular individual at a particular point in time; it involves a major act of conceptualization; the applicability of the new conceptualization has to be pointed out to other scientists, who would not have come to this conception by themselves; it solves problems which are of very considerable scientific significance; and it opens up new avenues of successful research. I suggest that discoveries which are depicted in a way which emphasizes such features *thereby* become explicable in terms of genius or awesome mental capacity or some equivalent turn of phrase. In this sense, 'genius' is one component of a particular kind of discovery account. It is an aspect of the textual methods which participants can use to depict a discovery in a particular way for a specific context or a specfic occasion (see Gilbert and Mulkay, 1984, chap. 3).

The occasion for Cunningham's text is, of course, the award of the Nobel Prize to Spencer. His article is a celebration of the Nobel Committee's judgement that the chemiosmotic theory is a major scientific contribution and that its discovery was accomplished by Spencer alone. Thus we must recognize that the account of this discovery contained in Cunningham's article is not *just* a discovery account; it is also a celebratory account. To put the point more generally, any discovery account will be embedded in a text which is engaged in additional interpretative work, such as celebrating a prize, contesting a claim, answering an interviewer's question, and so on. It seems reasonable to suppose that the form and content of each discovery account will be organized in a way which makes possible whatever further interpretative work is required (see the earlier discussion of originality and replication accounts).

In Cunningham's article, the work of celebration appears to be primary. For the article begins and ends with unqualified endorsements of the award of the Nobel Prize to Spencer. It is this, I suggest, which leads to the focus in this text on the uniqueness of the individual recipient, to the presentation of a discovery account organized exclusively around this individual's achievement and, consequently, to the creation of an account in which individual genius becomes an obvious explanatory factor, serving not only to explain and to objectify the discovery in question but also to justify the award.

It follows from this argument that in different contexts we would expect different interpretative work to be performed; and consequently, that we will find significantly different accounts of and different explanations of a given 'discovery'. Let us see how Spencer's account of the discovery differs from that of Cunningham, as he deals with the task of celebrating his own receipt of the Nobel Prize.

Spencer's Nobel Lecture

Spencer's Nobel Lecture is much longer and more complex than Cunningham's short article. Consequently, in order to prevent my analysis from becoming too unwieldy, I will have to be much more selective in examining its text. In this section, therefore, I will concentrate on just a few features which are particularly relevant to the preceding and subsequent discussion.

An immediately obvious and striking feature of Spencer's lecture is that it celebrates another man's genius, namely, that of his teacher, whom I will call King. This is made clear in the lecture's very title: 'King's respiratory chain concept and its chemiosmotic consequences'. This title is appropriate, because one of the main themes of the lecture is that Spencer's concept of chemiosmotic reactions followed fairly directly from King's prior conception of the nature of the respiratory chain. Thus, in the second paragraph, we find:

> Perhaps the most fruitful (and surprising) outcome of the development of the notion of chemiosmotic reactions is the guidance it has provided in work designed to answer three questions about respiratory chain systems and analogous photo-redox chain systems: What is it? What does it do? How does it do it? The genius of King led to the revelation of the importance of these questions. In this article, I hope to show that, as a result of the painstaking work of many biochemists, we can now answer the first two in general principle, and that considerable progress is being made in answering the third.

In his final paragraph, Spencer brings the speech to a close with another tribute to King:

> . . . it is especially noteworthy that King's chemically simple view of the respiratory chain appears now to have been right all

along – and he deserves great credit for having been so reluctant to become involved when the energy-rich chemical intermediates began to be so fashionable.

This presentation of the story of chemiosmosis is significantly different from Cunningham's. We are now told, not only that Spencer had a precursor of genius, but that Spencer's contribution was made possible by his having acquired a correct understanding of the nature of the respiratory chain from that precursor. In addition, elsewhere in the article, Spencer refers by name to seven other researchers who provided 'suggestive clues' during the 1950s leading towards the chemiosmotic theory. Moreover, Spencer describes the development of scientific understanding as an 'evolution', rather than as a revelatory, at a stroke, resolution of the mysteries of energy conservation.

Spencer's story, then, is of a slow, cumulative process, set in motion by King's genius in the 1950s and 'ending' in the 1970s, after painstaking contributions from many scientists, with the experimental confirmation of the four basic postulates which he had been largely responsible for formulating. The originating, explanatory factor in Spencer's text is King's genius and not his own. Compared with Cunningham's account, we can say that the concept of 'genius' has been displaced in the Nobel Lecture from Spencer to his predecessor King and with it the genesis of the historical process which culminated in the validation of the chemiosmotic theory. But why is this so? Is there something about the interpretative work required by the Nobel Lecture which is responsible for the marked differences between the two stories and the two attributions of genius?

One possibility is that, at least in public discourse among scientists, the explicit self-attribution of genius or extraordinary mental capacity is normally avoided. If this is so, then public attributions of genius will tend to be third person and not first person attributions. 'He is a genius' will be allowed and in some contexts preferred. 'I am a genius' will not usually be acceptable. On this assumption, any Nobel Lecturer is faced with the interpretative task of telling a celebratory story about his own work without using first person attributions of genius. In addition, as I will illustrate in the final part of this book and as I have shown in detail elsewhere (Mulkay, 1984b), the structure of Nobel discourse is organized in terms of a circulation of praise from non-Laureates to Laureates and back again to non-Laureates. In other words, the conventions of the Nobel ceremony appear to require Laureates to keep self-praise to a minimum and to emphasize the contributions made by others to the work being honoured by the award of the prize. The constant repetition of this pattern ensures that the Nobel ceremonies become celebrations of the accomplishments of the scientific community as a whole.

Spencer conforms to this pattern and elegantly solves the problem of avoiding excessive self-praise by using the lecture to celebrate King's work and by keeping to a minimum any explicit reference to his own originality. In this way, Spencer is able to retain the element of celebration, that is, the approbation of a specific scientist's exceptional achievement, and to use the accompanying notion of 'genius' as an explanatory factor in his history of the field, without ever attributing to himself any remarkable mental qualities. It is, of course, true that the 'correct' scientific views on the nature of the respiratory chain for which King is given credit in this text are also Spencer's own views. In this sense, Spencer's celebration of King is indirectly a celebration of his own work. However, by displacing the location of 'genius', he achieves this celebration with a minimum of self-congratulation. Thus, as in Cunningham's case, the attribution of genius is not *textually* vacuous. Not only does it furnish a point of origin for the work which eventually culminated in the discovery of chemiosmosis, but it also enables Spencer to celebrate his own scientific achievements with humility.

We have seen so far, then, that a speaker other than Cunningham, in a different interpretative situation, has provided a significantly different account of this particular discovery and has identified a different originating genius. Furthermore, although I will not demonstrate this point in detail, it is clear that Spencer's attribution of 'genius' to King is accompanied by and made appropriate by surrounding interpretative work which closely resembles that used by Cunningham to attribute 'genius' to Spencer. For example, recognition of the chemically simple character of the respiratory chain is depicted as being King's singular achievement; King's ability to recognize the truth is contrasted with the limited capacities of other scientists; the fundamental importance of the scientific problems in question is stressed; the experimental productivity of the right answer is copiously demonstrated; and so on.

Thus the underlying interpretative structure is very similar in the two instances we have examined. Both writers use the notion of 'genius' in a celebratory manner to tell a story of scientific development in which a unique contribution by a highly gifted individual eventually leads lesser men to an understanding of the truth. Furthermore both authors attribute 'genius' to some other person. In all these respects, the structures of the two accounts are parallel. In concrete detail, however, they differ sharply. These differences are produced, as we have seen, simply because Spencer is the central actor in Cunningham's story, and because Spencer chooses not to, or is perhaps obliged not to, attribute 'genius' to himself.

Before we move on to consider our third discovery account, it is necessary briefly to note one further feature of Spencer's Nobel Lecture. Because Spencer is textually engaged in linking the chemiosmotic theory directly to King's conception of the respiratory chain, he describes the essential elements of that theory in a way which emphasizes the connection with King's work. Cunningham, it will be recalled, brought out the nature of Spencer's basic innovation by contrasting Spencer's conception of directional (vectorial) chemical reactions with the scalar conception which other biochemists employed during the 1950s to understand the respiratory chain. Neither Spencer nor Cunningham suggest that King differed from other biochemists at that time in this respect. Thus, Spencer has to distinguish King and himself from all other contributors to the field by depicting his theory in a manner which is different from that of Cunningham. Spencer emphasizes that it was he and King alone who insisted that the redox processes of energy conservation occurring in the respiratory chain are chemically separate from the processes of phosphorylation whereby this energy is used to produce ATP (see Figure 1, p. 26). All other researchers, it is suggested, made the mistake of thinking that the respiratory chain was multi-functional, in the sense that it was directly involved in phosphorylation, where energy is used to make ATP, as well as in the process of respiration, whereby free energy is generated.

> This development caused King's chemically simple concept of the respiratory chain to be almost universally rejected in favour of a chemically duplex concept according to which respiratory chain components participated directly, not only in the known redox changes, but also in other chemical changes involving the energy-rich intermediates.

Spencer writes a few lines later that, 'By 1965, the field of oxidative phosphorylation was littered with the smouldering remains of numerous exploded energy-rich chemical intermediates.' It was, of course, the chemiosmotic theory which eventually helped to show that the supposed energy-rich intermediates did not exist and 'permitted a return to King's notion of a chemically simple respiratory chain'.

The point I wish to emphasize is that Spencer, in organizing the text of his lecture in a way which highlights the overlap between his own work and that of King and which contrasts their position with the views of those who thought in terms of energy-rich chemical intermediates, comes to portray the chemiosmotic theory rather differently from Cunningham. I am not suggesting that Cunningham's stress on vectorial reactions and Spencer's on the chemical simplicity of the respiratory chain are 'incompatible'. Nevertheless, they do differ in emphasis and they do so in accordance with the rather different interpretative themes which organize the two texts. Thus it appears, not only that accounts of the process of discovery can differ from one text to another, but so also can authors' descriptions of what has been discovered vary in accordance with the surrounding interpretative work. As this point has been documented in detail elsewhere (Gilbert and Mulkay, 1984), I will not dwell on it here. It will, however, take on greater significance in the next section.

Let us now explore what can be learned about the textual organization of discovery accounts by comparing the two cele-bratory texts examined so far with one which differs from them significantly, both in form and content.

Cultural Maturation and Multiple Discovery

The article to be considered here is entitled: 'The origins of proton-driven ATP formation: a personal analysis'. It was written by Dr Jennings in 1980 as a contribution to a collection of personal essays dealing with the development of research into bioenergetics. Such a collection of personal reminiscences imposes less of a constraint on the nature of the text than does a celebratory article or lecture. Thus the interpretative context for Jennings's historical account is essentially self-generated. It is provided by the central, organizing themes around which he chooses to weave his story. The main theme of Jennings's article can be described as a demonstration (or complaint) that a discovery which he in fact made has been wrongly attributed to Spencer alone. The following summary of this theme comes on the final page of the article.

> I do not hesitate when I state that I felt cheated from 1961 to 1978. I became caught in a race of self-justification. This was my reaction on the basis of the knowledge I have of the work I had done and which I have put down here in this admittedly subjective analysis. I did not feel cheated of £80,000 or of an honour – I do not think these things mean much to me. I felt however that a set of insights which had fallen into my lap, had been attributed to another, with whom I had not had a pleasant

relationship. I wondered 'Did the judges know the facts?' (How could they?) and 'Did the judges understand what they applauded?' (I doubt it)

Jennings's interpretative task, then, is to provide a convincing account of his own work and of the development of the field which, at the same time, both objectifies his own discovery and enables us to understand how the credit has come to be wrongly attributed.

A 'genius-type' story will not easily meet these requirements. 'Genius' is taken to be unique and extraordinary. Yet it is central to Jennings's account that he and Spencer both made virtually the same discovery at more or less the same time. Effectively, Jennings could only provide an account, not of an unprecedented individual achievement, but of something very close to a multiple discovery. The details of his intellectual biography must fall into the broader framework of the second folk theory of discovery identified by Brannigan, that of cultural maturation. Thus, in the first paragraph of his article, he writes as follows:

> I wish to stress the cooperative manner in which these 'new ideas' develop in one field from the coming together of new pieces of information from many fields. This development is in my view largely inevitable and the individuals who make given bits of progress happen to be distinguished simply because they are in the right place at the right time and have become involved with particular ideas and experiments. Given a few weeks, months or very few years the same answers would appear under other names. The idea of the great scientist in biochemistry, given the level of activity today, is a myth.

The details of Jennings's story of how he came to discover 'proton-driven ATP-formation' are depicted in a manner which gives substance to this overall view of scientific development. His version of events can be summarized as follows. During the 1950s, he moved between various areas of scientific research, each of which provided one of the elements necessary for an understanding of ATP-formation by proton-transfer. By the end of the 1950s he had put the various pieces together and had discovered that ATP was created by the translocation of protons in biological membranes. But other scientists were inevitably working along the same lines. Spencer, in particular, was developing an hypothesis similar to that of Jennings and, although Jennings was the first to grasp and the first to publish these essential ideas, Spencer was given the recognition and the rewards. This happened partly because Spencer adopted some of Jennings's conceptions, thereby improving his own initially rather inadequate analysis, and also because Spencer did not acknowledge the prior and parallel work of his competitor to which he was intellectually indebted.

In the following extracts, Jennings describes how he came to make the discovery.

> I had worked in all these fields [four areas have been listed] by 1957/1959 when the connection between proton gradients and condensation reactions of polyphosphate, ATP, first occurred to me.
>
> . . . by chance it can happen that one may acquire a variety of bits of knowledge and even though he is not aware of all the bits at any time they will constantly interact. . .
>
> The subjects clicked for me in 1957. . . At the time of becoming aware that the synthesis of ATP could be driven by a proton gradient, 1957 (published 1959), I did not know of parallel work on connecting such a gradient to ATP formation.

This account of Jennings's own experience is in accordance with his previous statement that scientific developments are largely inevitable, whilst any individual's contributions are to a considerable extent accidental. The existence of other scientists independently advancing similar ideas is treated as exactly what one would expect, given the impersonal forces at work. Whereas in Cunningham's account the 'rapid advances' occurring in many areas of biochemistry in the 1950s are mentioned as a way of emphasizing the intractability of the unsolved problems in oxidative phosphorylation and of indicating that their solution required an act of individual genius, Jennings draws upon the advances occurring in other fields to make the solution of the problems of oxidative phosphorylation appear imminent and potentially available to any researcher with the requisite background.

For Jennings, the rapid advances occurring elsewhere in biochemistry lead directly towards the discovery of proton-driven ATP-production. Thus the discovery process does not depend entirely on the activities of any one, peculiarly gifted individual. Discovery is, rather, the culmination of a gradual combination of diverse intellectual components which are coming to maturation in the minds of various scientists. Nevertheless, Jennings's account of cultural maturation does not force him to abandon the concept of a 'moment of discovery', nor does it weaken his claim to have been the discoverer. Jennings stresses that, for the individual who is in the right place at the right time, there comes an occasion where all the disparate elements suddenly coalesce into an integrated conception of how a particular segment of reality works. At this moment, implies Jennings, the individual discoverer feels like Cortez (as portrayed by Keats) looking out upon the Pacific Ocean for the first time.

> In discovering (or rediscovering) proton-driven phosphorylation I felt that I had found some secret of nature and I was deeply satisfied in a purely personal way. If I may wax lyrical it was as if I had stood 'on a peak in Darien'.

Jennings's cultural maturation 'theory', then, can textually objectify the act of discovery quite effectively, making the event appear as a recognition of something external to the discoverer and existing in the natural world independently of his complex interpretative work. It also enables Jennings to furnish a detailed description of how he, in particular, came to make the discovery as well as to provide a personal evocation of the unusual state of consciousness attendant upon the final act of discovery. At the same time, Jennings is able to repudiate the very concept of 'genius' and to dismiss it as no more than a myth, at least so far as biochemistry is concerned. In so doing, he challenges any account, such as that by Cunningham, in which the uniqueness of Spencer's or King's contribution to bioenergetics is objectified through the attribution of extraordinary mental powers. Finally, and perhaps most importantly in this text, Jennings's determinist form of historical interpretation allows for the possibility, even the probability, that several similar solutions to any major problems will be forthcoming at about the same time.

Jennings's general suggestion that all scientific discoveries are potential multiples is brought to bear upon his own case, in the following words, in the course of a single-paragraph section headed 'The Nature of Discovery':

> While I was working from an analysis of inorganic reactions in biological systems, another man was working on membranes – we were both heading for oxidative phosphorylation. The other man, Spencer, had been involved with general ideas as to how osmotic gradients could be linked to chemical reactions, chemiosmosis, e.g. how Na^+/K^+ gradients were due to ATP hydrolysis, in the period 1950–1960. . . I come directly to the standing of his work in August 1960, when Spencer gave a paper at a conference in Prague. In this paper the ideas of chemiosmosis are clearly put forth with no mention of how ATP-formation could be driven by protons. In the middle of September of 1960 Spencer gave his first version of oxidative

phosphorylation as the second half of a paper in Stockholm and he now included chemiosmotic driven ATP-formation. (Both papers are published in 1961.) The striking coincidence is that in the very month in which I submitted, August 7th, 1960, my paper to *Journal of Theoretical Biology* Spencer must have thought of proton sucked ATP formation. We had come to almost identical conclusions by two totally different routes. It was all a remarkable coincidence. The pity of it is that unlike Darwin and Wallace we failed to behave like old-fashioned gentlemen but behaved by the new rules of scientific races.

It is, of course, possible to read this passage ironically, that is, as implying that the 'remarkable coincidence' was not a coincidence at all and that, in reality, Spencer had taken the idea of applying chemiosmotic gradients to ATP-formation from Jennings. However, the literal effect of this passage is to show, in accordance with the theory of cultural maturation, how two independent researchers 'had come to almost identical conclusions by two totally different routes' and also to provide for the possibility of explaining how other scientists could subsequently, in their ignorance of what had actually transpired, mistakenly attribute the original discovery to Spencer: 'I wondered "Did the judges know the facts?" (How could they?).'

The concept of inevitable cultural maturation in science makes Jennings's particular story that much more convincing. If all scientific discoveries are potential multiples, it becomes more difficult to dismiss out of hand Jennings's complaints in this particular case. If there usually are a number of candidates for any major discovery, then any particular attribution of discovery must be settled by a careful examination of who said and wrote what, to whom. In his article, Jennings uses the cultural maturation approach to justify his own detailed examination of the published and unpublished documentary evidence. He concludes that he was the first to publish, in 1959, a basically correct description of the way in which proton gradients contribute to the production of ATP. Thus in Jennings's re-telling of the history of the field, he becomes the discoverer of the essential process of ATP-formation and Spencer becomes a man who actually got there just too late, but who nevertheless managed to reap the benefits.[2]

Who Said What, Where, When?

What I have documented in the last section has traditionally been described by sociologists as a 'priority dispute' (Merton, 1973).

But, as Brannigan emphasizes, the participants in such disputes are seldom arguing simply about who first discovered or published a given scientific formulation; they are usually also engaged in disputing which scientific formulation is correct (1981, p. 77). Priority disputes can have this cognitive dimension because, as we saw earlier, participants can formulate what has been discovered in different ways without ceasing to assume that they are referring to the same discovery.

We have already noted how Spencer's and Cunningham's versions of the scientific content of the discovery differed in emphasis. Jennings introduces a third formulation, in which the *central* notion is that ATP is created by the movement of protons through biological membranes. Jennings insists that it is this idea, common to both his and Spencer's schemes, which essentially constitutes the discovery; hence the title of his historical article, 'The origins of proton-driven ATP-formation'. The basic idea as described in Jennings's 1959 discovery article was that: 'Oxidative phosphorylation could be driven directly by using oxygen to generate protons and then absorbing the protons in the condensation of anionic phosphate groups (ATP-formation). We do not believe that this *alone* is the mechanism of oxidative phosphorylation but it serves to illustrate a part of the total scheme.'

Although Jennings accepts that both Spencer and he published the same basic concept of oxidative phosphorylation within a short period, he maintains that his publication alone contained this discovery, not only because he believes that Spencer may have taken over his (Jennings's) basic idea, but also because Spencer did not fully grasp the nature of proton-translocation. In other words, Spencer is said to have been scientifically wrong as well as being late. It is particularly significant that the feature of Spencer's chemiosmotic theory which Jennings rejects as scientifically incorrect is precisely that notion which Spencer takes to be central in his Nobel Lecture, namely, that the redox reactions of the respiratory chain are chemically and spatially totally *separate from* the ATPase enzyme where, according to the chemiosmotic theory, ATP is actually manufactured. In Jenning's view, this simply cannot be the case, for a whole variety of reasons. Jennings proposes, instead, that the protons which are used to make ATP do not cross to the outside of the membrane to form a diffuse proton gradient, as Spencer maintains, but pass from the respiratory chain through a local channel in or along the membrane directly to the ATPase.

. . . the Spencer mechanism of connecting a proton to the synthesis of ATP is undoubtedly wrong. It is the proton from oxidation that is passed through the membrane. . . [Chemiosmosis] has no proton channel to the ATPase. There is no question of a possible local circuit. Full equations are written to exclude any such scheme. Furthermore the same proton gradient is opposed later to chemical uptake of many chemicals in a totally reversible manner. It is inevitable then that all processes equilibrate across the membrane so that a cell has fixed states of redox activity, proton gradients, chemical synthesis (ATP), and ion and metabolite gradients. The system also runs into problems of buffering and capacity. I cannot believe this to be true. . . . is [chemiosmosis] also wrong in principle? For myself I believe that it is and that the Nobel Prize award was premature and could be damaging to further research in this area. . . I believe that all the data are consistent with proton-driven ATP-formation by a localised system within membrane confines and that chemiosmosis is only a useful way of looking at back-up storage.

In these passages, Jennings acknowledges that Spencer's scheme does have a distinctive element; and he identifies this element in terms somewhat similar to those used by Spencer in his Nobel Lecture. But this original conception, far from being the essential feature of Spencer's (or King's) contribution to our understanding of ATP-production, is treated as being simply wrong. As Brannigan has made clear, scientists accept as 'discoveries' only those knowledge-claims which are deemed to be correct. In Jennings's text, although Spencer is credited with having partly grasped how ATP is created by proton movement, his elaboration of this basic insight is taken to be misconceived. For Jennings, Spencer's notion of 'chemiosmotic reaction' may possibly be a discovery when applied to some biochemical phenomena, but it is definitely not the discovery of how ATP is formed.

Jennings's far from celebratory text enables us to see more clearly the interpretative work on which the accounts offered by Spencer and Cunningham depend. For instance, Cunningham maintains that Spencer's unique contribution to the field was his conception of vectorial reactions. He makes no mention at all of Jennings's work. Yet the latter had discussed the role of vectorial reactions by letter with Spencer before the publication of what Cunningham treats as Spencer's 'discovery paper', and Jennings has persistently maintained that his approach as well as Spencer's is vectorial. Of course, Cunningham could reasonably point out that it was impossible to deal with such historical complexities in a short article written to celebrate the award of the Nobel Prize and that his task was simply to reflect the common understanding of Spencer's scientific achievement. Such a reply, however, would clearly imply that the story of Spencer's discovery presented by an author on a specific occasion is designed to meet the needs and constraints of that occasion. Thus it becomes increasingly evident that the version of events given in Cunningham's article is but one of the stories that any given author could construct. In his celebratory article, by radically simplifying his account in such a way that there seems to be only one chemiosmotic theory, only one candidate discovery paper and only one conceivable discoverer, Cunningham offers a version which makes Spencer's achievement and the award of the Prize appear totally unproblematic.

In his Nobel Lecture, Spencer can hardly get by with such a skeletal account. In fact, Spencer describes developments in the field between 1950 and 1978 in some detail and he does refer in passing to Jennings's work at several points. However, Spencer's version of events is organized in a way which implicitly repudiates any claim that Jennings might make about having discovered the process of ATP-formation or even about having contributed in any significant way to this topic.

There are at least three features of Spencer's text which have this effect. In the first place, although seven scientists are cited as having furnished 'suggestive clues' in the search for chemiosmosis, Jennings is not mentioned in this context. The earliest paper by Jennings which is cited in the published text of Spencer's Lecture is dated 1962; that is, one year after Spencer's 'discovery paper' and three years after Jennings's 'discovery paper'. Secondly, although the lecture never explicitly deals with the issues of originality or priority, a series of dates are included 'as it happens' in the text in such a way that any close scrutiny of this single text would resolve the issue unambiguously in Spencer's favour.

> As it happened, the main protonmotive adenosine triphosphatase (ATPase) principle of this hypothesis was first outlined at an international meeting held in Stockholm in 1960. . .
>
> These postulates were almost entirely hypothetical and experimentally unexplored when they were given as the basis of the chemiosmotic hypothesis in 1961 . . . [the postulates] have now survived 17 years of intensive scrutiny [in 1978]. . . These, then, were the circumstances that led me to remark at a symposium in 1953: '. . . in complex biochemical systems, such as those carrying out oxidative phosphorylation the osmotic and enzymic specifications appear to be equally important and may be practically synonymous'.

Spencer's lecture provides a chronology of discovery which confirms his priority, even if we were to accept Jennings's claim to have hit upon basically the same idea. However, Spencer's text effectively demolishes this claim by the way in which Jennings's work is characterized.

By 1965, the field of oxidative phosphorylation was littered with the smouldering conceptual remains of numerous exploded energy-rich chemical intermediates. . . Nevertheless, the quest for the energy-rich intermediates continued through the 1960s and persisted into the 1970s with only a minor broadening of the conception of the type of coupling mechanism [linking respiration to ATP-production]. . . This conceptual broadening, stemmed from ingenious suggestions by Watson, Gowan, Huxley, Pugh, Fennell, Jennings and others . . . these workers assumed that coupling may be achieved through a direct conformational or other non-osmotic physical or chemical interaction – that might, for example, involve protons as a localized anhydrous chemical intermediate [Jennings's papers of 1962 and 1970 cited] . . . in the supposedly duplex respiratory chain system, often described as the 'phosphorylating respiratory chain'.

In Jennings's own article discussed above, he distinguishes himself firmly from the orthodox view that oxidative phosphorylation is brought about by a high-energy chemical intermediate. Not only does he avoid applying the term 'chemical intermediate' to his own conception, but he depicts his notion of proton-driven phosphorylation as a radical departure from this view. Spencer, however, places Jennings's conception within the same category as the now discredited (1978) high-energy chemical intermediate. Jennings's contribution is treated, not as a radical departure, but as a 'minor conceptual broadening' of a view which is fundamentally incorrect. Spencer treats it as irrelevant that Jennings, like himself, has proposed that proton-movement is a crucial part of ATP-synthesis. He also disregards Jennings's insistence on such features as charge separation, vectorial reactions, separation of phases by the membrane, and proton transport within the membrane, all of which they appear to have in common and all of which Jennings claims to have been advocating before 1960–1. Instead, Spencer treats Jennings's approach as equivalent to the more traditional conception of chemical intermediates located in the respiratory chain, on the grounds that Jennings insists that the protons generated within the respiratory chain are directly coupled to the process of phosphorylation in the ATPase. As we noted, it was precisely Spencer's failure to accept this aspect of Jennings's work which Jennings cites as his grounds for rejecting Spencer's theory.

Thus despite all they seem to have in common in their conceptions of oxidative phosphorylation, both authors focus on this distinguishing feature which they both use to assert their own originality and to deny that of the other party.

Other scientists, even in celebrating Spencer's Prize, have produced versions of chemiosmosis which ignore such fine distinctions and which seem to encompass both Jennings and Spencer. For example, Richards, another biochemist in the field, writes that the central fact in Spencer's discovery was that 'electron transport chains and the various devices they drive, are associated together as components in a proton circuit, in such a way that their reactions are coupled through a flow of protons flowing through the circuit'. Spencer and Jennings, however, formulate the supposed processes of oxidative phosphorylation so as to exclude the other from full participation in the discovery. Thus the texts of these two men, whether or not they claim to be concerned with the question of originality, are organized in a manner which endorses each author's priority. In both cases, the author's account of the discovery and his implicit or explicit attribution of priority varies in accordance with his substantive claims about the biochemical realities of ATP-production.

This means, of course, that if scientific opinion about the nature of oxidative phosphorylation were to change, say in favour of the view that the protons involved in phosphorylation move through a process of controlled diffusion through the membrane to the site of ATP-formation, then some of the existing discovery accounts would have to be retrospectively altered. Presumably Jennings's work in the late 1950s would be given greater prominence and it would become more difficult to treat him as indistinguishable from the advocates of energy-rich chemical intermediates. Moreover, the current portrayal of the field in terms of two simple historical phases, namely, before Spencer's discovery paper and after that paper, would have to be modified. At present, all work which came before 1961 is treated as 'leading towards' that date, the date of 'the discovery' (Woolgar, 1980); whilst all work since then is depicted as referring back to the discovery, for example, as either confirming the discovery or as being a failure to recognize the validity of the discovery.

This simple two-directional historical model would perhaps be replaced, if Jennings's views were to come into favour, by two or perhaps more phases. One of these would begin with the discovery of proton-translocation in 1961. But all phases would 'point forwards' to the eventual discovery of the complete mechanism of oxidative phosphorylation at some time in the future. Spencer, of course, does not depict the situation like this. As we saw in the

Nobel Lecture, he proposes that two of the three basic questions 'set by King' have now been answered and the third is also succumbing to the application of the chemiosmotic theory. In his texts, the journey of retrospective confirmation begun in 1961 is nearing completion, at least within the field of oxidative phosphory-lation. It is hardly surprising to find, however, that Jennings is already engaged in constructing a radically different, multi-phase conception of the field's long-term evolution.

> The future is now clear. We have a general scheme of controlled proton diffusion to an ATP synthesising site. *We have yet to discover* how the proton is generated, how the negative charge migrates, how the proton migrates, and how during its migration it causes ATP to be produced. All these problems are those of understanding proteins and especially organised proteins. In a recent article I have set out my thoughts on how some of the problems may be looked at and tackled, *but we are not very far along the trail* of relating the protein sequences, through the structures and dynamics of single proteins, to their functions. *We have only just started* on the study of proteins which combine to make machines. . . The nature of energy capture of the membrane machines remains a fascinating problem. [emphasis added]

Thus historical reinterpretation, along with opposing claims about the nature of prior discoveries and dispute over the allocation of the symbols of scientific honour, are likely to remain textual possibil-ities in this field as long as significant differences persist with respect to the biochemical processes of oxidative phosphorylation.

The Discourse of Celebration and the Discourse of Opposition

This chapter has provided further support for the major claims of recent sociological analysis of scientific discovery. It has also helped us to extend that analysis as well as to describe and document an instance of scientific discovery which has not previously been examined in the secondary, analytical literature.

In accordance with Brannigan's analysis, the debate over the discovery of the mechanism of oxidative phosphorylation focuses around the three constitutive criteria of proper motivation, originality and scientific validity. This is most evident in Jennings's attempt to challenge the accepted story of the chemiosmotic theory, where these three issues are examined explicitly and in detail.

Jennings challenges others' claims that Spencer's work on chemiosmosis constitutes a discovery on the grounds that it is not correct, not original and that the propriety of some of Spencer's actions may have been doubtful. In simple affirmations of the discovery, as in Cunningham's article, and to a considerable extent in Spencer's lecture, these issues are resolved with much less explicit interpretative work. Nevertheless, Spencer's validity, priority and proper motivation are endorsed in various ways in both these articles as other participants in the field are categorized and depicted in ways which make the unprecedented and unquestionable character of Spencer's scientific contribution appear unproblematic. In other words, as Brannigan suggests is likely to happen, the history of the field is retrospectively constructed through members' discovery accounts, in this case many years after 'the event', in ways which objectify the discovery and make it appear as something 'out-there-in-the-social-world'. Although alternative versions of events are never mentioned in the two celebratory texts, they are implicitly denied by the very organization and content of these texts.

Brannigan's analysis is further confirmed by the fact that the participants we have studied do make use of 'genius' and 'cultural maturation' in their discovery accounts. I have tried to extend Brannigan's work on these folk theories of discovery by suggesting that in order to understand the use made of these interpretative resources we must recognize that discovery accounts are often embedded in complex, multi-functional texts. Thus the conceptions of 'genius' and 'cultural maturation' are employed, not simply to furnish plausible explanations of discovery, but also to facilitate the additional interpretative work which is being carried out in a given text. Only if we pay attention to the textual complexity of discovery accounts can we begin to appreciate why more than one general-purpose folk 'theory' of discovery is required.

We have seen that the two conceptions of discovery are more than mechanisms for making sense of discoveries after the event. They are also an important part of the interpretative *method* by means of which members construe particular 'events' *as* discoveries. For a discovery is not only a properly motivated, original and valid contribution to knowledge; it is also known by ourselves and by participants to be an event which can follow inevitably from cultural maturation or creatively from an act of genius. By attributing a scientific contribution to one or other of these factors, we thereby make it appear more clearly to *be* a discovery.

In addition to helping to define events as discoveries, these two conceptions seem to provide explanations of the occurrence of discoveries which furnish an interpretative resting place. In other words, when a discovery has been explained in these terms, there is no point in asking further 'Why?' questions. To ask why Spencer was a genius or why Jennings happened to move between the areas necessary for him to develop his theory seems to be irrelevant to the explanation of why the chemiosmotic theory appeared when and in the form that it did. As we have seen, our three participants use these conceptions, without further clarification, as the points of departure for their historical reconstructions.

Although 'genius' and 'cultural maturation' can be used to account for and to constitute events as discoveries, neither is *essential* to the folk concept of discovery. The fact that there are two potentially incompatible folk 'theories' makes it obvious that neither of them is a necessary feature of what we mean by 'discovery'. For this reason, Brannigan is right to distinguish the two folk 'theories' of discovery from its constitutive criteria. 'Genius' or 'cultural maturation' are optional features of discovery accounts. Which one is chosen depends on the surrounding interpretative work that is being accomplished in a given text. The material we have studied above gives us some hints about the uses to which they can be put.

One distinctive characteristic of the 'genius account' is that it focuses on the individual scientist and on the uniqueness of his intellectual contribution. This is especially appropriate for celebratory texts, where the work of a particular scientist (or a small number of scientists) is being honoured. I have suggested above that it is the celebratory work of the two 'genius texts' which is primary. In other words, it may be that in the act of textual celebration scientists produce versions of events which stress, for example, the individual's remarkable ability, the radical significance of his reconceptualization, and the slowness of others to understand, and which thereby lead naturally to the attribution of genius. Although we have examined two instances where the word 'genius' is actually employed, the use of this particular term does not seem to me to be especially important. Were it not so clumsy, it might be better to refer to this kind of account as the 'remarkable mental capacity' account. Such accounts, by locating the prime mover of scientific discovery in the exceptional mind of an individual scientist, furnish explanations of discovery which are necessarily, at the same time, celebrations of creative individual achievement. As we know, the scientific community is very much given to honouring its eminent members (Merton, 1973). It may be that the folk theory of genius can be understood as one of participants' methods for bestowing such honour, along with eponymy and the award of prizes.[3]

The 'theory' of cultural maturation, in contrast, seems designed to bring about quite different textual outcomes. This 'theory' can, as we have seen, explain and objectify discoveries, as well as allowing each individual discoverer to describe the actual moment of discovery. But it does not encourage the celebration of individual achievement, for the obvious reason that it treats the individual's contribution as largely accidental and attributes the discovery to supra-personal forces. However, 'cultural maturation' has two important features which make it particularly appropriate in certain circumstances. The first is that it treats all discoveries as potential multiples; the second is that, unlike the notion of 'genius', it is easily self-applicable.

Consequently, where there is some dispute about priority and/or about whether an accredited discovery is genuine, the 'theory' of cultural maturation can be brought into play by the disadvantaged party to suggest *that* there are and to explain *why* there are, contrary to the dominant discovery account, several candidate discoveries. In this way, the concept of cultural maturation furnishes an interpretative context in which mistaken attributions of discovery seem distinctly possible.

I am in no way suggesting that scientists employing 'cultural maturation' in such circumstances consciously choose this theory simply because it suits their purpose. For a scientist constructing an account where he has to make sense, not of a unique contribution to the field but of what he takes to be two or more similar, overlapping conceptions, some variety of the 'theory' of cultural maturation will presumably seem to offer the only sensible interpretation. Such an approach has the added advantage of allowing the challenger to insist, as did Jennings, that he is not so interested in prizes or recognition. These by-products of discovery, he can consistently propose, are rightly his only by chance. Accordingly, a claimant adopting this perspective on discovery is likely to present himself, once again as Jennings did, as being concerned in the first instance to set the historical record straight. Of course, it inevitably follows that any revision of scientific history which ensues will suggest the need for an appropriate re-allocation of the symbols of scientific honour.

It may be that, whereas the 'theory' of genius is part of scientists' celebratory discourse, the 'theory' of cultural maturation is mainly a part of the *discourse of opposition* sometimes engendered amongst those who are unwilling to accept the dominant historical account within a given area of research. Because, as we have seen, the nature of scientists' histories and discovery accounts varies in accordance with their scientific claims about the natural world, attempts to reinterpret the past are likely to continue in any area as long as active intellectual disagreements persist. It may be that the 'theory' of cultural maturation is one important resource available

to scientists who are trying to alter what they take to be the
accepted body of scientific opinion and who are attempting to
rewrite scientific history accordingly.

Notes to Chapter 6

1 Spencer himself does not use the noun 'chemiosmosis' and objects to its
   use by others. He employs only the adjectival form, as in 'chemiosmotic
   hypothesis'. I have used the word 'chemiosmosis' occasionally because
   it is frequently employed by other bioenergeticists. Despite Spencer's
   objections, it is part of the linguistic culture of the area. This issue will
   reappear in the next chapter.
2 Anyone interested in the historical accuracy of the various accounts can
   consult the letters exchanged between Jennings and Spencer which
   have been deposited at The Royal Society. In order to identify these
   letters, allowance will need to be made for my use of pseudonyms.
3 Jennings commented as follows on this passage: 'Here you are very
   close I think but there is something more. The idea of "genius" in
   science adds a romantic depth. Science is then not just you and me
   slogging away but can be enlightened by hidden forms of mental
   activity. "Genius" is the reason why most of us fail although we are
   excellent analysts.' Earlier in the chapter, he wrote: 'Peculiarly I believe
   "genius" as used by a scientist means a man proceeding by a logic not
   open to ordinary inspection and therefore not given to explanation!
   Discovery is the ordinary process.'

7

The Helpful Analyst: an Analytical Invention

Both analysts and participants, in coming to concrete conclusions about the status of any particular discovery, have to provide answers, either explicitly or implicitly, to a network of potential questions. These questions are likely to include the following: did a discovery occur? If there was a discovery, what exactly was discovered? Was the discovery a unique, individual achievement by a particular scientist or did more than one scientist share in the discovery? When did the discovery take place? When did it come to be recognized to be a discovery? How sure are we that it was a genuine discovery and not a fraud, a plagiarism or a mistake? If there is disagreement among participants about the answers to such questions, how is it to be dealt with? How much agreement among participants is required to certify a discovery and is the testimony of all participants to be treated equally? If a discovery turns out in due course to have been scientifically incorrect, will it then cease to have been a discovery?

Most statements furnished by participants on the topic of a specific discovery will tend to treat such questions as having obvious and unproblematic answers. It is only when we consider and compare various texts that we begin to see how complex is the interpretative work on which they depend and how varied their answers can be. In order to explore the complexity of the interpretative task of 'discovery work', I have below used participants' texts as the basis for an imaginary discourse about the discovery of 'chemiosmosis'.

Although the situation textually created below is clearly fictional in the sense that, as far as I know, nothing like it has ever actually occurred, most of the statements attributed to participants are based directly upon the actual words of scientists involved in the field of bioenergetics. Thus any simple distinction between fact and fiction will not capture the nature of the present text. I suggest that it should be seen as an exercise in *verstehende sociologie* or sociological hermeneutics. It is an attempt to use the resources of scientists' discourse to explore the character of the interpretative practice whereby they construe events as discoveries. It is an attempt to represent that practice in a form accessible to those outside this particular area of research and especially to non-scientists. It is for this reason that I have simplified the technical discussions below so that they are, I hope, more or less understandable to non-experts. All the scientists' names are pseudonyms. The words spoken by Dr Spencer and Dr Jennings are closely based on statements made by particular scientists. The sources for each of the other characters are more diverse. The sociologist's remarks are loosely based on Brannigan (1981) and I have, therefore, given that author's name to this fictitious character. I must stress that, whatever their name and whatever the source of their words, all the characters below should be treated as figures in an analytical invention.

What follows is taken to be the transcript of a tape-recorded discussion which took place several years ago concerning the 'discovery' of chemiosmotic reactions. All but two of those taking part are chemists or biochemists who have contributed to research on the topic of oxidative phosphorylation. The two exceptions are, first, the sociologist, who has been invited to attend because he has written a major analysis of scientific discovery, and second, the auditor. The role of 'auditor' here is modelled on that of the auditor who is sometimes appointed by the 'powers that be' in science to investigate possible cases of fraud. Whereas a genuine auditor's job is to discover whether there was a fraud and, if so, who is to be held responsible for it, this auditor's job is to discover whether there was a discovery and, if so, who is to be given credit for it.

List of Participants

The Auditor   A researcher who, although he has never worked on oxidative phosphorylation, is technically competent and is accepted by all to be a scientist of acumen and unquestionable integrity. American.

Spencer   Normally taken to be the discoverer. British.

Jennings   An inorganic chemist who also claims to be a discoverer. British.

Elder   A mature researcher of the same generation as Spencer and Jennings who, in general, accepts the validity of chemiosmotic theory. British.

Critic	Another mature researcher who tends to deny the validity of chemiosmotic theory. American.
Younger	A younger man, who supports Spencer. British but now working in the USA.
Statesman	An older scientist who was a member of the committee which recommended Spencer for the award of the Nobel Prize. European.
Brannigan	A young sociologist who has written about the social construction of discovery. Canadian.

The Transcript

Auditor Gentlemen, we are here to find out whether or not there has been a major discovery in your field associated with the concept of 'chemiosmosis' and, if there has, to establish once and for all who was the discoverer and who deserves the credit. You have been asked to attend this meeting to give testimony and to represent the various generations and interests in the field. It seems to me to be most appropriate to begin by asking Dr Spencer to give his account of the origins of chemiosmotic theory. The rest of you will then be able to comment on Dr Spencer's statement.

Spencer Thank you for this opportunity to set the record straight. I have tried to make clear on several previous public occasions how chemiosmotic theory developed; see my Nobel Lecture, my CIBA Lecture and my chapter in *Of Oxygen, Fuels, and Living Matter*. But misunderstanding still seems to persist. So let me begin by stating unequivocally that I am certainly not the discoverer of 'chemiosmosis'. I myself have never used that word, except to recommend that it should be avoided. As I have explained in print, the use of the noun 'chemiosmosis' to describe the processes distinguished adjectivally as 'chemiosmotic' is semantically unsound. It's rather like suggesting that, because we study *chemical* processes, there must be some underlying, general process of 'chemation'. I sometimes wonder who was responsible for introducing this misleading word 'chemiosmosis', and why they did it.

I do not wish to deny that I have made a modest contribution to the understanding of chemiosmotic processes and to the establishment of the chemiosmotic theory. But I personally have made no major discovery. In my view, the development of chemiosmotic theory is best described as a gradual evolution of concepts and painstaking experimental activity. As a result of this long-term process, we now know much more than we did when I started research about the production of useable energy in living organisms. However, this growth in scientific knowledge has not been brought about at any stage by sudden, revelatory discoveries. Let me substantiate this claim in a little more detail. Although the chemiosmotic theory can now be seen to have a much broader range of applicability than was initially envisaged or is generally appreciated, for the sake of simplicity I will focus on the central field of oxidative phosphorylation in the cells of higher organisms, that is, on the production of ATP from the combination of ADP and inorganic phosphate within the organelles called 'mitochondria' located in living cells.

As you all know, one of the guiding ideas of chemiosmotic theory is that the chemical reactions occurring in the mitochondrial respiratory chain which contribute to the production of ATP are not directionless, but are organized in space; that is, they are what I have called 'vectorial reactions'. We must not think of the cell or the mitochondrion simply as a 'bag of enzymes' in which chemical reactions occur in a spatially disordered manner, but as a topologically structured entity within which chemical reactions are related to spatially organized features. A second crucial idea is that the inner membrane is a critical structural feature of mitochondria and that the vectorial organization of chemical reactions is brought about by enzymes which are plugged through the mitochondrial membrane. Thirdly, the enzymes of the respiratory chain within the membrane separate the constituents of hydrogen into electrons (negative particles, $2e^-$) and protons (positive particles, H^+). Fourthly, the protons are transported across the membrane to build up a proton gradient and an electrical difference which drive the transported protons back across the membrane through the ATPase enzyme, within which the free energy made available by proton movement (proticity) is used to create ATP.

Now I suggest that, although this particular combination of ideas was first brought together by myself around 1960 and published in 1961, nothing particularly new was involved. Take the idea of vectorial (directional) chemistry, for example. This can be traced back through the ideas of Guggenheim (1933) and Curie (1894) to the invention of the electromotive hydrogen-burning fuel cell by Grove in 1839. Grove's fuel cell for generating electricity breaks down hydrogen and separates electrons from protons. Whether the fuel cell is used to generate electricity or proticity simply depends where one opens the circuit to conduct away the power for external use. The idea of electrochemical cells and circuits was generalized by Guggenheim in 1933 to include the chemically motivated transport of any two species of chemical particle around a suitably conducting circuit. Guggenheim showed in rather abstract terms how the transport of a chemical component (e.g. H^+ or e^-) can give rise to what he called the chemicomotive forces directed across phase boundaries or membranes. This treatment was elegantly applied to biological transport by Rosenberg in 1948, at a time when I was working on my Ph.D.

In the early 1950s, I took over these ideas and applied them to several specific biochemical problems, including that of oxidative phosphorylation. As early as 1953, I proposed that the *transport* of chemical species across biological membranes and the *chemical reactions* responsible, for example, for the production of ATP, might be 'practically synonymous'. But I was not alone in developing such ideas at this time. My work progressed in parallel with that of various other researchers working on biological transport processes. Larsen in particular, Robson and Wynne, Fellows, Dale and Perch, and Phillips all contributed to a growing appreciation of the fact that biological membranes can be spatially organized in ways which bring about charge separation, electron translocation and proton transport across membranes. I must stress that the scientific content and value of what I was coming to think of as the 'chemiosmotic rationale' depended on the feasibility of mechanisms which are relatively orthodox biochemically, and which require little more than the addition of a spatial dimension to the well-established concept of chemical group potential. Had this not been so, I would not have thought it worth fostering the chemiosmotic hypothesis.

Finally, I have to mention the fundamental contribution of my friend and mentor, David King. King convinced me that the components of the respiratory chain were chemically simple; that is, the respiratory chain was involved in the breakdown of hydrogen but not directly involved in the synthesis of ATP. Thus, whereas most scientists investigating oxidative phosphorylation at that time were looking for a complex sequence of purely chemical reactions within the respiratory chain, requiring the existence of one or more unknown and observationally elusive chemical intermediates, in following King I was able to see that the respiratory chain functioned simply to break down hydrogen and to create a transmembrane proton gradient. There was no need, therefore, to search for further as yet unobserved chemical transformations; for it was the proton gradient operating across the functionally organized membrane which made possible the creation of ATP. It was King's chemically simple conception of the respiratory chain which enabled me to realize that this chemical simplicity was supplemented by the topographical complexity of the biological membrane.

We can see, then, that the basic concepts of the chemiosmotic hypothesis, as formally stated in 1961, were not new and that all the significant scientific innovations were made by my predecessors, some of whom were men of genius. Of course, what began as the chemiosmotic hypothesis has now been acclaimed as the chemiosmotic theory. The four basic postulates of the theory are now widely regarded as experimentally established facts. In this sense, we have discovered a great deal about the production of ATP and related processes. But there has been no single event which can be described as 'the discovery'. Since 1961, as well as before, development has occurred gradually and in a piecemeal fashion, with numerous small contributions being made by many different researchers and with much of the improvement in our understanding arising out of the recombination of existing ideas and information.

Once again, therefore, I want to stress that I make no claim to biochemical originality, except, perhaps, in as much as I have consciously endeavoured to invoke the least original and the most simple, ordinary, and orthodox types of biochemical concept to evolve working hypotheses which explain the real biochemical phenomena observed in the laboratory. The process can be summed up with the aphorism: 'The obscure we see eventually, the completely apparent takes longer.'

Auditor Thank you for that clear and, for me at least, rather unexpected statement. Your first point, then, is that the term 'chemiosmosis' is misleading in various ways. I take it that you regard my initial use of that term as particularly unfortunate in this context because it gave the impression that there exists out there some simple entity to be discovered corresponding to the noun 'chemiosmosis'. Secondly, your view is that much *has* been discovered in the field of bioenergetics, but that the accumulation of knowledge has operated over a long period of time and that no present-day researcher, not even yourself, deserves any particular credit for the discoveries that have been made. Well, if we can quickly get general agreement to that effect, we could all be home by tea-time [laughter].

Younger Perhaps I can just make a brief comment. I'm not too worried about the widespread use of the term 'chemiosmosis'. Science is, after all, a living language and new words are constantly introduced and old ones change their meaning. Dr Spencer himself has been a great terminological innovator and, although the noun 'chemiosmosis' is not one of his, I don't think that it causes much confusion among active bioenergeticists. I'd like to say a few words about the history of bioenergetics and about the part played by Dr Spencer in that history. I don't want to disagree with Dr Spencer about the historical facts. I'm sure that the concepts of chemiosmotic theory developed exactly as he describes. But I would like to suggest a slight change of emphasis in our interpretation of the historical sequence and a significantly different allocation of credit.

One of the difficulties facing Dr Spencer in talking publicly about his own research, it seems to me, is that, if he gives a proper estimation of his actual contribution to bioenergetics, he is likely to *sound* conceited. Perhaps, in trying to avoid that danger, he has underplayed his personal significance and, in my opinion, has erred on the side of excessive humility. The fact is that he has made a unique, unprecedented and scientifically fundamental contribution to the field which places him in the highest rank of scientific eminence.

The conception and development of Dr Spencer's chemiosmotic hypothesis has led to a revolution in the field of bioenergetics which has many similarities with the Copernican revolution of an earlier century. We can no more deny Spencer's right to be regarded as the discoverer of chemiosmotic reactions than we can deny the right of Copernicus to be regarded as the discoverer of the heliocentric planetary system. Before 1961, our field was dominated by the idea that electron-transport-linked phosphorylation was basically similar to well-understood substrate level oxidative phosphorylation. Not only did Spencer show that that orthodoxy was wrong (in the same way that Copernicus showed the Ptolemaic system to be wrong), but he replaced it, at a single stroke, with a theoretical framework which has since been shown to be correct in all essentials.

I want to emphasize that virtually everybody in the field during the 1950s and well into the 1960s adopted a classical, chemical view of oxidative phosphorylation. This view postulated the existence of high-energy chemical intermediates which linked together the processes of electron transfer in the respiratory chain and the production of ATP. But the supposed intermediates could never be isolated or identified, despite numerous attempts. Then, in 1961, Spencer radicalized things by suggesting that the reason why the postulated intermediates were elusive might be because they did not exist. At the same time, he proposed that the 'missing link' could well take the form of a proton gradient; which he went on to confirm experimentally. Nowadays, it is not possible to work on photochemical reactions, on electron transport, phosphorylation, structure, transport or any other aspect of bioenergetics, photosynthesis, bacterial metabolism or mobility without taking account of the fact that electron transport chains and the various devices they drive are associated together in a proton circuit, in such a way that their reactions are coupled through a current of protons flowing through the circuit.

I think it is clear that Spencer's 1961 *Nature* paper, which I read as a graduate student, set out a radically new mechanism for oxidative phosphorylation. Spencer is undoubtedly right to point out that his formulation of this mechanism draws heavily upon prior work. Nevertheless, nobody previously had put these various ideas together in the way that Spencer did and, perhaps most importantly, nobody previously had formulated this kind of conception in a way which made numerous clearly defined predictions about oxidative phosphorylation and closely related processes which were open to experimental investigation.

The novelty of Spencer's ideas can be gauged from the extremely hostile response which they elicited from most of the established researchers in the field for a decade or more after 1961. Spencer's conception was initially beyond the grasp of most scientists working on 'ox phos'. It was far ahead of its time and could only have been conceived, in my opinion, by a scientific genius. Thus we have to recognize that chemiosmotic theory was a remarkable individual accomplishment. The validity and experimental productivity of Spencer's hypothesis is evident in the unusually wide-ranging and cumulative body of experimental work which it stimulated and in the fact that the four basic postulates, which were originally proposed on purely theoretical grounds, have now been experimentally verified many times over in laboratories throughout the world. Difficulties remain, of course, over details of certain of the molecular mechanisms involved, but the broad outline of the hypothesis and its essential components of vectorial metabolism, group translocation and the proton current remain inviolate. It is these components and their integration in the chemiosmotic theory that constitute Spencer's discovery and which have justified the award to him of the Nobel Prize for his unique individual achievement.

Critic   Sir, I would like to respond to Dr Younger's assertions which are, in my judgement, incorrect and misleading in several important respects. In the first place, he did not enter the field until after 1961. He has probably not read the literature of the 1950s at all closely and, like many researchers of his age, he has a distorted perception of the extent of Dr Spencer's originality. I think that Spencer himself was right in playing down the novelty of his own scientific views. During the 1950s and 1960s numerous scientists, such as Larsen, Robson and others, were developing ideas about the importance of charge separation and ion transport in biological membranes. Spencer mentioned this work earlier. Undoubtedly Spencer's chemiosmotic hypothesis has been cited much more frequently than the work of these other scientists by those concerned with ox phos and so on, and in this sense Spencer has had a much more obvious scientific impact. But this in no way implies that Spencer's ideas were that unusual. Spencer's impact on the field and the recognition now accorded to his work have been due more to his active proselytization than to the originality of his ideas as such. Relative newcomers to bioenergetics, like Dr Younger, will tend to confuse Spencer's present-day prominence in the field with his originality, because they are simply unfamiliar either with the intellectual background out of which the chemiosmotic hypothesis emerged or with the contributions of earlier researchers whose work is not now remembered.

Dr Younger suggested that the strong resistance to chemiosmosis during the 1960s by established researchers is a clear indication of the novelty of that hypothesis. Let me suggest, however, speaking as one of those established researchers, that this resistance was in no way due to the novelty of this hypothesis, but to its flaws and incompleteness. Larsen, and other advocates of similar proposals, were careful to keep *their* ideas close to the experimental evidence. They proceeded slowly and gradually, and developed their theoretical concepts in accordance with experimental observation. Thus I, and my colleagues, had no particular quarrel with their claims. They made no exaggerated theoretical assertions and their ideas were consequently explored and refined without controversy. Spencer's 1961 hypothesis, in contrast, was a purely theoretical and speculative extension of such ideas. It went well beyond the evidence then available and, in my opinion, although it has certainly helped to generate heated debate and has provoked further experimental work, it has not yet been proven by overwhelming experimental evidence.

The resistance to the chemiosmotic hypothesis, then, was, and is, not a measure of its originality, but a proper response to its scientific inadequacies. I am, nevertheless, very pleased that Dr Spencer has been selected for the Nobel Prize. He espoused a very controversial hypothesis and stimulated a great deal of new thinking and active experimention about an important issue. The only question is whether he's right.

Spencer tells us that the processes of respiration and electron transfer create proton gradients which, in turn, contribute to the synthesis of ATP. Well, we *can* observe proton gradients under certain experimental conditions, but we have very little idea how such gradients are linked to the creation of ATP. The problem is that chemists like to write chemical structures, and the chemical structures in this case appear to be missing. So I think that it is misleading to claim, as Dr Younger did, that Spencer furnished a novel mechanism of oxidative phosphorylation. No *mechanism* has been identified. You can't go from ion gradients to ATP by a series of structures that are known. The chemist's mind boggles at the incompleteness of it. You can hardly call this a major discovery. It's a speculative, incomplete and as yet unproven hypothesis.

Jennings I agree with a great deal of what Professor Critic has said. Like him, I think that the so-called chemi-osmotic hypothesis is basically wrong. I also agree that few people now in the field properly understand how ideas developed twenty years ago. I think he's also right to point out that Dr Spencer has been a very active and persuasive advocate for his own theory and that, as a result, people have naturally enough come to give him credit for ideas which are his only by adoption. As both Professor Critic and Dr Spencer point out, most of the concepts to be found in the chemi-osmotic hypothesis had already appeared in various forms and in various areas of research during the 1950s. Yet I think that they are both wrong, in slightly different ways, in denying that there was an historically specific discovery. Let me explain.

In my experience, what are called 'new ideas' in any one field develop from the coming together of separate pieces of information from several other fields. Thus 'new ideas' are seldom intrinsically new, but consist of novel combinations of existing ideas in relation to phenomena which have previously been beyond their scope. This is what happened in the field of oxidative phosphorylation in the late 1950s and it is the reason why two outsiders, Spencer and I, were responsible for initiating at that time a significant reconceptualization of the field.

In my view scientific development, like that which occurred in ox phos, is largely inevitable and the individuals responsible for particular advances happen to be distinguished only by being in the right place at the right time and by being the carriers of the necessary bits of information. Given a few weeks, months or very few years the same answers would appear under other names. Consequently, the idea of the great scientist in biochemistry today, as proposed earlier by Dr Younger, is a myth. Nevertheless, this in no way implies that discoveries do not occur. It simply means that there are always likely to be several potential discoverers in any particular case.

In the case of oxidative phosphorylation, it is clear that both Dr Spencer and I had been exposed in the 1950s to some of the ideas which were necessary to achieve a breakthrough in our understanding of ATP-production. During that decade, I had worked on the redox properties of metal ion complexes, which had some bearing on the respiratory chain; on condensation polymerization, which helped clarify how ATP could be formed; and on diffusion through membrane spaces, which helped me to realize the chemical significance of the mitochondrial membrane. These subjects clicked together for me in 1957, when I came to see how they could be combined to provide a new answer to the problem of oxidative phosphorylation.

The curious progression of ideas which I am attempting to portray in a self-conscious way is that by chance it can happen that one may acquire a variety of bits of knowledge and even though he is not aware of all the bits at any one time, they will constantly interact. The several bits can come to form a pattern of connections and there is then in his mind a hypothesis – that the connections he has had the luck to make are a part of reality and not just vague imaginings or dreams. This is what happened to me in relation to ox phos. For it came to me in 1957 that there was a connection between proton gradients and condensation reactions of polyphosphate; in other words, that the synthesis of ATP could be driven by a proton gradient linked to the mitochondrial membrane.

This was for me a true revelation. I felt like Cortez when he stood upon a 'peak in Darien' and saw the Pacific for the first time. In discovering proton-driven phosphorylation I felt that I had found some secret of nature and I was deeply satisfied in a purely personal way. As we now know, proton-driven phosphorylation *is* a biochemical reality. That has been amply confirmed experimentally. Accordingly, I insist that I did make a genuine discovery. The fact that I discovered proton-driven ATP-formation is, I think, clearly documented in my 1959 article. In essence, I am saying that there were *two* separate events: Spencer's initial formulation of the chemi-osmotic hypothesis, which had to do with a particular type of metabolic phenomenon that was already known, and my identification of electron/proton/ATP reactions in 1959, which eventually became incorporated, by some means or other, into the chemi-osmotic theory. In my article, you will find the first statement of the central ideas which later appeared in Spencer's chemi-osmotic hypothesis. But it is also a fact that my priority has not been widely recognized and this requires some explanation.

Early in 1961, Spencer wrote to me about my published work on proton-driven ATP-production. As the correspondence developed, it became clear that our ideas had been progressing along similar lines. But it also became increasingly clear that there were significant differences of scientific opinion between the two of us. I became more and more suspicious of his motives and when he wrote claiming that all I had written was a 'partial restatement of his views', the exchange went very sour.

The subsequent publication in 1961 of what has been referred to here as Spencer's 'discovery paper' came as quite a shock to me. There was no need for him to acknowledge our correspondence, though that would have been courteous. But there remained for him a requirement to reference my published work about which he

knew more than anyone else. This he failed to do. Science must
have a code of conduct and scientists must insist on that code and
not turn a blind eye to it later. We must obey a set of unwritten
rules. Even in athletics, barging earns disqualification from a race.
So it should be in biochemistry races, if we must have races and
prizes. However, I think that I understand Spencer's actions now. I
surmise that I had stumbled on chemi-osmosis and as I had not
given any references to his work, he felt justified in deliberately
ignoring my papers and letters.

Now, although the basic ideas of proton-driven ATP-formation
had been published by Spencer and myself during the period
1959–61, it took another decade for the majority of bioenergeticists
to accept these ideas. And undoubtedly Spencer was much more
actively involved in demonstrating these ideas experimentally and
in converting the biochemical heathen than I was. I was responsible
for running an inorganic chemistry lab and it was impossible for me
to engage at all in biochemical experiments on ox phos. In contrast,
Spencer was able to set up his own private laboratory in the early
1960s and to devote all its resources to promoting the chemiosmotic hypothesis. It's hardly surprising, therefore, that my initial
theoretical contribution came to be largely forgotten or ignored. In
retrospect, it seems inevitable that Spencer should have received
the credit and the prizes. Given the complex origins of any
scientific discovery, there is no way in which discoveries can be
properly monitored. Frequently the person who is recognized as
the discoverer is not the first to say something or even to do
something, but is the one who appears to some outside authority to
be making the running when they declare that this or that
particular race is over. I do not hesitate to state that for a long
period of time I felt cheated. I felt that a set of insights which fell
into my lap had been wrongly attributed to another and I still
believe that to be the case.

Spencer I do not intend to follow Dr Jennings in making
emotional accusations based on wild surmises about other peoples'
motives and actions. We are unlikely to reach a satisfactory
conclusion here today by accusing each other of improper
behaviour twenty years ago. I prefer to deal in facts rather than
delusions.

To begin with, it is obvious that there is a basic contradiction in
what Dr Jennings has just said. He began by agreeing with
Professor Critic that the chemiosmotic hypothesis is fundamentally
wrong. But he then went on to claim that it was he, and not I, who
had discovered the existence of chemiosmotic reactions and that
this discovery had since received ample experimental confirmation.
So, according to Jennings, we both made the same discovery, for

which I have wrongly received all the credit; yet at the same time, he insists that my supposed discovery is not a discovery at all, because it is scientifically wrong. The confusion arises, I think, because Jennings disgrees with me about the nature of ATP-formation, yet wants to claim that we both made more or less the same discovery – although, of course, I am said to have been a little later than Jennings and, perhaps, to have borrowed some of his ideas. The fact is, however, that the views on proton-driven ATP-formation published by Jennings are not only different from mine, but they have also been shown to be wrong. Thus which of us published first is irrelevant. The chemiosmotic theory is the correct theory and, in so far as there has been a discovery, it is embodied in that theory, to which Jennings has in no way contributed.

Jennings's account of ATP-formation seems to me to be no more than a minor conceptual broadening of the long-discredited idea of high-energy chemical intermediates. Jennings's idea was that coupling between respiration and phosphorylation might involve protons moving through the mitochondrial membrane to the ATPase as a localized anhydrous chemical intermediate. This conception resembles the chemiosmotic hypothesis only in that it gives some indeterminate role to localized protons in the process of ATP synthesis. But this hypothesis entails much more than the recognition that protons are involved. The chemiosmotic hypo-thesis specified that the plug-through respiratory chain complex generates proticity across the coupling membrane, energizing the aqueous conductors on either side, so that the power created by the proton gradient can be drawn off and used by other plug-through complexes, such as the reversible protonmotive ATPase. These facts have never, I think, been part of Dr Jennings's view of ATP-production.

Jennings   Let me make it quite clear that I am not an opponent of the chemi-osmotic hypothesis. The point I want to bring out is that the chemi-osmotic hypothesis is only a special case of a more general idea. Moreover, this special case does not have acceptable experimental support in my view and I have therefore stressed at all times the more general approach. The general idea is that charge separation occurs in the mitochondrial membrane; that a proton concentration gradient between two regions of space is created; and that the controlled diffusion of the proton makes ATP. This general idea is common to chemi-osmosis and to my own views. It is this which constitutes the basic discovery and it was first formulated in my 1959 paper.

Now Spencer and I clearly differ about the details of the processes whereby the controlled diffusion of the proton operates. My view is that proton diffusion is controlled locally within the

membrane by specific catalysts. Spencer's view is that protons pass
across the membrane to the outside, where they create a delocalized
gradient. I believe that this latter interpretation of the general idea is
incorrect. Why do I say this, when much evidence and many voices
have been raised in support of chemi-osmosis? My opinion is that
while many experiments can be interpreted as being in its favour,
there are some that are in direct conflict with it. My view of a
theory is that it becomes unhelpful and even positively disadvant-
ageous once facts are known which conflict with it. It is then better
to look elsewhere for a theoretical framework. As I have stated
many times and for a number of reasons, I believe that all the data
are consistent with proton-driven ATP-formation by a localized
system within membrane confines.

Elder The trouble with Dr Jennings's view of oxidative
phosphorylation is that it isn't concrete enough. He sees it as being
to the credit of his hypothesis that it is 'consistent with all the
data'. But this is really its major defect. The localized proton
hypothesis is a good example of what Popper calls the 'self-
annealing myth'; that is, because it is so vague and unspecific, it
can be interpreted as being consistent with any and every
experimental observation. This is the main reason why Dr
Jennings's views have had so little impact on the field.

In contrast, Dr Spencer's hypothesis had considerable predictive
power and most of these predictions came off. It worked well in my
experiments and it worked well in other peoples' experiments and
gradually it came to dominate the field. Now Jennings is, in effect,
claiming that the whole thing is happening within a black box
which you can only ever look at with NMR, when you're clever
enough. And to some extent he may be right, but it's not helpful.
In discussing Jennings's work I always point out that the Greeks
used to spend hours talking about atoms. They had long debates on
it and they coined the word, and so on. But it never *led* to
anything, except the adoption of the word 'atom' when they were
finally shown to exist. And I think that really is very important in
science. You've got to do more than have ideas. They must be
testable. They must be ideas that people can do things with.

So, as regards the discovery, it's not that important who had 'the
idea' first. Clearly Spencer was thinking and writing along these
lines in 1953 and Jennings published a more developed statement
in 1959 and so on. But the significant question is: which published
statement first translated the basic idea into a scientifically
productive formulation? And the answer to that is unambiguous: it
was Spencer's 1961 *Nature* paper. This paper identified a whole
series of biochemical phenomena which could be, and were,
experimentally investigated and, on the whole, confirmed.

Thus, I see Jennings's ideas as a variant of Spencer's chemiosmotic hypothesis which is much more closed, much less accessible. Effectively what he's saying is that protons are involved in all this, there is indeed proticity as defined by Spencer, but the protons never *appear* anywhere, except in the microcircuits which are actually built into the mitochondrial membrane. It's useless.

Furthermore, neither Spencer's nor Jennings's conceptions would have become adopted by bioenergeticists without strenuous personal advocacy. And it was Spencer who made this personal commitment. He spent a lot of time drawing peoples' attention to the chemiosmotic hypothesis and explaining it to them. In fact, he made himself very ill doing it. He had to show, and I mean this, real personal courage. In the early days, he and I could well be in a room full of scientists in which the other people actually thought we were stark raving mad and treated us accordingly. Thus the discovery and validation of the importance of chemiosmotic reactions was a personal as well as a scientific achievement; and in both respects the credit has to be given to Dr Spencer.

Statesman   Sir, I think that the view of this affair taken by the Nobel Committee is similar to that of Professor Elder, at least with respect to the scientific merits of the chemiosmotic hypothesis. It was our view that the central ideas of vectorial metabolism, proton circuits and so on had been of seminal importance in bioenergetics. We were in no way implying that the details of Spencer's work had been conclusively proven, nor that the chemical structures were known. The actual molecular mechanism has yet to be clarified and, when it is known, many of the details of Spencer's work may have to be revised. But in our view and that of the bioenergeticists we consulted, Spencer's writings over a period of nearly twenty years had transformed our whole conception of the processes of biological energy production and use. Spencer led bioenergetics out of the cul-de-sac of high-energy chemical intermediates into a realm of multiple experimental possibilities. Moreover, Spencer did much more than theorize productively. He sustained a long-term experimental programme which helped to introduce into bioenergetics a new and more quantitative style of experimentation. I simply cannot see that there is any problem about the award of the Nobel Prize. It was awarded, not just for a particular discovery, but for prolonged scientific achievement in the field of bioenergetics. In this respect, there seems to be no comparison, on Dr Jennings's own admission, between himself and Dr Spencer. Dr Jennings suggested that the discovery of chemiosmosis around 1960 was more or less inevitable and that it was largely a matter of accident who happened to make the discovery. If this is so, the Committee were clearly right to award the Prize, not for the discovery of chemiosmotic reactions as such (for Dr Jennings's view of discovery seems to imply that it requires little scientific merit), but for a sustained experimental and theoretical exploration of one of the most important issues in biochemistry.

Critic　I am not convinced by either of the last two speakers. Nobody denies that Dr Spencer's writings have been very influential or that he worked very hard to convert people to his views. But they seem to me to dodge the central issue which I identified earlier: is chemiosmosis right or not? If it is right, then Spencer's influence will have been all to the good. Not only will he have stimulated experimental activity, but this activity will have contributed to genuine scientific knowledge. However, if he turns out to have been wrong, then this experimentation will have been more or less worthless. When the Nobel citation referred to Spencer's *seminal* influence, it was necessarily being implied, in my judgement, that the Committee thought that his hypothesis was basically correct. In my opinion, this has not yet been proven. I think, therefore, that we simply have to wait before we decide whether chemiosmosis was a discovery or a mistake. Similarly, I think that the Nobel Committee should have waited until they could have awarded the prize, not just for an influential theory, but for a chemically complete and validated formulation of the process of oxidative phosphorylation.

Jennings　I agree. I believe that Spencer's version of chemi-osmosis is wrong in principle and that the award of the Nobel Prize was premature and could be damaging to further research in the area. We could have a similar hang-up to that in the 1950–70 era in the study of ox phos, if chemi-osmosis is taken as dogma. In my view, although a significant discovery was made around 1960, most of the basic issues in this area are still unresolved. We have yet to discover how the proton is generated, how the negative charge migrates, and how during proton migration it causes ATP to be produced. All these problems are those of the understanding of proteins and especially organized proteins. With respect to Professor Elder's comment a few moments ago, it is simply impossible to predict in advance how these proteins are organized. We have to proceed by systematic and careful experimentation. In a recent article, I have set out my thoughts on how some of the problems may be looked at and tackled. But we are not very far along the trail of relating the protein sequences, through the structures and dynamics of single proteins, to their functions. In my view the field remains wide open and the nature of energy capture of the membrane machines remains a fascinating problem.

Spencer　Sir, I do think that these objections to the chemios-motic theory are very unrepresentative of informed opinion in the field. It seems to me now to be fairly generally agreed that we know what the respiratory chain system is, what is does and, to some extent, how it does it. It is a system of specific hydrogen and electron conductors, which generates proticity by virtue of the fact that it is effectively looped across the coupling membrane, and catalyses the spontaneous diffusion of hydrogen atoms and electrons in opposite directions, adding up to a net proton translocation across the coupling membrane. This and much more I have specified in detail elsewhere. The present position is that, with comparatively few dissenters, we have successfully realized a consensus in favour of the detailed chemiosmotic theory. What I find most remarkable and admirable is the altruism and generosity with which most former opponents of the chemiosmotic theory have not only come to accept it, but have actively promoted it to the status of a theory. According to their classically Popperian view, the chemiosmotic theory is worth accepting, for the time being, as the best conceptual framework available.

Auditor Thank you, Dr Spencer. Well, I think that all the bioenergeticists here have had a chance to state their position. Let me try to summarize what has been said, in order to make sure that I have properly understood the various positions. Dr Spencer's view is that there is now a firm consensus in favour of the chemiosmotic theory, the basic tenets of which can be taken as established fact and which provides the best available conceptual framework for the understanding of oxidative phosphorylation and related processes. Accordingly, the existence and operation of certain kinds of chemiosmotic reaction can be regarded as a genuine discovery; but not as his discovery. The discovery is, rather, a collective achievement brought about by numerous researchers over a long period of time. Even his erstwhile opponents, says Dr Spencer, have helped to promote and validate the chemiosmotic theory. From this perspective, I suppose, the award of prizes and other honours should not be regarded as recognition of Spencer's individual contribution or intellectual abilities, but as a celebration of the advance of scientific knowledge and of the accomplishment of bioenergeticists in general, for whom Dr Spencer merely acts as a representative.

Dr Younger agrees with Dr Spencer that the chemiosmotic theory is a major discovery; indeed, he regards it as a discovery of Copernican dimensions. However, Dr Younger sees the discovery as being very much Spencer's personal contribution to bioenergetics. Unlike Dr Jennings, who proposes that the basic idea was 'in the air' at the time and certain to be applied to ox phos before long by one person or another, Dr Younger believes that the chemiosmotic hypothesis was well ahead of its time and that its formulation was a remarkable personal accomplishment. For Dr Younger, the initial resistance of researchers in the field is a sign of the novelty of Spencer's solution to the mechanism of oxidative phosphorylation. He has no doubt that the award of the Nobel Prize was only right and proper.

Professor Critic's view seems to be diametrically opposed to that of Dr Younger. For Professor Critic maintains, even more vigorously than Dr Spencer himself, that the concepts of the chemiosmotic hypothesis were not original. In addition, he suggests that the chemiosmotic hypothesis is scientifically incomplete; at best it deals with only one part of the overall process and cannot, therefore, be said to have specified a mechanism for oxidative phosphorylation. Thus, even if the hypothesis were correct, there would be no reason to attribute any major discovery to Spencer. Moreover, in Professor Critic's judgement, the hypothesis has not yet been shown to be correct and, consequently, it is still too early to say whether research into chemiosmotic phenomena has revealed anything of lasting scientific value.

Like Professor Elder and Dr Jennings, Professor Critic has commented on Dr Spencer's enthusiastic proselytization on behalf of his theory. However, in contrast to Professor Elder who sees this advocacy as a proper response to entrenched resistance and as an essential part of Spencer's contribution to bioenergetics, Professor Critic argues that it merely created a false impression of the extent of Spencer's actual scientific originality and significance.

On the basis of the testimony provided by our first three speakers, it has seemed that if you accept the chemiosmotic hypothesis you say that there has been a discovery; and if you do not accept it, you reject the idea of discovery. If we were to treat Professor Critic as representing a fairly small minority, we could think in terms of accepting the majority opinion; namely, that chemiosmotic theory is substantially correct and that there has, therefore, been a discovery. This would leave us the question of deciding on the significance of Spencer's personal contributions. This issue is made rather awkward by the marked disagreement between Drs Spencer and Younger. However, Dr Younger pointed out how difficult it is for a major discoverer to claim full credit for his work. If we bear this in mind, and make allowance for a certain conventional humility in Dr Spencer's public statements about his originality, we can begin to see some possibility of deciding in favour of the discovery of chemiosmotic reactions around 1961 by Dr Spencer. This would, of course, reaffirm the award of the Nobel Prize, whatever the precise grounds for that award.

Critic I'm aware that you haven't finished and I'm sorry to interrupt. But I cannot let you dismiss my views as being irrelevant, simply because I am supposed to represent a minority. It is true that a majority of people in the field call themselves 'chemiosmoticists', but this doesn't make the chemiosmotic theory right. Furthermore, they all mean different things by 'chemiosmosis'. What sort of a discovery is it that means different things to different people? In fact, the largest single group with the same coherent view within the field is made up of those who reject the chemiosmotic hypothesis. So, if you intend to base your decision about the occurrence of a discovery in ox phos on the existence or otherwise of a current scientific consensus, you will have to examine that supposed consensus with some care. For in my opinion, it's a consensus about theoretical labels and not about biochemical reality.

Auditor Thank you for pointing that out, Professor Critic. I think that I was moving in that direction, anyway. I was about to say that Dr Jennings's testimony tended to undermine my initial, tentative conclusion, in several ways. In the first place, in line with what you have just been saying, Dr Jennings raised the issue of the scientific content of the discovery. Dr Jennings claimed that there had definitely been a discovery, yet he insisted that Dr Spencer's views on ox phos were largely mistaken and that we currently knew very little about the details of the supposed biochemical processes. This led me to wonder whether the very general basic insight that both Spencer and Jennings seem to have experienced in the late 1950s could be said to constitute a discovery. If Jennings and Critic are right in maintaining that we are unable to specify the detailed chemical processes at work, and even those unreservedly in favour of the chemiosmotic theory accept that the molecular mechanisms have yet to be ascertained, can we properly decide that there has been a discovery? Of course, for Spencer and others, that basic conception has now been elaborated and confirmed in considerable detail. But many people seem to have reservations about various parts of the detail. Until the detail of chemiosmotic theory has been unequivocally validated, there's always a possibility that further research will lead to radical reconceptualization. And if that were to happen, we might have accepted as a discovery what was in fact a fundamentally flawed conception of oxidative phosphorylation and related processes.

There are other problems raised by Dr Jennings. If we accept his view that the discovery consisted of the recognition of the critical role played by controlled proton diffusion in the formation of ATP, then we don't have to worry in the same way about the scientific details of what has been discovered. However, we are now faced with the problem of who had this basic idea first and who published it first; as well as that of deciding whether this rather broad insight constitutes, in itself, a major advance in scientific knowledge. If it doesn't, and I'm inclined that way, then we seem to have no discovery, despite the occurrence of Dr Jennings's 'discovery experience', and we do not need to bother with the question of priority. If, however, we decide that the basic insight *was* a major scientific advance, and hence a discovery, we have a priority dispute to resolve.

In Dr Jennings's statement, the 'discovery' is treated as something which occurred in the late 1950s. What happened later had nothing directly to do with the discovery as such. Subsequent events merely served to obscure his contribution and to ensure that the prizes and the recognition went solely to Spencer, instead of to Jennings or to the two of them. However, Professor Statesman has made it clear that the most important prize of all was not awarded to Spencer for his 1961 'discovery paper' alone, but for a seminal contribution to the field, experimental as well as theoretical, over a prolonged period. Thus, although the Nobel Prize is treated by Jennings, and presumably by others, as implying official recognition of Spencer's original formulation of the chemiosmotic hypothesis, in reality the meaning of the Prize is more complex than that. I take it that, even if the Nobel Committee had accepted that both men made more or less the same discovery around 1960, as indeed the Committee may have done, it would still have awarded the Prize to Spencer alone in recognition of his sustained contribution to the field. The fact that there were practical reasons why Spencer was able to concentrate on promoting his work and Jennings was not is irrelevant to the proper allocation of scientific recognition.

Jennings This reasoning all sounds very plausible, but the fact is that Spencer's publications added nothing that is correct to my first two papers on the subject. Chemi-osmotic theory gradually took over ideas which I first formulated and Spencer was given the credit for them. For example, in the early 1970s Spencer began talking of micro-chemiosmosis and a proton channel through the membrane was also incorporated by then. Spencer must have remembered that these possibilities had been examined in my papers a decade earlier. Yet he ignored my contribution; or when he did mention my work, he misrepresented it. Consequently, very few people in the field, particularly among the younger researchers, were aware that Spencer was gaining credit for my ideas. This has persisted until the present day and seems to be happening once again in the present discussion. I thought that the object of today's meeting was to establish what really happened and to attribute credit accordingly. It seems to me, however, that your reasoning, Sir, is simply leading towards another unjust affirmation of the status quo.

Auditor I think, Dr Jennings, that it is a mistake to get too heated about these issues. I'm sure that everyone here is concerned to get to the truth of the matter. Before your comments, I was merely exploring various lines of argument. I had not yet reached the stage of trying to propose conclusions.

The point that I was about to explore, Dr Jennings, actually follows from your own account of the discovery process. You suggested that new discoveries emerge more or less inevitably out of the existing stock of knowledge, that if one scientist doesn't make the discovery another researcher very soon will, and that no particular merit attaches to the discoverer. I think you said earlier that the idea of the outstanding thinker in biochemistry is no more than a myth. Now if this is so, it seems that your charge of 'injustice' is rather weak. Given your view of the discovery process, you can hardly be claiming that you have any remarkable scientific merit that should be rewarded. Nor can you be claiming that, without your contribution, research on ox phos would have been set back a decade or so. Indeed, it seems to me that neither of our candidate discoverers has furnished an account of the discovery process which would justify all the fuss of the Nobel Prize and so on. Perhaps we should abandon the idea of deciding upon the proper allocation of credit at this meeting and concentrate solely on the issue of whether or not there was a discovery.

Younger Sir, with all due respect, I don't think that's possible. The very word 'discover', that is, to expose to view, to replace ignorance with knowledge, implies an active human agency and also the value of the end product. Consequently, it is an evaluative concept and necessarily involves us in approving the responsible agent. It seems that, in the present case, we are divided over who is the active agent and what is the end product.

As far as the end product is concerned we seem to have three possibilities; that nothing of any significance has been discovered, that a rather general concept has been discovered or that a relatively detailed biochemical process has been discovered. If we decide that there has been a discovery, we also seem to have three possibilities with respect to the agent: either Spencer or Jennings or the community of bioenergeticists is the discoverer. If we decide that Dr Jennings is the discoverer, then clearly there has been a miscarriage of justice. If the research community is the discoverer, then the acclaim given to Spencer is not justifiable, except in so far as we treat Spencer as symbolizing the advance of scientific knowledge and as furnishing a model for young, aspiring researchers. Finally, if we accept that Dr Spencer is the discoverer, not only does the esteem given to him provide the symbolic and motivational benefits just mentioned, but it also properly recognizes his outstanding personal and intellectual merit as well as his courageous pursuit of the truth, and is a just and fitting tribute to the contribution which he has made to the discipline of biochemistry. It seems to me to be perfectly obvious, not that we should decide in favour of Dr Spencer's discovery, but rather that we should *confirm* that discovery by Dr Spencer which is already properly recognized by the scientific community at large—

[At this point the transcript becomes unclear. Several people speak rather loudly at the same time. Expressions of approval seem to overlap with heated objections. Those objecting appear to be accusing Dr Younger of turning what started as a reasonable summary of the outstanding issues into an eulogy for Dr Spencer. After several minutes, the Auditor regains control.]

Auditor   Thank you, gentlemen. Before Dr Younger got carried away by his own eloquence he did, I think, identify what seem to be the alternatives before us. I take his point that, although we are scientists and are therefore accustomed to dealing only with facts, on this occasion we cannot avoid making evaluations. 'Discovery' does seem to be both factual *and* evaluative. Perhaps at this juncture, therefore, it would be helpful if we were to invite Dr Brannigan to join our discussion. He will be more accustomed than we are to dealing with evaluative concepts and, in addition, he is an expert on the nature of scientific discovery. We have, I think, Dr Brannigan, provided you with several different perspectives on the discovery in question and outlined their differing practical implications. Can you help us to reconcile all these divergent viewpoints?

Brannigan   Thank you for inviting me to take part in this discussion. It has been a unique opportunity to observe the social construction of a discovery at first hand. However, I think that there may be some potential misunderstanding of the contribution that I can make. So I had better begin by trying to clarify that.

You referred a moment ago to the divergent viewpoints on the discovery which have been expressed here today and you asked me to help in reconciling them. Now the very nature of your statement and your request reveals a crucial difference between your conception of discovery, as a participant, and mine as an analyst. Your use of the term 'viewpoint' seems to pre-suppose that there was one series of events about which everybody has been talking here today, but which some people have interpreted as a discovery and other people have not. By suggesting that the various different claims about the discovery of chemiosmotic reactions are matters of *viewpoint*, your statement leads us to believe that the differences between the various accounts reflect not the availability of different but equally valid histories of ox phos, but differences between the various people furnishing the accounts. Your statement implies that each viewpoint reflects the position of the viewer and that my task, as a sociologist, is to take account of the effects of these personal differences, thereby extracting from their contradictory stories a correct description of what really happened.

These assumptions seem to me to be quite natural for a practising scientist. I imagine that everyone here, except myself, is of the opinion that either there was a discovery or there was not; hence this meeting, which has been convened to resolve precisely this issue. My position, however, is that all social actions are open to a variety of quite divergent interpretations, including those actions which come to be called 'discoveries'. There is nothing about an act in itself which makes it a discovery. Whether or not an act is deemed to be a discovery depends on the interpretative work carried out by participants. Consequently, from my analytical perspective, it is not appropriate to think of the discovery of chemiosmotic reactions as an event or process which occurred in 1959 or 1961 or whenever, the details and nature of which we are now trying to ascertain. 'Discovery' is not an event in the past, it is a *method* which you are using *now* to construe past events as discoveries.

You are actually engaged here today in the *practical* task of creating this particular discovery. I am concerned, in contrast, with the *analytical* task of making sense of discovery in general. You will want to come to a firm and, for you at this moment, a supposedly final decision of 'yes' or 'no'. But I have to bear in mind, for example, that in other research areas what are now known as discoveries were not always so defined and that what were previously said to be discoveries are not always treated as such today. Thus my sociological theory of discovery must come to terms with the fact that the categorization of a scientific contribution as a discovery is an interpretative and variable accomplishment on the part of those involved. So, as an analyst, I cannot tell you which actions were discoveries and which were not, because no action is a discovery until participants make it so.

Auditor Well, I feel rather disappointed by this reply. You were recommended to me by a well-known Professor of Physics as someone who had written an interesting book on scientific discovery. I haven't read the book myself, of course, but I thought that you would be more helpful than this. You seem to by saying that we scientists can take anything to be a discovery. When we do this, we believe that we've actually identified a discovery; but you, with your wider analytical concerns, can see that our supposed recognition of a discovery is arbitrary. So in the case of the chemiosmotic theory, the practical implication of your analysis seems to be that we can just as easily decide that there was or there wasn't a discovery and we can just as well take Spencer, Jennings, the research community, or even me, as the discoverer. Whatever we decide, once we've made our decision, you will be able to come along and say 'Yes, that's a discovery'. But you can offer us no counsel in advance. Your only advice is, 'choose whomever you like'.

Brannigan No, I don't think that the social world is as disordered as that. There *are* certain basic criteria which have to be fulfilled by any discovery; that is, when we say that an action is a discovery we *mean* that it meets certain criteria. Any action which could not be construed by those involved as meeting the criteria would necessarily be regarded as something other than a discovery. There are four criteria by means of which discoveries are recognized: possibility, appropriate motivation, originality and validity. Perhaps it will help if I give some examples.

A minute or so ago, you proposed yourself, ironically, as a potential discoverer of proton-driven ATP-formation. Now I knew immediately that that was an ironic, and not a serious claim, partly because it was obvious that you did not meet the four criteria. In this case, the clearest disqualifying criterion is that of 'possibility'. You yourself told me before the meeting started that you had never published any papers on ox phos. If this is so, if there is no textual evidence of your ever publishing any papers on ox phos, then it's impossible for you to have discovered the biochemical process of ox phos. Of course, in this instance, *I* have carried out the interpretative work necessary to apply the criterion of possibility. Normally, it would have been applied by researchers in the relevant area. It is by applying such criteria that participants distinguish between discoveries and other actions, and between discoverers and other kinds of scientists.

Although I quickly reached a firm conclusion about your discovery-claim, I could have been wrong. It *may* be that you were lying when you said that you had never written about ox phos. It *may* be that this meeting has been arranged, not to find out who discovered chemiosmotic reactions, but to make fun of a socio-logist. Consequently, it could be that you have all been playing a game with me and that the person I thought was the Auditor is really Dr Spencer or Dr Jennings, and vice versa. If that's so, then you may decide that I have improperly applied the criterion of 'possibility'. It *may* be that you could possibly be the discoverer. The point I want to make is that even apparently self-evident interpretations of the criteria of discovery depend on background assumptions, which may be wrong. When we are led to reinterpret the criteria, what before *was* a discovery may now be seen never to have been one, whilst what was not a discovery may well in fact have been one all along.

In this example, I've dealt with the changing status of a 'discovery-event' over time. But it is equally possible for participants to differ about their application at one point in time. This is what has happened in the preceding discussion. I suggest that virtually all of the prior discussion centred around the three other criteria of validity, originality and motivation plus the related issue of agency.

Consider 'validity' as an example. When I say that validity is a criterion of discovery, I mean that only knowledge-claims which are taken to be true, correct or valid can be regarded as discoveries. If one scientist is able to convince another that a scientific claim is wrong, the second scientist is obliged, by the very meaning of the words, to treat this claim as something other than a discovery; for instance, he may have to regard it as a fraud or a mistake. Consequently the earlier discussion today, like most disagreements about particular discovery-claims, involved contradictory assertions about scientific validity. Drs Spencer and Younger were able to treat chemiosmotic theory as a discovery because they maintained that the theory had been experimentally confirmed. Professor Critic, in contrast, denied that it was a discovery on the grounds that it had not yet been proven. Whilst Dr Jennings undertook the complex interpretative task of denying the validity of Dr Spencer's hypothesis, and thereby denying his discovery, yet maintaining that he *and* Spencer had both seen an essential truth about ox phos.

This 'essential truth', of course, was made to appear as Dr Jennings's and not Dr Spencer's discovery by Dr Jennings's reference to the two remaining criteria, namely, originality and proper motivation. In other words, Dr Jennings treated the discovery as *his* discovery because he was the first to obtain and publish what he took to be the basic idea of proton-driven ATP-formation and also because, in his view, Dr Spencer acted improperly. The reference to Dr Spencer's supposedly questionable actions, for example in not citing Jennings's work, contributed to Jennings's discovery account by depicting Spencer's actions as those of an opportunist rather than those of a genuine discoverer.

I imagine that these brief examples are sufficient to illustrate my general point, namely, that all discovery-claims and denials are organized around the four criteria that I have mentioned. Any action which is taken to satisfy these criteria *is* a discovery. However, the criteria are necessarily rather general in character and they can always be applied and interpreted in many different ways in any particular instance. This is why, in the earlier debate, although everybody seemed to accept a common definition of what a discovery is, they came to such radically different conclusions about this particular discovery. Thus whether or not a discovery is deemed to have occurred depends on participants' specific judgements about validity, originality, and so on, and, unfortunately, such judgements cannot be completely formalized. In other words, we cannot translate the criteria of discovery into a formal algorithm. The identification of discoveries must ultimately depend on participants' judgements. Because discoveries are *attributed* by social groupings and not *made* by individual discoverers, it is impossible for any outside analyst, like myself, to come along and sort things out by identifying the discoverer for you. The very nature of discovery as a participants' accomplishment means that you must do it yourselves. All that my sociological perspective enables me to do is to understand why disputes about 'discovery' occur and identify the four key parameters along which discovery-claims are negotiated.

Spencer If I understand you correctly, your analysis of the criteria of discovery amounts to no more than a re-statement of what all scientists know already. What you have done is to re-state the criteria which we use to define, recognize and constitute scientific discoveries. Thus your contribution is merely to confirm what we hold in common with respect to discovery and about which there is no dispute, and to pass back to us those questions where we disagree and where we actually need your help. Whereas we want you to say something substantive about discoveries, you insist on restricting your attention to the formal grammar which we use in referring to discovery. Can you do no more than this? Are all sociological theories equally bereft of practical implications? I would think rather poorly of a biochemical theory which could not, *in principle*, offer interested non-researchers some kind of practical guidance.

Brannigan My point is that the grammar of discovery generates the conventions by which we reason about specific discoveries. By understanding the grammatical basis of our everyday decisions about discovery, we make it possible to treat discovery-claims and counter-claims as moves in a social game. I think that realization of the grammatical or conventional nature of our common-sense conclusions about discovery and about other 'social facts' can be extremely *liberating*. It releases us, to some extent, from common usage. We come to realize that there is a difference between the World and the spectacles through which we view it.

In addition, I think that the sociological theory of discovery may be of *some* practical assistance. Sociological analysis has shown that discoveries do not simply 'occur' or 'happen' naturalistically, but are socially defined and recognized products. In other words, discoveries are those events which, in the judgement of those involved, are deemed to have met the basic criteria; and discoverers are those who are socially recognized to have been the responsible agents. For example, Columbus, although he never relinquished the belief that he had landed in the Indies, is credited in our culture as the discoverer of the 'New World'. It was only in the light of Vespucci's explorations, however, that the existence of this 'New World' came to be accepted and the 'true' nature of Columbus's discovery recognized. Thus the exact character of Columbus's original actions and beliefs are irrelevant to 'what we now know' to have been his discovery. When we say that Columbus discovered America (as opposed to St Brendan, Hoei-Shen, Vespucci or Leif the Lucky) we are exhibiting a structure of social recognition which has subsequently been accorded to his achievement by the European world. We see Columbus as the discoverer of America because we belong to the tradition that was initiated by his achievement.

Now it seems to me that a similar case can be made for your discovery, Dr Spencer. As I understand the situation, most of the researchers now working on ox phos and related fields would claim to be working within the chemiosmotic framework as defined and exemplified in your writings. Dr Younger and Professor Elder have both testified to this. In addition, it was suggested that present-day researchers are largely unaware of and uninterested in the detailed origins of the theory. Most researchers today are happy to regard you fairly unproblematically as the discoverer of chemiosmotic reactions and this is reflected in the award to you, not only of the Nobel Prize, but also of many other symbols of scientific recognition.

In my view, it is pointless trying to establish exactly what happened and what was discovered by whom in the period 1959–61. To attempt such an historical reconstruction is to treat discovery as an intrinsic attribute of events as such, instead of as a quality attributed *to* events by social actors. All that will be generated by such a procedure is the kind of diverse medley of incompatible accounts that we have heard today. In contrast, if we ask: 'How do most of the scientists involved regard the discovery today?', we obtain a fairly clear answer: 'It was a genuine discovery made in 1961 by Dr Spencer.' For all those scientists who belong to the tradition of research which has been initiated by your achievement, your discovery is no more problematic than Columbus's discovery of America. In so far as participants in ox phos recognize Dr Spencer as the discoverer of chemiosmotic reactions, that is what he is.

Critic I thought that sociologists were mostly radicals! The guidance you are offering us, however, seems remarkably conservative, if not reactionary. Your analysis, it seems to me, will inevitably support the status quo. You deal with the issue of evaluation that we raised earlier by saying that whoever has got the prizes and the recognition thereby deserves them. I'm not willing to accept that. Anyway, your argument is logically fallacious. The fact that many people *say* that Spencer is a discoverer and chemiosmosis a discovery doesn't *make* it so. You said yourself that a genuine discovery has to be scientifically valid. Well, the validity or otherwise of the chemiosmotic hypothesis will be decided in the long run by the experimental facts. If those facts show the theory to have been wrong, as I confidently expect, then it will have been wrong from the start and it will never have been a discovery, whatever the current generation of bioenergeticists happens to believe or say. One of the basic errors in your approach is that you don't distinguish carefully between genuine discoveries and what people *believe* to be discoveries. What people *believe* can of course vary over time or from one person to another. But whether or not something *is* a discovery is not variable. It's logically contradictory to maintain, as you do, that something is both a discovery (at one time or for one person) and not a discovery (at another time or for another person). The chemiosmotic theory is either a discovery or not a discovery; and this is to be decided, not by counting how many researchers vote for it, but by assessing it on the basis of controlled experimental results.

Brannigan   As an outsider, trying to understand science and scientists, I cannot adopt the same 'realist' view of the natural world as you do. If I were to adopt your realist approach, I would have to base my conclusions about every discovery in which I was interested on some prior assessment of the scientific facts. As a result, I would have to become a bioenergeticist, a high-energy physicist and so on, in order to carry out analysis of possible discoveries in these fields. Not only is this impossible in practical terms, but it would mean that my judgements about scientific validity would significantly influence the shape of my sociological analysis. Accordingly, the views about discovery of those scientists with whom I agreed in scientific terms would be analysed differently from those with whom I disagreed. Thus my whole analysis would be linked to, and biased by, my relatively incompetent scientific conclusions.

Clearly, for reasons of sociological methodology, I cannot operate in this way. I must take an impartial view of the realities of, say, the biochemical processes of ox phos, and therefore of the validity of the chemiosmotic or other competing hypotheses. For the sociologist, a valid theory is whatever participants take to be a valid theory and a discovery is whatever participants take to be a discovery. Only if we adopt this kind of cognitive impartiality can we recognize that what matters for scientists as social actors is not validity in some ultimate sense, but validity as it is locally interpreted here and now.

If I were to adopt your 'realist' approach to scientific knowledge, and to allow as discoveries only those achievements which meet what I take at present to be the ultimate criteria of scientific validity, I would constantly find myself in the position, at least implicitly, of telling past generations of scientists that what they thought were discoveries were not really so. The progressive character of science means that all our current 'orthodoxies' will be superseded or tempered by better theories in the future; although each generation seems to suffer amnesia on this point. Consequently, while at any time contemporary theories will be held as objective and valid, this validity has a provisional or conventional character. Like discovery itself, theoretical validity is socially constructed and is likely to be superseded by later social constructions. The only tenable sociological position is that both validity and discovery are what particular scientists at particular times take them to be.

Younger I'm not sure that you can escape so easily from telling scientists that they're wrong. For one thing, you said a few minutes ago that, in sociological terms, Dr Spencer seemed to have become the discoverer. This seems to contradict what Dr Jennings and Professor Critic have asserted. So maybe we need to rephrase your point more carefully. Let's make it: 'Dr Spencer has been widely recognized as the discoverer.' But there are several problems with this version. First, it's a rather weak and uninteresting claim. It says nothing about 'discovery', only about the recognition of discovery. Moreover, it seems to imply that *my* claim about Spencer's actually being the discoverer is too strong to be acceptable. In retreating to your weak sociological claim about the recognition of the chemiosmotic theory, you seem to imply that my claim, and indeed *all* participants' claims about the *actual* discovery, are exaggerations and unsatisfactory in some way. In rejecting what you called 'naturalistic' accounts of discovery, you seem to me to be claiming superiority for your own non-naturalistic analysis. You said something like, 'sociologists have shown that discoveries do not occur naturally in the way that people normally think of them occurring, but are socially defined products'. Are you not, therefore, competing with our understanding of discovery and claiming a rather remarkable interpretative privilege for your own analysis? Given that our accounts tend to be naturalistic accounts which treat discovery as something 'out there' in the social world, are you not claiming to know better than us?

I don't intend to be rude, but your view seems particularly astonishing, given your inability to say anything concrete about the way that scientists interpret the criteria of discovery. I suggest that the underlying problem which you are unable to overcome is your lack of scientific competence. If you were a trained researcher, you would be able to decide upon issues of scientific validity and, consequently, to distinguish genuine from false discovery-claims. In this way, you would be able to say something concrete and interesting about particular discoveries, instead of offering us an abstract account of what we know already, masquerading as a superior form of analysis.

Brannigan I don't think that becoming a trained scientist would help *very* much. You are just as much an outsider to high-energy physics as I am. So training to be a bioenergeticist couldn't help me to carry out sociological analysis on any area other than bioenergetics. And even here, how would it help? Presumably Professor Critic, Professor Elder and Dr Jennings are all competent researchers, yet they assess scientific validity differently in this instance and they come to different conclusions about discovery. Moreover, even you and Dr Spencer do not agree about the present discovery, despite being in apparent agreement about the validity of the chemiosmotic theory. As I pointed out previously, although validity is an important criterion of discovery, it is not the only one. Acquiring technical competence would not enable me to reach assured conclusions about priority or proper motivation. So I think that your remark about scientific competence is a red herring. Scientific competence doesn't enable you to solve your own interpretative problems; nor would it help me.

However, your other point is rather more interesting. I'm not, in fact, claiming that my non-naturalistic account of discovery is more appropriate or superior for *all* purposes. I'm only suggesting this in relation to sociological analysis. For your practical purposes as a participant in science, it is clear that discovery has to be treated as a natural fact and, indeed, that to you the discovery *appears to be* an objective historical fact; just as to Dr Jennings and Professor Critic and so on, it appears, just as objectively, to be a different kind of historical fact.

What I think happens is that each participant adopts a particular stance towards a candidate discovery and interprets the events surrounding that candidate discovery accordingly. Thus for Dr Jennings the basic conviction seems to be that he made the discovery, but didn't get the credit for it. All preceding and subsequent events are interpreted accordingly. For instance, his proposal that all scientific discoveries arise from an inevitable process of scientific development helps him to explain the almost simultaneous discovery by Spencer and himself of proton-driven ATP-formation. This, in turn, makes the subsequent 'misunderstandings' about the discovery 'only to be expected'. Similarly, Spencer's actions and motives are interpreted in a way which helps to explain why Jennings received no recognition, despite having made the discovery. And so on. All of this interpretative work by Jennings is projected upon the world. Although the uninvolved outsider may recognize that these events may be quite differently interpreted to tell a different yet equally plausible story, for Jennings, his account is a description of what actually happened.

This is true, of course, not just of Jennings's story, but also of your own and of the others that we heard earlier. One indication that these accounts are stories, rather than literal descriptions of events, is that they tend to take highly conventional forms. Thus Dr Jennings used a recurrent form of interpretation which I call the 'folk theory of cultural maturation', whilst you used the 'folk theory of genius'. Now these theories are quite inadequate, when you look at them closely. Your attribution of genius to Dr Spencer, for example, is a mere tautology. The only evidence that can be adduced of his genius, as distinct from the kind of high intelligence which all of you display, is the very discovery which it is used to explain. People who, unlike you, do not treat his discovery as a fabulous triumph by a creative individual over dogmatic ignorance, make no mention of Spencer's genius. Thus 'genius', I suggest, is no more than a useful part of the conventional story which seems most appropriate to you, as a younger researcher whose own success has been accomplished within the research tradition attributed to Spencer.

Dr Jennings's folk theory of cultural maturation is no more convincing. For instance, the idea that discoveries are produced by an inevitable and cumulative advance of scientific ideas seems to imply that new ideas will emerge in a context where they will be favourably received. Yet much of the testimony given earlier emphasized that the chemiosmotic hypothesis was not well received and that it actually took a decade or so before many people would give it serious consideration. Thus both these folk stories seem to me to be conventional forms of interpretation which are defective as proper explanations of events, but which are appropriate for the particular purpose of the story-teller.

One important consequence of the use of these familiar and plausible scientific folk stories is that the particular version of discovery which is embedded in each of them thereby comes to seem more objective. In making sense of a discovery in a particular way, scientists make it appear 'obvious' that their version of the discovery is the correct one. For example, if Spencer has been a genius all along, then it's not surprising that he should have made a major discovery in due course. Similarly, if any important new idea is likely to occur to several people at about the same time, then it's not surprising that there is often confusion about who has actually made a particular discovery.

In short, the point of participants' talk about discovery is not a detached description of events, but rather an engaged depiction of events. Whereas the analyst, who is not actively involved in the social world of science, simply tries to observe the various ways in which events can be construed by participants, scientists themselves are necessarily involved in devising evaluative accounts of what they take to have happened. Accordingly, sociological analysis of scientific discovery is a distinct form of discourse from participants' interpretation of discovery. The latter is designed to objectify discovery, to turn it into a 'natural fact' within the social world of science. The former is designed to describe how this objectification is accomplished. Because these two forms of discourse are linked to these different outcomes, I am unable to help with the practical objective of deciding who really made the discovery. Because my aim is to encompass and to understand the full range of discovery accounts produced by scientists with respect to any given discovery, my stance is bound to be seen by the scientists concerned as a rejection of and a criticism of their own particular versions of the discovery-event in question. The non-naturalistic character of sociological analysis will inevitably appear to you to put in question your naturalistic endeavours—

[At this point, several people begin talking at once. Normal conversational decorum breaks down. It may be that speakers' patience in waiting for long periods without being able to contribute had at last become exhausted. What follows is a transcription of what could be extracted from the jumble of sound. Copies of the tape can be provided for any conversation analysts who are interested.]

'I don't think that it's a tautology to refer to Spencer as a genius at all. You only have to read his papers to see that he is head and shoulders above everyone else in the field. Only a mind of remarkable quality could have. . . I've always thought it silly to talk about genius in this connection. A genius would have been better at chemistry. . . I've never claimed to be particularly original. If there has been a genius in the field it was David King who . . . I definitely had a discovery-experience. It was a genuine feeling of revelation. . . The people in ox phos responded unfavourably because the ideas came from other areas and were rather strange to them. . . The point is that there are many *scientists* who are scientifically incompetent. It's really a select group of researchers who are properly qualified to make reliable judgements about validity and discovery. . . Popper has identified the criteria which we use to assess the validity of competing theories. Of course, one must always regard currently accepted theories as permanently open to falsification. But in practice, very few well-established theories ever get completely overthrown. . . Smacks of relativism to me. . . It is true that Spencer has come to be accepted as the discoverer. His name is always given great prominence in the textbooks. I read one the other day which said that, although controversy was still raging over the localized or delocalized proton, the author would invoke Occam's razor and adopt the simpler, delocalized interpretation. So, you see, that sociologist was right to say that the research community is inclined in Spencer's favour. . . I think that it was a waste of time inviting him here. He just confused matters. We'd reached a point where we had some fairly simple decisions to make. If we'd excluded Jennings and Critic, who are obviously biased against Spencer because they are envious of his receiving the Nobel Prize, and if we allow for Spencer's natural reluctance to press his own claims. . . He did seem to me to be claiming that, whereas we rather simple-mindedly *thought* there was such a thing as discovery, he in his wisdom could see that this was an illusion. . . He seemed to be suggesting that our statements were no better than fairy-stories. I accept that there's bound to be a few odd-balls about. But scientists in general are trained to be objective and to give you the facts as they really happened. . . There must be discoveries, otherwise science wouldn't advance. . . Could we have some order, *please*. . . Yet the only contribution he could make was to tell us what we already knew, that is, that a discovery is an original contribution to knowledge and that Spencer discovered the existence of chemiosmotic reactions. . . I tell you, Spencer did *not* discover. . .'[1]

At this point the tape stops. I have contacted participants in order to find out what happened, but the accounts I have obtained seem confused and contradictory. Brannigan informs me that there was an undignified scuffle, during which the tape-recorder was knocked to the floor and broken. But he is unable or unwilling to say who was responsible. He also tells me that he is never going to try to help scientists again and that in future he is going to concentrate on less dangerous activities, such as beekeeping and research on the criminal fraternity.

Note to Chapter 7

1 The debate presented in this chapter took place several years ago.
   Professor Jennings asked me to include this brief postscript referring to
   the current situation:

   > 1985. The arguments have continued. The reader is encouraged to
   > ask a friend conversant with the standing of local and delocalized
   > theories within the frame of chemi-osmosis which of these theories is
   > dominant today. Then it might be appropriate to re-read this play.
   > The effect of time on one's vision of discovery is sometimes most
   > perplexing.

PART 4

Celebrations

8

Noblesse Oblige: an Analytical Parody

One of the central themes in this book has been that sociological analysis can benefit from adopting new literary forms. In this chapter I am going to complete, and in my own way celebrate, this preliminary exploration of new forms by turning my attention to parody. My starting point is the proposal that all (sociological) analysis is a form of parody and, therefore, that parody can be a form of (sociological) analysis. This argument can be sustained, I think, in relation to any kind of analysis. I will concentrate, however, on the particular case of sociology.

All sociological analysis makes use of and builds upon what I will call 'original texts'. These texts are 'original' in the sense that they precede and are necessary for the production of the analytical text. Such original texts are sometimes produced by the analyst himself; for example, an observer's field notes in which he describes the actions of those under study. Sometimes they are produced by the actors under investigation; for example, letters exchanged among participants and subsequently collected by the analyst. Sometimes these original texts are jointly produced by analysts and participants; for instance, the interview schedules devised by an analyst and answered by a respondent. There is also a form of sociological analysis which relies almost entirely on previous sociological writings for its original texts. The analyst's task, put as generally as possible, is to make sense of a particular batch of texts (the original text) by formulating a secondary text of his own. The objective of the secondary text is to show any reader, including the analyst, how the original text is to be read or understood.

One necessary feature of the secondary, analytical text is that it differs from the original text. If the secondary text did not differ from the original text, it would be a mere repetition of that text and would be analytically empty. The secondary text inevitably selects from the original text, summarizes it, ignores parts of it, rephrases it, puts it in a new context, identifies its important and unimportant features, simplifies it, and so on. In other words, the analytical text systematically deviates from and, in this sense, distorts the original text as it performs analytical work on that text and re-presents it for analytical purposes. This systematic distortion is captured in the frequently used distinction between raw data (original text) and results or findings. The raw data are manipulated, re-ordered and re-presented in the analytical text to reveal their sociological meaning.

There is one word in particular in the previous paragraph which may seem inappropriate, namely, the word 'distort'. For whereas 'distort' is equivalent to 'misrepresent', 'twist out of shape' or 'falsify the meaning of', the secondary analytical text customarily claims to be true to the original text and to be doing only what is necesary to bring to light the underlying meaning of that text. Thus sociological analysis changes the shape of the original text, yet it does this in order to reveal its actual structure and its true sociological significance. In this sense, the secondary text necessarily bears an ironic relationship to the original text. As Woolgar puts it: 'To do irony is to say of something that appears one way, that it is in fact something other than it appears' (1983, p. 249). The secondary text, in transforming the original text yet claiming to reveal that text's meaning, inevitably asserts the kind of interpretative privilege over the original text which is the essential element in textual irony. The original text is denied the right to speak for itself. It is the secondary, analytical text alone which can properly convey the reality of the original text.

But what does this have to do with parody? In order to establish the connection, it will be helpful to consider the origin of this word. It is derived from 'para', which is Greek for 'alongside of', and 'oide', a 'song' (Funk, 1978). Thus, a parody is literally a song written alongside another song. In time, the second song came to concentrate on identifying the central features of the first song and, by the artful combination of re-statement and variation, to undermine the standing of the original song in some way, often by means of irony or humour. The word 'song' was appropriate in the Greek context owing to the nature of Greek dramatic and literary forms. But subsequently parody has come to be used in relation to a wide variety of textual forms. Accordingly, we can replace the word 'song' with the word 'text'. Linking this definition to the preceding discussion, I suggest that a parody is a secondary text which is closely based on (alongside of) an original text, but which differs from the original text in ways which reveal the true nature of the original text (its central features) and at the same time the superiority of the secondary text (undermine the standing of the original text).

We seem to have arrived at the conclusion that parody and analysis can be defined in virtually identical terms. Thus, I claim to have demonstrated my initial proposal that sociological analysis is a form of parody and that parody can be a form of sociological analysis. I have to admit that this conclusion depends upon some rather careful textual work carried out above. Consequently, some readers may feel that the argument presented here is itself a parody of proper analysis. But all analysis depends on such careful textual work. If this were not so, writing analytical texts would not require such detailed attention to wording, so many revisions and so many wasted pages (see Westfall, 1980, for a discussion of Newton's copious and minute revisions). Moreover, to maintain that my analysis is a parody only adds further support to my argument that analysis is a parody. The only criticism that might, at first, appear to weaken my case would be that my argument is *not* a parody. But if my analysis is not a parody, then I can assume that it stands as valid analysis; that is, I can assume that analysis *is* a parody. Hence, whichever of these responses the reader decides to adopt, he will be forced by iron logic, as the author has been, to accept that sociological analysis is a form of parody and, therefore, that parody can be a form of sociological analysis.

At this point, the Reader, the Textual Commentator or other characters who have appeared earlier in this text and who may be prejudiced against the conclusion rigorously demonstrated above are probably preparing a trap for me and for my argument. Clearly I am going to suggest that, now that we have established that parody *can* be a form of sociological analysis, we should actually employ parody as a form of analysis. But once I have put forward this recommendation, the trapdoor will be slammed shut with: 'But if analysis already *is* a form of parody, the recommendation to use analytical parody is redundant. Analysts are already using parody.' Fortunately for me, however, the door closed too quickly, leaving me safe outside. For my recommendation is not that sociologists should take up analytical parody, but that they should recognize, acknowledge, even celebrate their involvement in parody, instead of denying it, and begin to explore the possibilities opened up by cultivating parody as an analytical form.

One advantage of explicitly recognizing and presenting one's own analysis as a parody of others' texts is that the secondary text claims no interpretative privilege with respect to parallel secondary texts. An explicit parody does not claim to offer a definitive reading of the original text. It is offered as but one reading among many possible readings. In addition, it allows for the possibility of some kind of rejoinder on behalf of the original text. A secondary text which is an explicit parody invites further parody (analysis) of its own text.

As a result, explicit analytical parody enables us to treat our own work as one more contribution to a continuing series of texts; to treat our own work as a textual artefact which uses selection, simplification and exaggeration along with humorous contrast and incongruity to propose new readings of and inform third parties about other texts (Woolgar, 1983).

It is important, I think, to recognize that parody is not simply a textual form designed to make fun of original texts. Rather, ridicule and humour, as well as exaggeration and condensation, selection and paraphrase, are all used as a means of informing the reader about the nature of the original text. In this sense, explicit parody conforms to what is normally said to be the main objective of ordinary sociological analysis. At the same time, however, parody differs from ordinary analysis in drawing attention to its own textuality. Analytical parody says, in effect: 'What I have to offer is, I think, a viable conclusion, but it is not the original text (the real world) itself. Furthermore you, the reader, will have to perform the same kind of interpretative work on my text, in order to extract its meaning, as I performed on my original text.'

Analytical parody, then, differs from standard forms of analysis in openly inviting the reader to perform her own interpretative work on the analytical text and/or on the original text, and in encouraging the reader to explore alternative avenues of textuality in order to discover what they can reveal. Whereas conventional sociological analysis claims interpretative privilege for its own text, analytical parody directs attention to the possibility of carrying out diverse kinds of sociological analysis, that is, saying various new and interesting things about the production of the social world, by means of any and every conceivable literary form (including of course, as *one* textual form, conventional analysis). We have already seen some of these forms in operation. I now offer an attempt at analytical parody.

The focus of this analytical parody is the Nobel Prize ceremonies. Like a true sociologist, I will try to use parody to illuminate how the Nobel Prize ceremonies are socially constituted. Various symbolic domains are used to make the arrangements of the awarding of the Nobel Prizes properly ceremonial, including music, painting, eating and apparel. But I suggest that the critical sybolic realm is that of language; and that the various non-linguistic accoutrements are given their specific ceremonial meaning by being embedded in a particular kind of spoken discourse. This discourse takes the surface-form of presentations, formal lectures, banquet speeches, and so on. However, all of these surface-forms rely upon the same recurrent smaller-scale interpretative forms to accomplish the overall effect of a ritual celebration of human achievement at the highest level. It is through the regular use of these fine-grained forms by all those taking part in the Nobel ceremonies that the ceremonies become recognizably a celebration (Mulkay, 1984b).

The forms themselves, I suggest, are wholly conventional. It is the concentrated use of these conventions that creates the celebratory context. Any significant departure from these forms, any recourse to discourse which contradicts these forms, will disrupt the ceremonies and detract from their celebratory import. In the following pages, I will parody the discourse of Nobel Prize ceremonies and contrast it with forms of discourse which I believe are potentially available to, yet never actually used by, participants during the ceremonies. Thus I will construct a secondary text which is fictional, in the sense that I stress that the events it reports did not happen; yet which is factual in that it expresses in a concentrated way, and therefore with greater clarity and economy than could any original text, the interpretative forms through which Nobel Prize ceremonies are actually constituted.

I have used as my basic sources *Les Prix Nobel* for the years 1978–81. These are the original texts for the statements made by the Laureate, the representative of the Nobel Foundation, the presenter and the student representative. Most of these speakers' words are taken from these four volumes. The other speakers' words come from interviews with scientists collected over many years, from published responses to particular Nobel awards in various fields, and from my own informed invention. None of these characters is based upon, or intended to represent, any particular persons, nor any of the characters who have appeared elsewhere in this book. The actors in the parody below are composite figures representing typical features of scientists' discourse.

The Nobel ceremonies are made up of five kinds of textual component: speeches by non-Laureates leading to the award of a prize, return speeches by Laureates at the formal banquet, a speech addressed to all Laureates by a student representing the younger generation of researchers and scholars, formal lectures by each Laureate about their own contribution to knowledge, and a biographical account of each Laureate's career, usually written by the Laureate concerned. I have drawn on the full range of this material in devising a series of speeches supposedly given at a celebratory banquet. I have assumed that an unaccustomed intake of celebratory champagne has weakened the inhibitions of some of those who take part; particularly those who join in later in the sequence.

The Nobel Banquet Incident

REPRESENTATIVE OF THE NOBEL FOUNDATION Your Majesties, Your Royal Highnesses, Ladies and Gentlemen. It is my privilege and pleasure to begin the round of after-dinner speeches in honour of this year's Laureates. Honoured Laureates, the Nobel Foundation takes special satisfaction in welcoming you. You have already spent a few days in Sweden. I do hope that even this short time has enabled you to assess the magnitude of our appreciation for the stimulating scientific and personal contacts which have been made possible by the presence here of your honoured selves and your esteemed families. I also trust that you all feel that our traditional formalities are part of a friendly and cheerful celebration of your magnificent achievements.

Alfred Nobel stipulates in his will that his prize go to those who have conferred the greatest benefit on mankind. The Nobel Prizes in physics, chemistry and medicine have often recognized pioneering research achievements at the frontiers of our knowledge: enterprises, therefore, that usually can only be understood and judged by a small group of specialists. This is in keeping with Nobel's wish that principal encouragement go to basic and pioneering research, whose results can be expected to lead to practical, significant developments of benefit to mankind.

A great number of scientists from all over the world are involved as nominators for the Nobel Prizes, and thereafter the proposals are subjected to a careful analysis by experts. It is well known that receipt of a Nobel Prize is still considered to be one of the finest honours in the world. This opinion is based partly on the knowledge that the right to propose in the matter of prize awards is reserved to scientists throughout the entire world, and partly on awareness of the occurrence of the word 'discovery' in Nobel's will. It is easy to understand what a change the general assessment of the Nobel Prize would undergo if one did away with the thought-association 'Nobel Prize – discovery'. The prize would lose its singular character.

Nobel Prize Day plays more and more the role of an annual reminder to those in power in the world of the quickly exhausted and irreplaceable assets which people of the remarkable calibre of our prizewinners represent. Such outstanding figures must be granted the conditions they require to develop and exploit their immense intellectual capacity and industry in their ineluctable pursuit of further knowledge. What is more enticing or important than seeking the crown of truth wherever the search may lead?

If the Nobel Prizes can contribute to increasing political and public understanding for what research and creative and enterprising individuals can mean for the improvement of society, not only will Alfred Nobel's hopes of stimulating research within clearly defined areas be fulfilled, but the prizes will also contribute to the creation of the more peaceful world he dreamt of.

REPRESENTATIVE OF SWEDISH STUDENTS Your Majesties, Your Royal Highnesses, Honoured Nobel Laureates, Ladies and Gentlemen. Ever since the first Nobel Prize ceremony, we students have had the privilege of meeting once a year with the most distinguished representatives of science and literature, who by their brilliant achievements have earned the attention and admiration of the entire world. Today, we have the great pleasure of sharing this happy occasion with you.

On an evening such as this, research and higher education may seem glamorous and exciting occupations. Under the circumstances this is quite fitting, but as many of you know from personal experience a different reality is waiting around the corner tomorrow, when the festivities have ended.

One aspect of this other reality is that an increasing degree of control over scientific research has in many countries been accompanied by a growing reluctance to allocate funds. In a world blessed with a steadily increasing number of politicians and a steadily decreasing number of statesmen, long-term scientific effort is regretfully having to make way for the greater popular appeal of more short-term action. However, in a democratic society, free and independent research effort will always benefit all of mankind. For most scientific research has beneficial applications. Your important achievements have made an outstanding contribution to this process.

Each generation broadens and deepens the fund of knowledge possessed by mankind. You, the Nobel Prize Laureates gathered here today, represent pinnacles of achievement in your respective fields. We hope the younger generation of today will have the opportunity to develop your results, to take one more step up the steep ladder of knowledge. We hope the politicians of the world will provide the resources necessary to develop a flourishing base of higher education from which coming generations of researchers as able and as dedicated as you can be recruited.

Honoured Nobel Laureates, the students of the world pay homage to you today, because of your priceless contributions to the foundations upon which future generations of scientists are going to build. We wish to express our great respect for your brilliant results, our congratulations for the prizes you have received, and our esteem and tribute to you for being, not only the foremost representatives of science, but also the humble servants of our culture.

REPRESENTATIVE OF THE NOBEL COMMITTEES Your Majesties, Your Royal Highnesses, Ladies and Gentlemen. I have the great honour this year of speaking on behalf of the subject committees for physics and chemistry.

The prize for physics this year goes to Professor Purple for his great discoveries in the borderland between a strange but known country and the probably large unknown territory of the innermost structure of matter. Our way of looking at this structure has changed radically in the last decade. Purple's theory of strong–weak, or weak–strong, interaction has been one of the most important contributions to bring about this change of outlook.

The epoch-making theory which is awarded this year's physics prize has extended and deepened our understanding of the strong force by displaying its close relationship to the weak force: these two forces merge as different aspects of a unified strong–weak, or weak–strong, force. This means, for example, that the electron and the neutrino are intimately related. We now know, as a result of Purple's theory, that the neutrino is the electron's little brother. Similarly, it follows from the theory that the proton is, surprisingly, the electron's elder sister and also, therefore, the *neutrino's* elder sister. In other words, the theory predicts that they are all members of the same family. These dramatic predictions have been fully confirmed by experiments carried out during the 1970s. Further research will undoubtedly reveal, in due course, the full extent of the previously unimagined kinship network which lies hidden behind the superficial characteristics of the physical world and will open up new possibilities for collaboration between physicists and the previously under-valued discipline of social anthropology.

Professor Purple, the scientific world was shocked when you first announced your amazing discovery. Nobody, absolutely nobody, had anticipated anything like it. You pursued your demanding and difficult investigations with outstanding skill and determination and showed the impossible to be possible. You stand out as one of the greatest scientists of our time; the uncontested pioneer, original genius and founding-father of 'particle sibling research'.

I now turn to the prize for chemistry. The body and soul of man is the most complex and refined chemical machine that we know. Even the simplest forms of life, for example bacteria, are almost immeasurably intricate systems compared to the dead matter that we find on our Earth and in the rest of the Universe. However, modern biology has taught us that there is no vital force, and that living organisms consist wholly of dead atoms.

The machinery of life is made possible by a unique interplay between two groups of biological giant molecules, nucleic acids and the proteins, in the form of enzymes. These molecules form the orchestra that plays the various melodies which, in combination, create the harmony of life. DNA is the carrier of the genetic traits in the chromosomes of cells, and it governs the chemical machinery, it regulates the music of life, by determining which enzymes a cell shall manufacture.

The scintillating investigators who have been awarded this year's Nobel Prize for chemistry, Drs Frank and Stein, have brought about a new era in our understanding of the relationship between the chemical structure and biological function of the genetic material. Drs Frank and Stein carried out the immensely difficult task of constructing a recombinant-DNA molecule, that is, a molecule which contains DNA from different species, for example genes from a human being combined with part of a bacterial chromosome. It was their awe-inspiring privilege, and their great gift to mankind, to set in motion the new epoch of genetic engineering and to put flesh upon the Faustian dream of constructing new forms of life and perhaps, thereby, putting Man in the driving seat of evolution.

As we all know, there has been extensive debate about the need to control these new techniques, after an initiative as one would have expected from Dr Frank himself, warning of possible dangers. Continued research has shown, however, that the concern for hypothetical risks has been unwarranted. Scientists never forget to fasten the seat-belt.

Drs Frank and Stein, with incomparable ingenuity, great personal courage and unflagging persistence, you have innovated and brought humanity closer to a blithe new world. Your ideas and techniques have produced a breakthrough that has opened up major new insights into the fundamental processes of life and creation as well as infinite new practical possibilities. It is in recognition of these brilliant and pioneering contributions to science and to the benefit of mankind that we honour you today.

PROFESSOR PURPLE Your Majesties, Your Royal Highnesses, Ladies and Gentlemen. I have the great privilege and distinct pleasure to reply on behalf of the three Laureates in physics and chemistry. I wish humbly to express our deep appreciation and intense gratitude to Your Majesty and to all those who have made of Alfred Nobel's legacy a unique tribute to human achievement. We thank you for the very high honour and warm hospitality that have been bestowed upon us in Sweden.

During my career, the nature of science has changed dramatically. But despite these great changes, one thing still remains constant – it is the Nobel Prize. Its significance as the greatest scientific award on an international scale is universally recognized. This must be regarded as a unique achievement of Swedish scientists, because awarding prizes correctly requires great wisdom.

I do not mean to imply that you have been wise in awarding me the prize for physics; far from it. My personal contribution to science has been small. But I recognize the outstanding qualities and achievements of my fellow-Laureates here tonight and of those famous men and benefactors of mankind who have received this honour in the past. Their brilliant accomplishments lead me to reflect on the fact that scientific knowledge is cumulative; each individual stands on the shoulders of others, many of whom are giants, like those facing me across this table.

The completed body of scientific knowledge in any particular area is an integral work of art. It is like a patchwork quilt, built up from many separate pieces, which has become a golden tapestry. Tapestries are made by many artisans working together. The contributions of individual workers cannot be discerned in the finished work, and the loose and false threads have been covered over. So it is in the fields pursued by myself and by Drs Frank and Stein. The development of the strong–weak, or weak–strong, theory was not as simple and straightforward as it might seem. It did not arise full blown in the mind of any one physicist, nor even two or three. It, too, is the result of the collective endeavour of many scientists, both experimenters and theorists. This prize, therefore, is not awarded to me for *my* contribution to physics. I stand here today as the fortunate representative of that creative community of researchers who have pushed back the boundaries of physical knowledge. I have been chosen by Providence to receive the honour on their behalf.

Whilst I have the opportunity, I wish to give voice to the debt which we owe our teachers. My deepest impulse is to treat this year's prize for physics as having been awarded to my teacher and mentor, Professor Moon. When I became Moon's student, I gained access to a superior mind. Moon possessed clarity of thought, powers of concentration, encyclopaedic knowledge of physics, and an aesthetic sense unparalleled in modern research. He taught me, and I have taught others. It is the genius of Professor Moon which led to the original fundamental idea of the strong–weak, or weak–strong, force. The award of this year's

Nobel Prize for physics to me is a direct outcome of the light shed by Moon on the basic structure of matter. Every aspect of my work reflects the penetrating scientific vision with which Moon illuminated everything he touched.

I am also particularly indebted to my many students and co-workers who have contributed so much to our common goal and whom I hold responsible in the largest measure for my achievements. Without their genius, perseverance and stimulation our work would not have flourished. I want to express my deep appreciation and my profound affection for my students and associates who have shared with me in the toil and should share equally in the honour. Now is not the moment to mention particular names, but I owe a great debt to the many wonderful people with whom it has been my privilege to work in relation to the strong–weak, or weak–strong, force.

As many of you will know, the theory of the strong–weak, or weak–strong, force was initially received with incredulity and fierce rejection by those already working in the field. In the long run, however, they have all come to accept the validity of that theory. Thus, what I find most remarkable and admirable is the self-abnegation and devotion to truth with which my former opponents have not only adopted my original hypothesis, but have actively promoted it to the status of an established theory. I would like to pay a most heartfelt tribute to those who were formerly my strongest critics, without whose altruistic and generous impulses I feel sure that I would not be at this banquet. It is their untiring commitment to the basic scientific ideal of rigorous experimental testing which has ensured that our theoretical explorations have come to such great fruition. It is they who are honoured here today.

As I look back from this moment upon the last few decades of my life, I am struck by the good fortune that has come my way. Throughout my schooling, there was an abundance of opportunity and encouragement. Several of my teachers were remarkable individuals, scholarly and dedicated, who had a lasting influence on me. At every stage of my career I have been surrounded by stimulating and amazingly gifted colleagues, most of whom are my close friends. I entered research under the guidance of a kind and benevolent master, and my own endeavours have been enriched by exceptionally talented students and collaborators, and validated through the rigorous, but scrupulously fair, appraisal of other outstanding researchers in my field. Finally, and most important, my wife and children have created in my home an atmosphere of joy and harmony. They have loved and supported me with a selfless devotion without which my labours in pursuit of knowledge would have been impossible. My family has provided the bedrock on which all else has been built. They, above all, are honoured by the award of this year's Nobel Prize for physics.

I thank them. I thank you all. God bless you!

PROFESSOR BLACK Your Majesties, Your Royal Highnesses, Honoured Laureates, Ladies and Gentlemen. I have been asked to say a few words on behalf of the non-Laureates here tonight. I hope that nobody will mind if I change the tone of these proceedings just a little, by making one or two objective comments. I have listened with growing interest to the praise heaped upon Professor Purple and the other Laureates this evening, and to Purple's humble protestations that he personally does not deserve this praise. As scientists, we are all committed to the truth. It seems to me, therefore, that we must ask: who is right? If Purple is right in saying that the credit belongs to others, then the Nobel Foundation has made a mistake; the prize should have gone to Moon or it ought to have been shared with all those said by Purple to have made essential contributions to the strong–weak, or weak–strong, theory. If the Nobel Committee was right in honouring Purple, then Purple himself seems not to have understood the nature of his own achievement or he has been deliberately misleading us in his remarks tonight.

We seem, then, to be faced with rather a difficult choice. If we agree with the Nobel Foundation, it seems that we must regard Purple either as deceitful or as, at least, somewhat lacking in perception. If we agree with Purple, we must conclude that the Nobel Committee is incompetent. One might think that the problem is resolved by the manifest inconsistency of Purple's speech this evening. Thus, if the strong–weak, or weak–strong, theory was really Moon's idea, as Purple says, then it cannot be credited, as Purple also says, to Purple's students and collaborators. On the other hand, if the body of knowledge in Purple's area is a tapestry so intricately interwoven that individual threads cannot be distinguished, to paraphrase Purple again, it is inappropriate to award the prize either to Moon or to Purple or to Purple's co-workers; the award must be witheld or awarded to the whole 'creative communtiy' mentioned by Purple. It is clear, then, that Purple's various assertions are incompatible and his remarks are too internally inconsistent to be given more than a moment's serious consideration.

It appears that we have no alternative but to reject Purple's account and to accept the decision of the Nobel Committee. At first, this may seem to be an ideal conclusion. Apart from anything else, it would be convenient in allowing us to get back to the celebrations. But, unfortunately, we seem to have been left with a paradox, namely, we have concluded that the Nobel Committee was right to award the prize to a scientist who is unable even to give a brief speech about his own achievements without getting into a disastrous logical tangle. Can such a mind deserve what has been described tonight as 'the greatest scientific award' and 'a unique tribute to human achievement'?

PROFESSOR PURPLE   I must reply to these charges. Professor Black is, as usual, making a mountain out of a molehill. He is following his customary scientific procedure of erecting an elaborate, yet flimsy, structure of interpretation upon shifting sand. What would his reply have been if I had stood up this evening and claimed sole responsibility and the entire credit for recent advances in the understanding of the kinship relationships among elementary particles? He would have accused me of megalomania, of massive self-advertisement, of refusing to recognize the basic contributions made by others. He would have said that I was trying to deny Moon's seminal influence on the field, that I was seeking to put Moon into an eclipse, and that this was clear evidence of a deranged mind. Thus he would have ended up at the same putative paradox by another route.

Professor Black has chosen tonight to disrupt these celebrations by disregarding the proprieties which normally govern such occasions. He knows full well that it is simply inappropriate for a Laureate to engage in excessive self-congratulation on receipt of the prize. Laureates are expected to acknowledge the help they have received from others and to allow as many as possible to share unofficially in the honour. Professor Black has electd to take my partly conventional, but nonetheless sincere, remarks literally, under the guise of a scientific concern for the objective truth, in order to bring me into discredit and to spoil what would otherwise have been the most gratifying moment in my career.

As many of you know, Professor Black has been one of my most persistent critics and dogmatic antagonists. He has refused to accept the validity of the strong–weak, or weak–strong, theory, whilst at the same time maintaining that his own earlier weak–strong, or strong–weak, theory contains my theory as a special case. Thus Professor Black's personal attack this evening is due to his desire to stand here in my place. May God forgive him for the harm he has done.

PROFESSOR BLACK   There is a grain of truth in Purple's suggestion that I intended to remove the patina of convention which has shrouded most of the speeches here this evening. The student representative properly drew our attention earlier to that other reality which exists outside these walls. It was also my aim to make sure that this reality was not forgotten, not buried under the celebratory words required by the Nobel ritual.

Contrary to what Purple says, however, I don't mind about his getting the prize. But I do mind when the award of the prize is taken to mean that his theory must be correct and that it is universally accepted. In my view, and that of many others, Purple's hypothesis is incorrect and has certainly not been concusively confirmed by experimental evidence. In addition, there *is* an alternative theory, the weak–strong, or strong–weak, theory, which preceded his hypothesis and which already included those aspects of his hypothesis which have proven to be fruitful. I do not claim this alternative theory as my own. It evolved as part of the cumulative growth of scientific knowledge. Nevertheless, its existence puts in doubt the award of this year's prize to Professor Purple; for this theory was published before Purple began to work on the topic of particle siblings.

Finally, there is the issue which is normally discussed only in whispers, behind closed doors, but which I feel obliged to raise now: why has Delia Son not been included in the Prize? Dr Son studied with Moon before he retired, after which she transferred to Purple. She was very much the rising star of particle kinship research and her writings clearly foreshadow Purple's hypothesis. Yet she disappeared without trace from Purple's lab. I suggest that this is another example of a female graduate student being exploited by, and denied credit by, a senior male colleague. Given that this year's prize has been awarded for the strong–weak, or weak–strong, theory, then it should not be Purple facing me through the candelabra, but Dr Son and Professor Moon.

PROFESSOR PURPLE Your Majesties, Ladies and Gentlemen. I realize that this exchange between Professor Black and myself is becoming increasingly embarrassing. The topics raised by Professor Black should not really be discussed here. But I feel that I cannot let his slanderous accusations pass unanswered before this august assembly, whose respect I believe I deserve and which I wish to retain.

The fact is, as all who know me well can testify, that I strive constantly to maintain, and have succeeded in maintaining, an intimate accord with all my graduate students and post-docs. Delia Son was no exception to this. She worked closely with me for a short while, but there was neither exploitation nor plagiarism on my part. Nor was there any mystery about her departure from my lab. She left to have a baby; an eventuality which we have to face when we allow young women into research. She was a competent researcher. But she made no special contribution to our work. She simply followed my instructions and her research could always have been, as it eventually was, carried out by another young researcher. If she, or any other of my students, had made a distinctive and significant contribution, they would be alongside me this evening. My students are treated like members of my own family. They form part of a caring relationship which—

MRS PURPLE   This is too much! I've listened patiently to a lot of nonsense this evening, but I can't hold myself back any longer. My husband described our family life earlier, just as all the other Laureates described theirs, as a kind of earthly paradise which has been the source of all his success. Well, I think it's true that, without my constant labour and attention to his needs, his career might well have floundered. But the point is that it has not been an earthly paradise for me or our children; whatever it has been like for other Laureates' families. Indeed, when the children were younger, they would sometimes ask who their father was. They saw him so seldom, you see. He would either come home long after they were asleep or he would visit us briefly for dinner and then cycle back to his beloved lab.

He's still like that to this day; obsessed by his research. In my opinion, we have been sacrificed to his frenzied striving for success. In addition, I've had my suspicions about the reasons for all these conferences abroad. I'm not suggesting that these meetings are *just* a cover for marital infidelities, but the opportunities are certainly there, and if I know my husband—

PRESIDENT OF THE NOBEL FOUNDATION   My dear Mrs Purple, Professor Purple and Professor Black, I think you will agree that the realities of the world outside have become too obtrusive and are in danger of spoiling what is, after all, an occasion of joy and celebration; an occasion in which we all share in the honour associated with the outstanding cultural achievements of our time. I'm sure that these personal and scientific differences of opinion are important to those centrally involved. But they are of no interest to the rest of us gathered here to recognize some of the major accomplishments attained by the human intellect in recent years and to praise those responsible.

I suggest that it is time for music. If the orchestra is ready, let us now listen to the next item on the programme, which is the overture to George Gershwin's 'Of Thee I Sing'.

Last Words

Reader Is that it?

Textual Commentator I think so. He's stopped writing and has left the study looking pleased with himself.

Reader I don't think that he has any reason to feel pleased. That last sketch was more like *Monty Python* than a serious analysis.

Textual Commentator Well, I realize that academic analysis is traditionally serious, but do you think that we can learn to understand the world only by means of serious discourse? Do you not feel that you've learned a lot about social situations from the comic exaggerations of *Monty Python* and of other humorous representations of social life?

Reader Yes, I suppose so. But couldn't he have formulated his conclusions about the Nobel ceremonies more clearly and economically by using the conventional empiricist format? And doesn't that apply to all the other unconventional forms used in previous chapters? Couldn't they all be translated without loss into quite ordinary sociological analysis?

Textual Commentator There's no doubt that you could, as you say, *translate* these analyses into more conventional forms. But I suspect that translation always involves some loss and change of meaning. In particular, these new forms have in common that they draw attention to their own textuality, they emphasize the interpretative exchange through which texts are given meaning and they draw attention to the multiplicity of potential meanings. These things are done by the form itself and not by any particular statements that the author makes. Consequently, to restate these analyses in conventional form would, I think, greatly reduce the extent to which the author's basic claims about textuality are recognized and exemplified in the nature of his own text. In addition, it is my impression, from watching the author at work, that many of his analyses would have been significantly different if he had not employed textual forms involving multiple voices. Thus, although you could try to restate his conclusions, if you wished, in a more conventional way, the new analytical forms would nevertheless have played an indispensable generative role.

Reader You refer to 'conclusions', but what *are* the conclusions? We have not been told what this 'analytical parody' means; nor is there any summary of findings in any of the previous parts of the book. Perhaps there's another chapter yet to come.

Sociologist 1 I hope you don't mind my joining in. I agree that there are no conclusions. But I don't think it would matter to sociologists if there *were* any conclusions. Because this book is simply not sociology. For example, no mention is made of Marx, Durkheim or Weber; and although the subject matter is supposed to be the social world of science, there's no discussion of Merton or Kuhn. This is not sociology, but a rather whimsical examination of certain aspects of language and textual organization.

Spencer Well, I'm not a sociologist, so I cannot judge whether or not the book is 'truly sociology'. But I *was* able to draw some personal conclusions from it. By taking part in the discussion represented in Chapter 3, I became more clearly aware of the limitations of dialogue among scientific researchers and, having read the chapters on discovery, I felt that I had begun to understand how I and others come to be defined as 'discoverers' despite our own emphatic denials. I think that the book does offer some hope, in the long term, of a more fruitful exchange between sociologists, if the author really is a sociologist, and practising scientists.

Professor Black I agree that definite conclusions can be drawn, at least from the parody. I found that the opportunity to participate in a rather unusual, imaginary Nobel ceremony helped to reveal the basic character of normal ritual celebrations among scientists. I was also led to wonder how far such celebrations among ourselves resemble parallel rituals among other groups; for example, among film actors when Oscars are being awarded. The possibility of this parallel was, for me, an unexpected insight.

Sociologist 2 Any extended analysis of empirical material is bound to generate the occasional insight. But, in my view, the author's constant concern with the nature of his own textuality serves only to obscure his findings and to make his analysis less accessible. As a result, I don't think that it's possible for us to decide what he is trying to tell us about dialogue, replication and so on. I think there are empirical findings hidden within the book about the nature of discourse among scientists. But the, in my view quite unnecessary, attempts to make the text self-referential and self-exemplifying divert our attention away from these findings.

Student Representative One possibility that occurred to me is that the kind of creative dialogue advocated in this text might introduce rather interesting new possibilities into teaching. For example, instead of requiring students to reproduce as closely as possible the facts and interpretations of their teachers, one could encourage them to learn about the social world by means of an 'active re-creation' of various socially located discourses. This kind of active engagement with 'real' or 'imaginary' texts would probably engender a deeper understanding of the social world, as well as being more fun than the traditional learning situation.

Mrs Purple I like that positive response to the text. I was beginning to feel that this discussion was going to develop in the manner that is typical of what I call 'masculine discourse', with each speaker insisting on the exclusive validity of *his* position, *his* interests and *his* interpretation. We saw earlier, in the examination of epistolary dialogue, where such discourse tends to lead (see also Easlea, 1983). Now the present author, in my view, moves some way towards constructing an alternative, more feminine form of analytical discourse. Of course, women, as such, are treated as badly in this text as in most other academic texts. We're given only walk-on parts. But, almost despite himself, the author is trying to create a new form of discourse which is more collaborative, less exclusive, more able to allow for interpretative diversity, less committed to maintaining analytical privilege and is, therefore, a more feminine form of discourse. The main conclusion I draw from the book is that such discourse is possible; that supposedly scientific, masculine discourse is not the only possibility.

Sociologist 3 My interpretation of the book is not exactly the same as that, but we are not too far apart. I saw the central underlying theme as power and domination, not just of men over women, but more generally. Scientific discourse is clearly a discourse of power and domination over nature. When such a discourse is employed in the social realm, it inevitably becomes the basis for the exercise of social power. I think that earlier remarks about this analysis not really being sociology were quite misleading. True, it does not use the old sociological repertoires associated with terms like 'power', 'social structure' and so on. But maybe it's time we brought to bear on the problems formulated in terms of those old-fashioned concepts an analytical discourse which is more sensitive to the relationship between power and discourse and less naive about the domination implicit in empiricist forms of sociological analysis.

Sociologist 1 This is becoming ridiculous. There has been no discussion at all in the preceding text of feminist discourse or discourse and power, yet we're now being offered interpretations which treat these issues as central to the book's meaning. It seems to me quite clear that the book is not concerned with power or domination, but with remedying what the author sees as defects in the dominant, empiricist forms of analytical discourse in sociology. Because the possibility of using new kinds of analytical discourse is explored through the study of scientific dialogue, replication, discovery and celebration, the book also offers various sorts of claims on these scientific topics. *This* is what the book is about. There may well be particular ambiguities owing to the author's stylistic peculiarities, but the overall scope of the book and its broad conclusions and recommendations were clearly stated by the Book in the opening chapter.

Borges Remember, my friends, there can be many different readings of the same arrangement of words. Perhaps there is *no* proper reading of the book. Even the Book's own reading is but one among others. In that sense, there are no firm conclusions and the book has no single meaning. Maybe the text in which we are playing our part is no more than an opportunity for others to perform their own textual work.

Sociologist 1 The only person who can settle this for us is the author. Only he knows what he intended. Unfortunately, he seems to have disappeared.

Sociologists, 1, 2 and 3 Author! Author! Author!

Reader It appears that the author is unwilling to come back and bring this book to a proper conclusion. I suppose it's up to me, as the only potentially independent textual producer, to finish it off by responding with a text of my own. Let me see. Perhaps I'll begin: 'If only you were with me now, dear Author. . .'

References

Some of the sources listed here are not cited in the previous text, but have nevertheless had some influence on its development.

Ashmore, M. (1983), 'The six stages or the life and opinions of a replication claim', mimeo, University of York.

Atkinson, J. M. (1983), 'Two devices for generating audience approval: a comparative study of public discourse and texts', *Tilburg Studies In Language and Literature*, vol. 4, pp. 199–235.

Barth, J. (1979), *Letters* (London: Secker and Warburg).

Bloor, D. (1976), *Knowledge and Social Imagery* (London: Routledge).

Borges, J. L. (1970), *Labyrinths* (Harmondsworth: Penguin).

Bradley, M. (1982), *The Mists of Avalon* (London: Sphere).

Brannigan, A. (1981), *The Social Basis of Scientific Discoveries* (Cambridge and New York: Cambridge University Press).

Burdett, P. (1982), 'Misconceptions, mistakes and misunderstandings: learning about the tactics and strategy of science by simulation', MA dissertation, Institute of Education, University of London.

Collins, H. M. (1975), 'The seven sexes: a study in the sociology of a phenomenon, or the replication of experiments in physics', *Sociology*, vol. 9, pp. 205–24.

Collins, H. M. (1981a), 'The role of the core-set in modern science', *History of Science*, vol. 19, pp. 6–19.

Collins H. M. (1981b), 'Stages in the empirical programme of relativism', *Social Studies of Science*, vol. 11, pp. 3–10.

Collins, H. M. (1981c), 'What is TRASP? The radical programme as a methodological imperative', *Philosophy of the Social Sciences*, vol. 11, pp. 215–24.

Collins, H. M. (1982a), 'Scientific replication', in W. Bynum and R. Porter (eds), *Dictionary of the History of Science* (London: Macmillan), p. 372.

Collins, H. M. (1982b), 'Knowledge, norms and rules in the sociology of science', *Social Studies of Science*, vol. 12, pp. 299–308.

Collins, H. M., and Pinch, T.J. (1982), *Frames of Meaning: The Social Construction of Extraordinary Science* (London: Routledge).

Coulter, J. (1979), *The Social Construction of Mind: Studies in Ethnomethodology and Linguistic Philosophy* (London: Macmillan).

Culler, J. (1981), *The Pursuit of Signs* (London: Routledge & Kegan Paul).

Derrida, J. (1977), 'LIMITED INC a b c. . .', *Glyph*, vol. 2, pp. 162–254.

Easlea, B. (1983), *Fathering the Unthinkable* (London: Pluto Press).

Filmer, P., Phillipson, M., Silverman, D., and Walsh, D. (1972), *New Directions in Sociological Theory* (London: Collier-Macmillan).

Friedrichs, R. (1970), *A Sociology of Sociology* (New York: The Free Press).

Funk, W. (1978), *Word Origins* (New York: Bell).

Garfinkel, H. (1967), *Studies in Ethnomethodology* (Engelwood Cliffs, NJ: Prentice Hall).

Gieryn, T. (1983), 'Boundary-work and the demarcation of science from non-science', *American Sociological Review*, vol. 48, pp. 781–95.

Gilbert, G. N. (1976), 'The transformation of research findings into scientific knowledge', *Social Studies of Science*, vol. 6, pp. 281–306.

Gilbert, G. N., and Abell, P. (1983), *Accounts of Action* (Aldershot: Gower).

Gilbert, G. N., and Mulkay, M. (1984), *Opening Pandora's Box: A Sociological Analysis of Scientists' Discourse* (Cambridge and New York: Cambridge University Press).

Goffman, E. (1974), *Frame Analysis: an Essay on the Organization of Experience* (New York: Harper & Row).

Goffman, E. (1981), *Forms of Talk* (Oxford: Blackwell).

Gouldner, A. (1970), *The Coming Crisis of Western Sociology* (New York: Basic Books).

Habermas, J. (1970), 'Towards a theory of communicative competence', in H. P. Dreitzel (ed.), *Patterns of Communicative Behaviour* (New York: Macmillan).

Hanson, N. R. (1969), *Perception and Discovery* (San Francisco: Freeman, Cooper).

Harvey, B. (1981), 'Plausibility and the evaluation of knowledge: a case study of experimental quantum mechanics', *Social Studies of Science*, vol. 11, pp. 95–130.

Hofstadter, D. R. (1979), *Godel, Escher, Bach: An Eternal Golden Braid* (New York: Basic Books).

Holton, G. (1973), *Thematic Origins of Scientific Thought* (Cambridge, Mass.: Harvard University Press).

Holton, G. (1978), *The Scientific Imagination* (Cambridge and New York: Cambridge University Press).

Knorr, K. (1977), 'Producing and reproducing knowledge: descriptive or constructive?', *Social Science Information*, vol. 16, pp. 669–96.

Knorr, K. (1979), 'Tinkering towards success: prelude to a theory of scientific practice', *Theory and Society*, vol. 8, pp. 347–76.

Knorr-Cetina, K. (1981), *The Manufacture of Knowledge* (Oxford: Pergamon).

Latour, B. (1980), 'The three little dinosaurs or a sociologist's nightmare', *Fundamenta Scientiae*, vol. 1, pp. 79–85.

Latour, B. (1981), 'Insiders and outsiders in the sociology of science; or, how can we foster agnosticism?', *Knowledge and Society Studies in the Sociology of Culture Past and Present*, vol. 3, pp. 199–216.

Latour, B., and Woolgar, S. (1979), *Laboratory Life: The Social Construction of Scientific Facts* (Beverley Hills and London: Sage).

Les Prix Nobels, published annually (Stockholm: Almquist & Wiksell).

Levinson, S. C. (1983), *Pragmatics* (Cambridge and New York: Cambridge University Press).

Lynch, M. (1982), 'Technical work and critical inquiry: investigations in a scientific laboratory', *Social Studies of Science*, vol. 12, pp. 499–533.

McHoul, A. W. (1981), 'Ethnomethodology and the position of relativist discourse', *Journal of Theory of Social Behaviour*, vol. 11, pp. 107–24.

McHoul, A. W. (1982), *Telling How Texts Talk* (London: Routledge).

MacHugh, P., Raffel, S., and Blum, A. F. (1974), *On the Beginning of Social Inquiry* (London: Routledge).

Merton, R. K. (1973), *The Sociology of Science* (Chicago: University of Chicago Press).

Mulkay, M. (1979), *Science and The Sociology of Knowledge* (London: Allen & Unwin).

Mulkay, M. (1984a), 'The scientist talks back: a one-act play, with a moral, about replication in science and reflexivity in sociology', *Social Studies of Science*, vol. 14, pp. 265–82.

Mulkay, M. (1984b), 'The ultimate compliment: a sociological analysis of ceremonial discourse', *Sociology*, vol. 18, pp. 531–49.

Mulkay, M., and Gilbert, G. N. (1984), 'Replication and mere replication', mimeo, University of York. Forthcoming in *Philosophy of the Social Sciences*.

Mulkay, M., Potter, J., and Yearley, S. (1983), 'Why an analysis of scientists' discourse is needed', in K. Knorr-Cetina and M. Mulkay (eds), *Science Observed: Perspectives on the Social Study of Science* (Beverley Hills and London: Sage), p. 171–203.

Pickering, A. (1981), 'Constraints on controversy: the case of the magnetic monopole', *Social Studies of Science*, vol. 11, pp. 63–93.

Pinch, T. J. (1981), 'The sun-set: the presentation of certainty in scientific life', *Social Studies of Science*, vol. 11, pp. 131–58.

Pomerantz, Anita (1984), 'Agreeing and disagreeing with assessments: some features of preferred/dispreferred turn shapes', in J. M. Atkinson and J. Heritage (eds), *Structures of Social Action* (Cambridge and New York: Cambridge University Press).

Popper, K. (1963), *Conjectures and Refutations* (London: Routledge).

Popper, K. (1972), *Objective Knowledge: An Evolutionary Approach* (Oxford: Clarendon Press).

Potter, J. (1983), 'Speaking and writing science', D.Phil. thesis, University of York.

Potter, J. (1984), 'Flexibility, testability: Kuhnian values in psychologists' discourse concerning theory choice', *Philosophy of the Social Sciences*, vol. 14, pp. 303–30.

Potter, J. and Mulkay, M. (1983), 'Making theory useful', *Fundamenta Scientiae*, vol. 3, pp. 259–78.

Potter, J., Stringer, P., and Wetherell, M. (1984), *Social Texts and Contexts: Literature and Social Psychology* (London: Routledge).

Sacks, H., Schegloff, E., and Jefferson, G. (1974), 'A simplest systematics for the organisation of turn-taking for conversation', *Language*, December, pp. 696–735.

Sandywell, B., Silverman, D., Roche, M., Filmer, P., and Phillipson, M. (1975), *Problems of Reflexivity and Dialectics in Sociological Inquiry* (London: Routledge).

Saussure, F. de (1974), *A Course in General Linguistics* (London: Fontana).

Schegloff, E., and Sacks, H., (1974), 'Opening up closings', in R. Turner (ed.), *Ethnomethodology* (Harmondsworth: Penguin), pp. 233–64.

Schutz, A. (1972), *The Phenomenology of the Social World* (London: Heinemann).

Sharratt, B. (1982), *Reading Relations: Structures of Literary Production* (Brighton: Harvester Press).

Silverman, D. and Torode, B. (1980), *The Material Word* (London: Routledge).

Stehr, N. and Meja, V. (1984), *Society and Knowledge: Contemporary Perspectives on the Sociology of Knowledge* (London: Transaction Books).

Travis, G. D. (1981), 'Replicating replication? Aspects of the social construction of learning in planarian worms', *Social Studies of Science*, vol. 11, pp. 11–32.

Van't Hoff, J. H. (1878), *Imagination In Science*, translated by G. F. Springer (Berlin: Springer-Verlag, 1967).

Westfall, R. S. (1980), *Never At Rest: A Biography of Isaac Newton* (New York and Cambridge: Cambridge University Press).

Whyte, W. F. (1955), *Street Corner Society* (Chicago: Chicago University Press).

Woolgar, S. (1976), 'Writing an intellectual history of scientific development: the use of discovery accounts', *Social Studies of Science*, vol. 6, pp. 395–422.

Woolgar, S. (1980), 'Discovery: logic and sequence in a scientific text', in K. Knorr, R. Krohn and R. Whitley (eds), *The Social Process of Scientific Investigation* (Dordrecht: Reidel), pp. 239–68.

Woolgar, S. (1982), 'Laboratory studies: a comment on the state of the art', *Social Studies of Science*, vol. 12, pp. 481–98.

Woolgar, S. (1983), 'Irony in the social study of science', in K. Knorr-Cetina and M. Mulkay (eds), *Science Observed: Perspectives on the Social Study of Science* (Beverley Hills and London: Sage), pp. 239–66.

Wynne, A. (1983), 'Accounting for accounts of the diagnosis of multiple sclerosis', mimeo, Sociology Department, Brunel University.

Yearley, S. (1981), 'Textual persuasion: the role of social accounting in the construction of scientific arguments', *Philosophy of the Social Sciences*, vol. 11, pp. 409–35.

Yearley, S. (1982a), 'Analysing science and analysing scientific discourse', mimeo, Department of Social Studies, Queen's University, Belfast.

Yearley, S. (1982b), 'Demotic logic: the role of talk in the construction of explanatory accounts', mimeo, Department of Sociology, Queen's University, Belfast.

Yearley, S. (1984), *Science and Sociological Practice* (London: Open University Press).

Zipes, J. (1983), *The Trials and Tribulations of Little Red Riding Hood* (London: Heinemann).

Zuckerman, H. (1977), 'Deviant behaviour and social control in science', in E. Sagarin (ed.), *Deviance and Social Change* (London and Beverley Hills: Sage), pp. 87–137.

Index